T5-CVI-015

by J.A. Haxby and R.C. Willey

Editorial and Pricing Committee
Charles Moore and Bill Boynton

Printed and Bound in Canada

THE UNITRADE PRESS

91 Tycos Drive, Toronto, Ontario   M6B 1W3
Tel: (416) 787-5658   •   Fax: (416) 787-7104

IMPORTANT NOTICE

The editors have attempted to provide the most accurate, up-to-date retail prices for all Canadian coins, tokens and paper money. Our pricing is based on information from across the country. Collectors should note that prices shown in any catalogue should be taken as a guide only.

While every care has been taken to ensure accuracy, the publisher cannot accept responsibility for typographical errors.

ACKNOWLEDGEMENTS

The authors wish to express their sincere thanks and appreciation to the following individuals for assistance and contributions, both direct and indirect, to this and past volumes.

Walter D. Allan, Larry Becker, R.C. Bell, G.H. Bishop, R.F. Blandford, George Blenker, Al Bliman, Fred Bowman, Bill Boynton, K.E. Bressett, Patrick Brindley, Major Sheldon S. Carroll, Freeman Clowery, Myron Cook, Brian Cornwell, Michael Curry, Earl Davis, R.H.M. Dolley, Stephen Dushnick, Graham Dyer, Harry Eisenhauer, J. Douglas Ferguson, R.P. Findley, Guy Gibbons, Robert J. Graham, E.C. Grandmaison, Friederich D. Grosse, Leslie C. Hill, Klaas Hirsch, Dr. Douglas D. Hunter, Dr. J.P.C. Kent, James D. King, Andrew Kossman, Glen Lacey, Daniel Langlais, Wilf Latta, Michael Levy, Yvon Marquis, C.F. Martin, Ruth McQuade, Michele Menard, Charles Moore, Eric P. Newman, Walter Ott, Gary Patterson, Alfred E.H. Petrie, Major Fred Pridmore, R.K. Robertson, Douglas Robins, Dick Robinson, K.S. Sargent, Neil Shafer, Thomas Shingles, Thomas S. Shipman, Ed Solski, F. Stewart Taylor, Richard Thompsen, Pierre Van Wissen, Don Wainwright, Holland Wallace, Randy Weir, Harold Whiteneck, Warren X, G. Gordon Yorke
Special thanks to the Royal Canadian Mint for illustrations and technical information.

THE UNITRADE PRESS

TORONTO, CANADA

TABLE OF CONTENTS

Contents

3   Canadian Collectors' Issues (Continued)

4   Canadian Bullion Issues, 1979 to date 131

5   Ottawa Mint Sovereigns, Gold, 1908-1919 135

6   Pre-Confederation Provincial Decimal Issues 137

7   The French Regime 153

8   Pre-Confederation Colonial Issues 157

9   Trade, Advertising and Transportation Tokens 216

1
INTRODUCTION

HISTORICAL OUTLINE
For British North American Colonies

England was the first European power to explore the North American area, following John Cabot's discovery of the rich fishing regions off Newfoundland in 1497. The promise of good fishing drew other Europeans, including the French, into the area during the early years of the next century. The French initially concentrated on the area around the Gulf of St. Lawrence, founding settlements in Acadia (later Nova Scotia) in 1605 and Quebec City in 1608. During the next 150 years, France and England fought over the North American possessions. Gradually, England took control. The Hudson Bay region was ceded in 1713. In the 1750s most of the Acadians moved out and New Englanders moved in. Quebec and Montreal fell in 1759-60 and British control of the entire Maritimes region was confirmed by the Peace of Paris in 1763.

The area along the St. Lawrence River, formerly called New France, was renamed Quebec under English rule. The American Revolution (1775-83) had an important effect upon the northern colonies. About 50,000 Tories (English sympathizers) from the 13 colonies migrated to Canada, to the east and west of the French area. Most went to the Nova Scotia region, where the separate colony of New Brunswick was formed in 1784. Those who migrated to the west did not like the lack of democracy inherent in the old French order of Quebec and agitated for separation. This was effected by the Constitutional Act of 1791 in which Quebec became Lower Canada and the western region Upper Canada. Each was provided with its own governing body, consisting of a governor, executive council and legislative council appointed by the Home government and a legislative assembly elected by the people. The seeds were thus sown for later conflicts. Similar situations existed in the Maritime colonies.

The War of 1812 was a temporary interlude in Canadian history. It was essentially a successful defense by the British against American expansionists. The battlegrounds lay in Upper Canada for the most part.

The Canadian constitutional conflicts continued rising in intensity after the war, especially in Lower Canada, where the Catholic French-Canadians bitterly resented their tyrannical domination by a few Protestant English-speaking officials. The Lower Canadian power movement was fundamentally a "radical conservatism"; the desire was to keep life as it had always been by obtaining the power to assure it. The leader of this movement was Louis Joseph Papineau.

In Upper Canada, under William Lyon Mackenzie, the power movement was more directed toward change. In 1837 armed rebellions broke out in both the Canadas, but they were not well coordinated and were easily put down. Following the rebellions, Lord Durham was dispatched from England to examine the situation. His 1839 report is one of the most famous documents in British Imperial history. His two fundamental suggestions for correcting the causes of the uprising were to reunite the Canadas and to provide the British North American colonies with "responsible" government: the executives would hold office at the discretion of the colonial representative assemblies. Sovereignty was to be divided without disintegration of the colonial empire. This new system of responsible government was first applied in 1848 to Nova

Scotia and to the Province of Canada (formed from Upper and Lower Canada in 1841) and by 1855 was in operation in the other colonies.

Confederation was slow in coming. Prior to 1864 the Colonial Office favored a union of the Maritime provinces, but feared a larger union involving Canada. They secretly backed a conference of Maritime delegates in Charlottetown, P.E.I., in September 1864. Meanwhile, Canada was increasingly encumbered by a constitution dictating equal representation in the legislature for Canada West and Canada East (the new designations for what were formerly Upper and Lower Canada). Canada West wanted representation by population, and a federation of the two Canadas was sought by Canada West liberals. When word of the impending P.E.I. conference was received in Canada the Canadians asked to be unofficially included. A formal conference to consider the union of all the provinces was held in Quebec in October 1864 (unknown to the Colonial Office) and a series of resolutions set forth. The resolutions were received well only in Canada West. In Canada East, Nova Scotia and New Brunswick they were contested and in Newfoundland and Prince Edward Island the resolutions were soundly defeated in the legislatures. The union movement was saved by the potential economic boons of such a union and by increasing fears of possible fresh American attempts to annex British North America. The BNA Act was passed by the English Parliament, taking effect on 1, July, 1867. Newfoundland and Prince Edward Island did not participate in the initial union, but joined later with the more western areas.

The Pre-Confederation Coinages of Canada

One of the greatest hindrances to trade during the early days of the settlements in North America was a lack of coined money. What coins were used trickled in from all over the world. Prior to the English conquest in the 1700s, France endeavored to keep her colonies in coins with special colonial issues and some French Imperial issues, but the balance of trade always caused a net loss of coin from the colonies. The situation was not much better under the British.

One of the major coins circulating in the British North American colonies was the Spanish milled dollar, which was being produced in considerable quantities in several mints to the south. These coins gained wide acceptance and the colonial monetary systems came to be expressed in terms of them. The value of the Spanish dollar varied from colony to colony; in New York it was rated at 8 shillings and in Nova Scotia it was worth 5s. The New York rating was called York Currency and the Nova Scotia rating was called Halifax Currency. Halifax Currency was extended to old Quebec in 1777 during the American Revolution and to Upper Canada, superseding York Currency, in 1822. In English money (sterling) the Spanish dollar was worth 4s, 2d.

The local non-sterling ratings of the Spanish dollar had a profound effect upon the colonial copper currency. While it was possible for British shillings to circulate at the lowered ratings (by giving them a value in local currency of 1 shilling and a certain number of pence, and then giving coppers in change), the smaller valued pieces could not pass for more than their face (sterling) value. There was no way to make change for their additional increment of value in local currency. Thus the importer of British regal coppers incurred a significant loss while the exporter incurred a significant profit. Obviously, the net flow of these coins had to be out of the colonies.

As the situation grew worse, local merchants decided to import tokens from England. They were usually of halfpenny size, with a smaller number of penny pieces and a few farthings. Some tokens were anonymously issued. Others had the name of the issue, for example, PAYABLE AT THE STORE OF J. BROWN. Soon there were a number of attractive, generally well made, coppers in circulation.

However, the element of profit caused some to import lightweight pieces and in time the copper currency became too voluminous. New laws were passed to deal with the problem. In 1817, the Nova Scotia government forbade importation of private copper pieces and directed that the ones already in circulation be withdrawn within three years. In the Canadas an 1825 law was passed to prohibit the private issues, but it had no clause for the withdrawal of those in circulation and was worded so that the importation of tokens dated 1825 or earlier was not illegal. Hence the appearance of private coppers, many of light weight, and antedated, continued in the Canadas.

Meanwhile, the Nova Scotian government stepped in and assumed the responsibility for providing that colony's copper currency. Semi-regal pence and halfpence were issued in 1823 and intermittently until 1856. The people were thereby spared the deluge of metallic trash that was to continue to harass the Canadas, particularly Lower Canada.

The continued and growing presence of spurious coppers, many of which were struck locally, finally forced Lower Canada to take steps to correct the situation. In the absence of action on the part of the government, the Bank of Montreal issued one sou pieces in 1835, followed in 1837 by Banque du Peuple sous. These were of mediocre quality, however, and were immediately buried under an avalanche of counterfeits.

In 1837, four major Lower Canada banks participated in the issue of the *habitant* one- and two-sous pieces. After the Canadas reunited in 1841, three banks issued copper pence and half-pence. All four of these later bank coinages were of high quality and were not counterfeited to any significant degree. Gradually, the low quality pieces disappeared from circulation.

The semi-regal and bank issues paved the way for regal issues, based upon a decimal system of dollars and cents. They were struck at the Royal Mint in London or its prime sub-contractor, Heaton's Mint in Birmingham, England. Just as there had been individual colony's currency pounds, each colony's dollar was rated in its own particular way.

The province of Canada, New Brunswick and Prince Edward Island all set their dollar equal to the U.S. gold dollar, so the £ sterling was worth $4.86⅔. Nova Scotia set its currency at $5.00 to the £ sterling and Newfoundland's dollar was initially equal to the Spanish dollar, which made the £ sterling worth $4.80. The first decimals were for the Province of Canada in 1858, followed by issues for Nova Scotia and New Brunswick in 1861, Newfoundland in 1865 and Prince Edward Island in 1871.

Coinages for the Dominion of Canada

Following the formation of the Dominion of Canada, decimal coins were issued in 1870. The British North American colonies which had entered into the Confederation ceased to issue their own distinctive coins and a single coinage was issued for all. Newfoundland's coinage continued until 1947 and Prince Edward Island had a single issue of cents in 1871 prior to its entry into the Dominion in 1873.

MINTS, MINT MARKS
AND QUANTITIES OF COINS STRUCK

The pre-decimal colonial issues (tokens) were struck at many different mints. Most of the better quality pieces emanated from private mints in England, the foremost of which were *Boulton and Watt*, and *Ralph Heaton and Sons*. The bank tokens of 1837 (*habitants*) to 1857 all were struck at one or the other of these mints. Another prominent producer of tokens, *Thomas Halliday*, of Birmingham, struck the Tiffin pieces (Nos. 115-120), and many of the SHIPS, COLONIES & COMMERCE and Wellington tokens.

The only tokens to bear mint marks are the 1846 Rutherfords of Newfoundland (No. 4), which have RH (for Ralph Heaton) above the date, and some SHIPS COLONIES & COMMERCE tokens which were struck with an additional incuse H (for Heaton) on the water (No. 14c). Whenever known, the maker of each token issue is indicated in the text. Prior to 1908, all decimal issues for British North America were struck in England. The matrices, punches and dies were prepared at the Royal Mint in London and, when time permitted, the coins were struck there. As the Mint's work load increased, it was necessary to sometimes send the dies to the Heaton Mint (after 1889 called The Mint, Birmingham), where coins were struck on contract.

With the exception of the 1871 Prince Edward Island cent, all Heaton-struck coins bear a small H mint mark. The last Heaton issue for British North America was the Canadian cent of 1907. Locations of the H are as follows: *Canada:* 1¢ (1876-90, 1907): below date; (1898, 1900): below bottom leaf; 5-50¢ (1871-1903): below bow of wreath; *Newfoundland:* 1¢ (1872-1904): below bow of wreath: 5-50¢ (1872-76): below bust; (1882): below the date; $2. (1882): below date.

Late in the 19th century, the Canadians began agitating for a domestic mint with the power to coin sovereigns. Such an institution was authorized by the Ottawa Mint Act of 1901. However, construction was not begun until 1905 and was finally completed in time for commencement of coinage on 2 January 1908.

The name of the new mint was The Royal Mint, Ottawa Branch, but this was changed to The Royal Canadian Mint on 1 December 1931 when it became part of the Canadian government's Department of Finance, and has been a Crown Corporation since 1969, reporting to parliament through the Minister of Supply and Services. In November of 1973 the Mint's preparatory facility at Hull, Quebec received satellite mint status with the striking of the first Olympic coins. A completely new and separate mint at Winnipeg, Manitoba became operational in the Spring of 1975 to relieve some of the increasing demands for domestic coinage at Ottawa.

Certain of the 20th century Newfoundland coinages have been struck at the Ottawa Mint; and are designated with a C (Canada) mint mark on the reverse: 1¢ (1917-20): below bow of wreath; (1941-47): above 'T' of CENT; 5-50¢ (1917-47): at bottom reverse below oval. In addition, Ottawa-struck British type sovereigns of 1908-19 have a raised C mint mark centred on the base of the design above the date.

In many cases the mintages of tokens are not known, but when known are indicated in the text. The reader should be cautioned that, since many of the tokens were eventually melted, mintages are not necessarily reliable guides to scarcity today.

The quantities struck for the decimal coins are known with more certainty; nevertheless, those for the period 1858-1907 must, for the most part, be considered approximate. This is because the Royal Mint often attempted to use up all good dies, even if they bore the previous year's date. Hence, while the reported number of coins struck in a given year may be quite correct, one cannot be certain what proportion actually bore that date. A good example of the problem is the Canadian ten cents issue for 1889. Research results have pointed to the scarcity of that date (reported mintage 600,000) because 1888 dies were used to strike most of the pieces.

The reliability of mintage figures for the decimal coins is further complicated by the fact that portions of some issues were officially melted. This has turned what would otherwise be a readily available issue into a scarce or rare one. Where it is known or strongly suspected that such a melt has occurred, we have preceded the figure for *quantity minted* with *originally:* and placed the whole in parentheses.

VARIETIES AND OTHER DIFFERENCES

Collectors have long been interested in differences between coins of the same date or series. There can be variations in the precise details of portraits, the style or size of lettering or date, and so on. Such items have become increasingly popular, and a study of varieties can transform an otherwise placid series into an exciting one.

Together with the rise in variety interest has come a group of terms to describe these differences. Two coins are different *types* if their designs show some *basic* difference. For example, the Elizabeth II 1953-64 and 1965-89 obverses represent separate types. The critical distinction is the presence of a laureated bust on the former and a diademed bust on the latter. Conversely, the "broad leaves" and "small leaves" Canadian 10¢ reverses of George V are of the *same* type. The designs certainly differ in fine details; however, the basic appearance was unchanged.

The above mentioned George V 10¢ examples are *major varieties*, meaning that there is an obvious and deliberate alteration without changing the basic design. Less apparent varieties are termed *minor varieties* or *variants*. When the difference was actually prepared in the dies, the resulting coins will show variations called *die varieties*. There can also be *non-die varieties*. Examples in this category include deliberate changes in planchet composition or thickness.

Not all coins that differ from each other are varieties. The latter designation is reserved for coins differing as a result of some deliberate action by the issuing mint. Any variations arising from such causes as deterioration of dies or malfunction of mint machinery are not true varieties. They are known by names such as *freaks, mint errors* or *irregularities*. The term *mint error*, however, is usually inappropriate and its use in most cases should be avoided.

In order to understand varieties and the place they hold in numismatics, it is important to have at least a casual knowledge of how they came into being; that is, of how coinage dies are made.

THE MANUFACTURE OF COINAGE DIES
Development of the Matrix-Punch-Die System

Working punch and die

The usual method of making coins is to place a flat metal disc (the planchet or blank) between two *dies* bearing the designs and impart the designs to the blank with a sharp blow. A die has at its top the flat or slightly convex surface that will become the field of the struck coin. The design elements (e.g., portrait), which are *cameo* (raised) on the coin are *incuse* (sunken) and face the opposite direction in the die. If the reader has difficulty grasping this concept, he should press a coin onto a piece of clay. The image left in the clay is a model of what the top of the die which struck that side of the coin looked like.

In the beginningn and for many years thereafter, dies were individually hand engraved. This system was extremely laborious, and once any given die wore out, its precise design was lost for future coinages. Gradually, more complex systems arose, with the ultimate result of preserving a design for an essentially indefinite period.

The first refinement in die-making technique was to engrave the device (e.g., the portrait) in the form of a *punch*. A punch is a steel intermediate that has its design in cameo, in the same sense as on a coin. The design of the punch would then be impressed into blocks of steel, each of which would become a die. All secondary details (legends, rim beads, etc.) were hand engraved into each die, as previously. The effect of the punch-die system was to extend the life of those parts of the design borne on the punches, because each punch could make (sink) multiple dies.

The transition to the period of modern die-making occurred in the 1600s with the introduction of a third kind of intermediate, the *matrix*. A matrix has its design in the same sense as a die; however, it is used to make (raise) punches instead of to strike coins. The addition of the matrix step offered two advantages over the previous system. First, a design could be better preserved (a matrix can be used to raise several punches). Second, instead of adding the legend and rim heads at the die stage, these details could be incorporated into the matrix. With only slight modifications, the matrix-punch-die system of die making has persisted to this day.

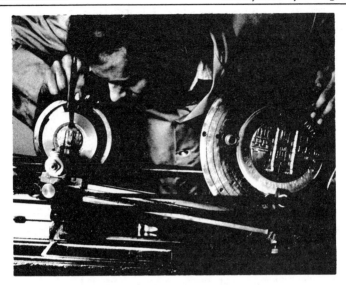

Initiation of a New Coinage Design

In modern die-making one of the fundamental problems is how to produce a matrix for a new design. The most direct way, but also the most difficult, is to engrave it by hand. After the outlines are scratched on the face of a steel block, the design elements are painstakingly hand cut to the exact size they are to appear on the finished coins. Lettering and other secondary features are often engraved as individual hand punches and punched into the matrix. Only a highly skilled engraver is capable of hand engraving a matrix, and this once common practice has largely disappeared today. The Canadian issues produced by this method are the Victory 5¢ of 1943-45 and the Newfoundland commemorative dollar of 1949. Both were by Thomas Shingles, formerly the chief engraver at the Royal Canadian Mint.

The alternative method for making a matrix of a new design is to use a "reducing machine." This machine was inventedaround the beginning of the 19th century by a Frenchman, Contamin, and was first used in London's Royal Mint in 1824. While initially rather crude, reducing machines have gradually evolved into a very important part of the engraver's tools. Briefly, it functions as follows: An 8" diameter three dimensional model of the design is produced in some hard substance such as plastic (formerly electroplated metals). At one end of the arm is a rapidly revolving cutter that faithfully duplicates the movements of the tracer, cutting the design on a reduced scale into a steel block. The reduction from the 8" model to coin size is usually made in two steps. Using the 8" model as a pattern, a steel *intermediate model* (about 3" in diameter) is made using the machine. This intermediate model is then similarly used to make a second reduction to coin scale. The second product of the machine is almost always a punch, called the *reduction punch*. The perfected reduction punch is placed in a powerful press and its design used to sink the matrix. Any details absent from the original model are then punched into the matrix. during the Vic torian period reduction punches bore only the portrait or reverse device; now only the rim denticles are lacking.

Alteration of Existing Designs

The creation of a partially new design from one already used for coinage can be accomplished by a number of methods. During the Victorian and Edwardian periods, the commonest means was to re-engrave a punch or matrix bearing the old design. In some cases the change was slight, in others very pronounced. The Victorian portrait modifications are an elegant example of such a process.

In the George VI and Elizabethan series, changes have been made more often by re-engraving at some point prior to the matrix stage. For example, the famous 1953 modification of the Canadian obverses was made by re-engraving the intermediate model for the reducing machine (see above section).

Dating of Coinage Dies

The dating of dies for the decimal coins has been accomplished by two methods. During the Victorian period it was common practice to employ reverse punches which had only a portion of the date (the first two or three digits). Dies sunk from such punches would then be finished by punching in, one digit at a time, the missing portion of the date. Occasionally, the date was completed at matrix stage.

Post-Victorian dies have usually been prepared from fully dated matrices. Notable exceptions, however, are the 50¢ and dollars for part of the 1940s and the early 1950s, where the date was once again completed in the dies.

Chromium Plating of Coinage Dies

During World War II, an attempt was made to increase die life. The most important advance was the development of an electrolytic process whereby a thin coating of pure chromium was deposited on the die faces. This gave the desired increase in die life and imparted a better finish to the coins. Following limited use in 1942-44, chromium plating was finally adopted for all coinage dies in 1945.

The process, for all its advantages, has also led to the creation of two kinds of trivial differences between coins. First, it sometimes happens that tiny pieces of the plating chip away, leaving pits in the die faces. Such pits are manifested on the struck coins as tiny, irregular "dots," (e.g., the 1947 "dot" coins). Second, during the late 1940s and part of the 1950s, serviceable dies with degenerated plating were replated and put back in the presses. One danger of this was the inadvertent removal of delicate design details when the dies were repolished. The 50¢ 1950 "no lines in 0" and 1955 and other so-called "Arnprior" dollars are doubtless traceable to this practice. Replating of dies is no longer done at the Mint.

COMMEMORATIVE CIRCULATION COINS

Canada is a country with a rich history and many of its important events and occurrences have been featured in special coinage designs.

The 1935 silver dollar, Canada's first commemorative circulation coin, was issued to celebrate the Silver Jubilee of King George V. This was also the first official dollar coin of Canada and introduced the symbolic "Voyageur" reverse design.

A special reverse design on the 1939 silver dollar depicts the centre block of the Parliament Buildings in Ottawa and celebrates the visit of King George VI to Canada that year. The 1949 silver dollar commemorates Newfoundland's entry into Confederation with a reverse design depicting John Cabot's ship, the *Matthew*.

In 1951 a special 5¢ piece depicting a nickel refinery on the reverse was issued to commemorate the 200th anniversary of the isolation and naming of the element nickel. This was the first instance of a commemorative and "regular design" version being issued for a circulating coin in the same year.

The 1958 silver dollar bears a totem pole on the reverse to commemorate the centenary of the gold rush and the establishment of British Columbia as British Crown Colony. The 100th anniversary of the meetings at Charlottetown, P.E.I. and Quebec City, Quebec, which paved the way for Confederation, was celebrated with a special reverse design on the 1964 silver dollar.

In 1967 the entire issue of circulating coins, 1¢ through $1.00, bore Canadian wildlife designs to honour the 100th anniversary of Confederation.

Commemorative circulation dollars were issued in 1970 (Manitoba Centenary), 1971 (B.C. Centenary), 1973 (P.E.I. Centenary), 1974 (Winnipeg Centenary), 1982 (Constitution), and 1984 (Jacques Cartier). A commemorative 25¢ piece was also issued in 1973 for the centenary of the R.C.M.P.

COMMEMORATIVE COLLECTORS' ISSUES

In 1967 the Royal Canadian mint inaugurated a policy of producing commemorative coins as collectors' pieces only, the first such piece being the $20 gold coin, issued to commemorate Confederation, although it lacked a specific commemorative legend.

With the exception of 1972, when a silver voyageur dollar was struck, cased silver commemorative dollars have been issued for collectors every year since 1971. Prior to 1981 the coins were of specimen quality but since 1981 the mint has issued each dollar in two qualities, uncirculated and proof.

Commemorative $100 gold pieces have been issued annually since 1977, and $200 gold pieces since 1990.

Collectors' coins are not issued for circulation and are sold by the mint at a premium over the nominal face value. The themes of the silver dollars and the $100 and $200 gold pieces are listed in the following table.

DATE	SILVER DOLLARS	$100 GOLD PIECES	$200 GOLD PIECES
1971	British Columbia	—	—
1973	Royal Canadian Mounted Police	—	—
1974	Winnipeg, Manitoba	—	—
1975	Calgary, Alberta	—	—
1976	Library of Parliament	—	—
1977	Silver Jubilee	Silver Jubilee	—
1978	11th Commonwealth Games	Canadian Unity	—
1979	The Griffon	International Year of the Child	—
1980	Arctic Territories	Arctic Territories	—
1981	Trans-Canada Railway	'O Canada'	—
1982	Regina, Saskatchewan	Canadian Constitution	—
1983	World University Games	St. John's Newfoundland	—
1984	Toronto, Ontario	Jacques Cartier	—
1985	National Parks	National Parks	—
1986	Vancouver, British Columbia	International Year of Peace	—
1987	John Davis Expeditions	XVth Winter Olympics	—
1988	Industrial Pioneers	Bowhead Whale	—
1989	Mackenzie River	Sainte-Marie Among the Hurons	—
1990	Henry Kelsey	International Literacy Year	Spirit of Canadian Youth
1991	Frontenac	Empress of India	Hockey
1992	Kingston-York stagecoach	Montreal	Niagara Falls

In 1973 an ambitious fund raising endeavor to help finance the 21st Olympic Games was begun. That year saw the first of seven silver four-coin sets; by the time the Games were held in 1976 at Montreal, 28 different silver $5 and $10 coins and two $100 gold pieces had been released.

The complete Canadian commemorative series, including the foregoing examples, is fully illustrated and identified in this book. Pertinent background information is provided for each issue.

CONDITIONS OF COINS

In very general terms, the condition of a coin indicates the amount of wear it has sustained since the time it was minted. Coin conditions are distinguished from each other by a series of coin grades. A coin's grade is important to know because it determines the coin's value; the better a coin's grade, the higher will be its value. Coins are classified as belonging to one of two groups, that is, circulated or uncirculated coins. Each of these groups is further divided into many grades.

To properly understand the factors which influence a coin's grade, it is first necessary to appreciate that older coins were manufactured to be used quite simply as *money* in the world of commerce. Secondly, these business or production strike coins were made on high speed presses, run through counting machines, and dumped into bags where they were scraped with other coins as they were being shipped to various banks across the country. Needless to say, they were handled with little regard to their numismatic posterity. Consequently it is the rule, not the exception, that these coins had marks and other signs of coin-to-coin contact even before they were placed into circulation and used as money. These marks show on the surface of the coin as bright spots or streaks against the soft sheen of the coin's mint lustre. They are called bagmarks or bag scratches and are easily distinguished from ordinary wear. Once placed into circulation, all coins begin to show signs of physical wear, i.e., a gradual destruction of the fine details that were originally present on a new coin.

Those coins that were used the most tend to have the fewest details remaining. Today the Mint makes many coins specifically for the collector. These coins are carefully handled and packaged in plastic holders by trained Mint personnel. Unless they are removed from their holders, it is unlikely their grade will change over time.

Until the mid 1970s, coin grades were described by adjectives such as Very Good, Fine, and Uncirculated. Since then the industry has adopted an alternative grading system using a numerical scale from 1 to 70. This system was originally attributed to Dr. Wm. Sheldon who devised it as a means of grading and relating prices for early U.S. copper cents. In his numerical scheme, the circulated grades use the range from one to 59; the uncirculated range begins with 60 and progresses to a perfect coin which is 70. In general, the higher the number assigned, the better the grade or quality of the coin. While the numerical scale is a continuous one, not all of its numbers are used. Grading simply is not that precise, but rather a mixture of both science-like methods and human judgements. Today it is quite common to see coins described using both the adjectival and numerical systems as in the example Extra Fine-40.

GRADING UNCIRCULATED COINS

An uncirculated coin must show absolutely no signs of wear or loss of detail (due to wear) when examined by the naked eye. To properly grade an uncirculated coin, it is necessary to assess three different qualities of the coin in relation to the typical mint state characteristics seen on a coin of that particular type. These three factors are the qualities of the coin's lustre, surfaces, and strike. A coin that has lustre that is dazzling and 'alive' is much to be preferred to lustre that is dull and lifeless. A coin that has surfaces that are free, or nearly so, of marks is preferable to one that shows obvious marks that are very distracting to the overall appeal of the coin. A well struck coin that shows all of the detail intended by the coin's designer is preferable to one that is very poorly struck with the resultant loss of detail in some area of the coin. Each of these factors are equally important in determining the grade of an uncirculated coin. In some cases, one of the factors may be so superior to that normally seen in a particular series that it can make up for a slight deficiency in the quality of one of the remaining factors which by itself would lower the grade.

There are currently five recognized grades used to describe uncirculated coins. These, along with their numerical designations, are: Typical Uncirculated (Mint State-60), Select Uncirculated (MS-63), Choice Uncirculated (MS-65), Gem Uncirculated (MS-67), and Perfect Uncirculated (MS-70). A brief description of each follows:

Perfect Uncirculated-70: The finest quality available. Such a coin under 4 power magnification will show no marks, lines or other evidence of handling or contact with other coins. The lustre quality will be of the highest quality possible, with no impairment of any sort. The strike will be perfectly sharp and of a quality very unusual for that series. The strike will show all of the detail intended by the coin's designer/engraver.

Gem Uncirculated-67: A more select example of a Choice Uncirculated coin by virtue of the coin's overall qualities of lustre, surfaces, and strike. The coin is essentially perfect in all respects to the naked eye.. Only after extensive study is there likely to be any fault or criticism of the coin.

Choice Uncirculated-65: This grade is reserved for coins that have an overall unquestionable quality look to them. Each of the factors of lustre, surfaces, and strike will be well above average for that normally seen on a typical mint-state coin of the series. The strike will be nearly full except for a slight weakness in a very localized area, the lustre will be almost completely free from impairments, and the surfaces generally free of marks except on the largest coins and those made of softer metals such as gold. Any slight imperfections present in no way distract from the overall beauty of the coin.

Select Uncirculated-63: A more select example of a typical uncirculated coin but lacking the quality appeal of a full Choice Uncirculated-65. Any faults with the surfaces, lustre or strike may be readily seen with the naked eye but they collectively are not a major distraction to the overall appearance of the coin.

Typical Uncirculated-60: Shows absolutely no signs of wear on any part of the coin's surface. This grade refers to a typically seen uncirculated coin and is expected to have a moderate but not excessive number of bagmarks or rim nicks, although none of a serious nature. The coin's lustre may be somewhat impaired by spotting or dullness. The strike may be weak enough to show a generalized weakness in detail in several areas. Usually the impairments to any of these three factors will be obvious at first glance and will continue to be distracting to the overall appeal of the coin.

GRADING CIRCULATED COINS

Once a coin enters circulation, it begins to show physical wear on its surfaces. As time goes on the circulating coin becomes more and more worn until, after many decades, only a few of its original details remain. The extent of this wear is the primary factor that determines the grade of circulated coins. There are ten regularly used grades for circulated coins. A brief description of each, along with its numerical grade assignment, follows:

Choice About Uncirculated-55 (AU-55): Only a small, localized trace of wear, at the highest relief points of the coin's design, is visible to the naked eye.

About Uncirculated-50 (AU-50): Traces of wear on nearly all the highest areas. Much of the original mint lustre is still present.

Choice Extremely Fine-45 (EF-45): Light overall wear can be seen on the highest parts of the coin. All design details are very sharp. Mint lustre is usually seen only in sheltered areas between the inscription letters and around the edges.

Extremely Fine-40 (EF-40): With only slight wear but more extensive than the preceding, the coin still has excellent overall sharpness. Traces of mint lustre may still show.

Choice Very Fine-30 (VF-30): With light even wear on the surface: design details on the highest points are lightly worn, but with all lettering and major features still sharp.

Very Fine-20 (VF-20): As preceding but with moderate wear on the high parts.

Fine-12 (F-12): Moderate to considerable even wear. Entire design is bold. All lettering is visible but with some weaknesses.

Very Good-8 (VG-8): Well worn. Most of the fine details of the hair and leaves are worn nearly smooth.

Good-4 (G-4): Heavily worn. Major designs remain visible but are faint in some areas. Other major features visible only in outline form without the central details.

About Good-3 (AG-3): Very heavily worn with portions of the lettering, date, and legends being worn smooth. The date is barely readable.

While these general definitions of grades are quite useful for most coins, the exact descriptions of circulated grades vary widely from coin type to coin type.

The use of intermediate grades such as EF-42, EF-43, and so on is not encouraged. Grading is not that precise, and using such finely split intermediate grades is imparting a degree of accuracy which probably cannot be verified consistently by other numismatists.

TONING

Often a coin will develop a toning or tarnish on its surfaces. This toning can be particularly colourful and attractive on uncirculated coins because they tend to be free of dirt and grime that will surround the surface of a circulated coin. Silver coins may tarnish in blues, purples, reds, greens, and other colours of the rainbow. Copper or bronze coins may develop dull red, purplish-brown, olive, and chocolate brown toning. However, just because a coin has attractive toning, it should not be concluded that the coin is necessarily a strictly uncirculated example. Numismatists have often fallen into this trap.

These toning features, while an integral part of a coin's price, do not form part of its grade assignment. That is, a coin is first graded as if it were a fully brilliant example and the quality of the toning present, if any, is described by a separate adjective. For example, a Choice Uncirculated-63 coin that is fully brilliant, or possibly with just a hint of toning, may be called Choice BU for Choice Brilliant Uncirculated. On the other hand, that same coin with very dark toning is referred to as being Choice Toned Uncirculated. Some toning descriptions are prefaced by the word "Original" as in Original Toned Choice Unc. This additional adjective refers to those coins that are thought never to have been cleaned (i.e., dipped) since the time they were first minted. As a result, the quality of the toning has a very special pristine look to it which is of considerable appeal to certain connoisseur collectors.

Toned coins must be considered with caution, especially if high price premiums are being demanded. Toning that is darker can obscure very fine marks on the coin's surfaces and therefore make it appear in better condition than it really is. Toning can also hide the fact that a coin has very slight signs of wear and in fact is not the uncirculated coin that it at first appeared to be. The best protection when examining toned coins is to ensure adequate lighting, lots of study time, and use of a magnifying glass. Because collectors have begun to pay premiums for toned coins, it has spawned an increase in the number of people attempting to "artificially" tone coins through chemical reactions. Most specialist in the colour field can tell artificial toning from that of Mother Nature. When in doubt, it would be wise to seek the opinion of one of these specialists.

MARKS ON COINS

There are many, many adjectives that are used to describe the various marks and other imperfections seen on coins. These descriptions tend to be confusing and make it difficult to properly describe the condition of a coin to others. The following scheme is simple and recommended for describing all marks, rim nicks, and other coin imperfections whether man made or caused by the minting process.

Major: Immediately obvious at first glance to the naked eye. Very distracting.

Minor: Still immediately noticed on first glance to the naked eye but not a major distraction considering the other qualities of the coin.

Slight: Can be seen by the naked eye but usually discovered only after a more detailed study (more than just a glance). Not distracting.

Very Slight: Really only clearly discernable when using low power magnification (4-5 power). Have to search to find it.

Very, Very Slight: Likely not even observable with the naked eye after the closest of study. The details will become clearly defined only under stronger magnification of 8-10 power.

SOME USEFUL GRADING CAVEATS

A grading caveat is, in simple terms, a warning of something to be sensitive to, or careful about, when evaluating the condition of a coin. A healthy respect for each of the following caveats is as important to being a consistently successful grader as is a knowledge of the rules that distinguish a VF coin from an EF and so on.

1. Scarcer dates within a coin series are graded no differently than the more common dates of the same series.

2. There is no such grade as 'commercial' grade. Coins are either strictly graded or they are sliders.

3. Expect the largest coins to have more and larger bagmarks than the smallest ones. Also expect to see larger and more numerous marks on coins made of softer metals such as gold.

4. The higher the grade of a coin, the greater the amount of time that should be taken to arrive at that conclusion.

5. Toned coins must always be studied more carefully to see what problems are being obscured.

6. Grading uncirculated coins requires an assessment of three of the coin's factors: the lustre, surfaces, and strike. On the other hand, grading a circulated coin basically involves only one factor, that being, the amount of wear of the surfaces of the coin.

7. There is a natural human tendency for the owner of a coin to overgrade his coin and for the purchaser to undergrade someone else's coin.

8. While a coin's grade and price are inter-related, a coin can only be priced once its grade has been determined. Furthermore a coin cannot be reliably graded by only knowing its price.

9. It is impossible to accurately grade an uncirculated coin of a given series without first understanding the typical minstate characteristics for coins of that series.

10. Grading is not, and never will be, an exact science. It involves a great deal of human judgement too.

11. It is the rule, not the exception, that business or production strike coins will have bagmarks and other possible manufactured imperfections.

12. Grading only by "eye appeal" is not really grading at all. Eye appeal grading can be deceptively inaccurate because the grader is tricked into overlooking the problems that may exist on the coin.

RARITY AND VALUE

When one inquires as to the rarity of a coin, it is not really sufficient to specify merely the date and denomination. Varieties exist for several issues, and where they are particularly noteworthy, they are often widely collected as distinct entities — that is, as if they were separate dates. It is also best to specify the condition of the coin. There is always a marked difference between the rarity of earlier issues in uncirculated and well circulated conditions. Compare values for the various conditions of the Canadian 1911 50¢. In Very Good (well circulated) it lists at $20, but in uncirculated it jumps to $3600!

Because determining rarity by the direct method of examining a large number of coins is often impractical, it is usually deduced by other means. A common practice is to compare prices. This method, while certainly a reasonable starting point, can sometimes be very misleading. For example, the Canadian 1921 50¢ in uncirculated condition lists for $50,000 while the 1870 50¢ without the designer's initials has been valued at nearly $15,000 in the same condition. Is the latter coin, then, three times commoner than the former. The mint state 1870 is in fact twice as rare as the 1921. Why the inverted price relationship? The 1870 is part of a series not widely collected by date and variety, and its rarity is much less appreciated than that of the famous 1921.

The other usual way to ascertain rarity is by comparing mintage figures. Here too, caution is in order. First, reported figures especially for the Victorian period (see above), are not always reliable. Second, in the case of varieties, the mints rarely know what proportion of a given year's issue was of a particular variety. And third, mint figures tell one nothing about the number of pieces preserved in the better conditions. Example: the mintages for the Canadian 1937 and 1938 50¢ are almost identical, yet the uncirculated valuation for the 1937 is $95.00 while that for the 1938 is $370. The 1937s were saved in quantity because they were the first date of a new series. On the other hand, most of the 1938s went into circulation.

The value of a coin is determined by the law of supply and demand. Some very scarce items change little in value from year to year simply because they are not widely collected, whereas commoner dates that are part of a very popular series can show great differences.

The approximate market values listed in this catalog are only indications of probable average worth. In an individual transaction a coin may sell for more or less than what is indicated here. Every attempt has been made to quote values that realistically reflect the market. These values were determined by a panel of several individuals, most of whom are in close contact with retail sales. In some instances, particularly for previously unpublished varieties, the prices are either theoretical or omitted.

THE SCOPE OF LISTINGS IN THIS CATALOGUE
Pre-decimal Colonial Issues

The well-known reference on Canadian tokens, Breton's 1894 work, is a hodge-podge of several different kinds of items which can be divided into seven basic categories:

1. Items that are not really Canadian.
2. Patterns.
3. Merchant and other advertising cards, tickets, etc.
4. Trade tokens, redeemable in goods and services only (e.g., transportation tokens) and only to a very limited extent money.
5. Fabrications made to deceive collectors.
6. Pieces that were used as money, with relatively unrestricted validity throughout the colony issue.
7. Contemporary counterfeits of (6).

The approach used in this catalog is to list only those pieces falling in classes (6) and (7). Careful note should be made of the distinction between contemporary counterfeits and those made to deceive collectors. Contemporary counterfeits, or imitations as they are often called in the listings, are of the same period as the production and circulation of the originals. They were made to circulate and serve as money along with the originals. Being of lighter weight and often containing less pure copper, the imitations brought a tidy profit to their purveyors. The contemporary counterfeits have traditionally been collected along with the originals and some can even command a higher premium to day. The inclusion of contemporary imitations in this catalog is quite logical, for they, too, for at least a while, served as Canada's money.

The collectors' forgeries or concoctions are another matter. They are usually made long after the originals circulated, with the intent to deceive coin collectors into paying substantial premiums for them. These items are not worthy of listing in a catalog of this kind.

Over the years, many token die varieties and freaks have been described. Men like *Lees* and *Courteau* have devoted considerable energy to the study of varieties in this series. An important reason why such studies are possible has to do with how the dies were made. Most (but not all) of the token dies, including the devices, were engraved entirely by hand. This made every such die distinct from each of the others, creating a large number of die varieties. In a general catalog it is not desirable to list every known difference, even when true die varieties are involved. Therefore, we have surveyed the varieties and have se lected for separate listing those that seem to us to be the most interesting and easy for the average collector to recognize.

Decimal Issues

Although most pattern pieces have been excluded from the listings (see the comments above on token patterns), two decimal coins that might be called "semi patterns" are included: the 1965 medium beads obverse and 1967 flat dies dollars. These coins are the products of trial production runs of several thousand each and are from regular dies. True patterns are almost always proof and are struck in very small quantities.

Varieties in the decimal series have been very popular with collectors and traditionally have been included in Canadian catalogs. Unfortunately, the treatment of varieties has not always been consistent; some have been listed while others, at least as important, have been omitted. In this work an effort has been made to list all noteworthy varieties, regardless of how rare they might be.

It has also been deemed necessary to include a small number of items that are either trivial varieties or not varieties at all. That is because the particular items involved have been touted as differences of importance (through advertising campaigns, etc.) for so long that many collectors have been misled into thinking they really are important. At this date it would seem unwise to remove such things as the "Arnprior" dollars from the catalog. Each of these "objectionable" listings is explained in the appropriate place in the main body of the catalogue.

As a final comment regarding those varieties which have been listed, it is stressed that this book is only a guide. By the inclusion of a given item the authors do not necessarily suggest that it should be part of a "complete" set. Each collector is urged to decide for himself the extent of his interest in the sub listings.

LOCAL AND NATIONAL NUMISMATIC ORGANIZATIONS

Throughout Canada and the U.S. are located many local coin clubs that include in their memberships those interested in any and all phases of numismatics. Becoming involv ed in such an organization offers important advantages to beginner and more experienced collector alike. One can acquire needed coins, dispose of extras, gain valuable knowledge and enjoy the good fellowship of others with like interests.

Similarly, anyone seriously interested in Canadian numismatics should join and support Canada's national numismatic organization, The Canadian Numismatic Association. Its members have access by mail to the association's impressive library and receive the official monthly periodical, the *Canadian Numismatic Journal.. The Journal* provides a medium for publishing and disseminating numismatic knowledge, so important for progress in the hobby. Those interested in membership should contact:

The Canadian Numismatic Association
General Secretary
P.O. Box 226
Barrie, Ontario, Canada L4M 4T2

There is also an organization for those interested in paper money:

Canadian Paper Money Society
P.O. Box 356
Fredericton, N.B., Canada E3B 4Z9

The principal national U.S. numismatic association (the largest in the world) is:

The American Numismatic Association
P.O. Box 2366
Colorado Springs, Colorado 80901
(Membership inquiries should be directed to the General Secretary)

Numismatic Publications

Weekly and bi-weekly (every two weeks) tabloid-type publications fill another need for the collector, that of providing an up-to-date view of hobby activity. Dealer advertising offering coins, paper money and related numismatic items can be found in abundance, as well as special sections devoted to features and events of interest. Many coin shops carry these informative periodicals, or subscriptions may be entered by writing directly to the publications listed below:

Canadian Coin News
103 Lakeshore Rd., Suite 202
St. Catharines, Ontario
Canada L2N 2T6
(Bi-Weekly, sample copy $1.00)

World Coin News
700 East State Street
Iola, Wisconsin 54990
(Weekly, sample copy $1.00)

2
DECIMAL COINAGE 1858 TO DATE

Although the early 19th century coinage of commerce in all the British North American colonies was ostensibly that of England, the actual coins were scarce and issues of a number of countries were used. They were primarily those of France, Portugal, Spain, Mexico and the United States. Furthermore, as outlined in other chapters, large numbers of privately issued base metal pieces circulated for pence and halfpence. The need for unified currencies was clear-cut. The ultimate result was a distinctive decimal currency for each of the colonies.

The principal leader in the Province of Canada's struggle for its own coinage was Sir Francis Hincks, Inspector General (1848-54), Prime Minister (1851-54) and later Minister of Finance for the Dominion of Canada. Legislation establishing the Province's decimal coinage consisted of several steps that took almost a decade. Initially there was strong British opposition.

In 1850 an act was passed which empowered the provincial government to have its own distinctive coinage, struck in denominations of pounds, shillings and pence. The British government disallowed the act, however, partly because it was felt that the regulation of coinage was the prerogative of the Sovereign and the use of English currency facilitated trade with the Mother Country.

In a second act passed in 1851, the Canadians continued the fight for control of their own currency. For the first time a decimal system was suggested; public accounts were to be kept in dollars, cents and mils. The English Treasury also viewed the second act with disfavour, but did not disallow it. Instead, it was proposed that the province have its own pound and that it could be divided into decimal units if necessary.

The 1851 act paved the way for an act of 1853, which established a Canadian currency consisting of pounds-shillings-pence and dollars-cents-mils, the public accounts being kept in the latter. The striking of coins was left to the Queen's prerogative and none was issued under this act.

Finally, in 1857, the dollar alone was established as the unit of money and all accounts, public and government, were to be kept in dollars and cents. The Canadian dollar was given the same intrinsic value as the U.S. dollar; the English sovereign (pound sterling) was worth $4.86⅔. An issue of decimal coins followed in 1858-59.

LARGE CENTS
Victoria, Province of Canada, 1858-1859

Diameter: 25.40 mm; weight: 4.54 grams; composition: .950 copper, .040 tin, .010 zinc; edge: plain

G: *Braid worn through*
VG: *No detail in braid around ear*
F: *Segments of braid begin to merge into one another*
VF: *Braid is clear but not sharp*
EF: *Braid is slightly worn but generally sharp and clear*

The basic obverse design, a bust separated from the legend by a beaded circle, is said to have been copied from the Napoleon III bronze coinages of France (1853-70). The Canadian obverse shows a very youthful Victoria with a laurel wreath in her hair and was designed and engraved by the Royal Mint's famed engraver, Leonard C. Wyon.

The reverse was also by L.C. Wyon and has a serpentine vine with 16 maple leaves. There are numerous slight variations involving recutting of some of the leaf stems or the vine stalk.

The coins were conceived to be used also as convenient units of measure; the diameter is exactly 1 inch and 100 (unworn) pieces weigh 1 avoirdupois pound. Nevertheless, they were not very popular at first and were discounted, sometimes by as much as 20%, to get them into circulation.

Wide, bold 9
over 8

Early form   Late form
Narrow 9

No. 1   No. 2
Double-punched narrow 9
(No. 1 is often erroneously
called a narrow 9 over 8)

1859 date varieties. Although the Province of Canada placed its single order for cents in 1858, insufficient time forced the Royal Mint to strike the bulk of the coins in 1859. Two distinctly different 9 punches were used for dating the dies. A number of dies (at least 11) were originally dated 1858 and have the final 8 altered by overpunching with a wide, bold 9, this 9 was apparently used only for overdating (we cannot confirm the claims that the wide 9 occurs on a non overdate). A second figure, used for non-overdates, is narrow and initially rather delicate. Some narrow 9 specimens have the 9 somewhat broadened; these are thought to be from dies dated late in the issue when the narrow 9 punch had distorted from extensive use (rather than two different styles of narrow 9 punches being used). Both the delicate and broadened narrow 9s are illustrated because the latter is sometimes confused with the wide, bold 9. The so-called "narrow 9 over 8" is not a true overdate but a double-punched narrow 9 with a small piece out of the die at the lower front of the 9s. A second double-punched narrow 9 has traces of the original 9 to the left of the second figure. The latter double-punchings are considered trivial by these cataloguers; however, they are included because of the current wide acceptance by collectors.

Date	Qty. Minted	G-4	VG-8	F-12	VF-20	EF-40	AU-50	UNC-60	BU-63
1858 421,000		30.00	50.00	65.00	90.00	125.00	175.00	300.00	700.00
1859 (incl. all var.) 10,000,000									
9 over 8, wide 9		20.00	35.00	45.00	66.00	90.00	130.00	225.00	450.00
narrow 9, all forms		1.25	2.50	3.50	6.00	10.00	20.00	45.00	225.00
dble-punch, narrow 9 .. No. 1		100.00	250.00	350.00	500.00	800.00	1,100	1,600	2,200
dble-punch, narrow 9 .. No. 2		30.00	45.00	60.00	85.00	120.00	175.00	250.00	500.00

Victoria, Dominion of Canada, 1876-1901

Diameter: 25.40 mm; weight: 5.67 grams; composition: .955 copper, .030 tin, .015 zinc; edge: plain

G: *Hair over ear worn through*
VG: *No details in hair over the ear*
F: *Strands of hair over the ear begin to run together*
VF: *Hair and jewels are clear but no longer sharp*
EF: *Hair over the ear is sharp and clear. Jewels in diadem must show sharply and clearly*

Because of the large issue of 1858-59 cents by the Province of Canada and later the Dominion of Canada governments, this denomination was not issued again until nearly ten years after Confederation. The Provincial cents had been unpopular because of their weight, so the Dominion cents were struck in the same weight as the British halfpenny.

The obverse type of the Dominion cents was changed to one with a diademed Queen, although a pattern piece with the 1876 reverse and 1858-59 obverse suggests that the laureated type may have been considered. The diademed obverse type is composed of four distinctive portrait varieties, differing in the facial and certain other details. The portrait for the initial obverse (Obv. 1) was created by modifying one of those used for the Jamaican halfpenny. Later obverses were revisions to those previously used: Obv. 2 being derived from Obv. 1, while Obv. 3 and 4 were derived from Obv. 2. All designs were by L.C. Wyon except for Obv. 4, which was probably by G.W. de Saulles. The portraits are distinguished as follows:

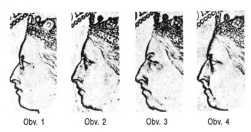

Obv. 1   Obv. 2   Obv. 3   Obv. 4

Obverse 1: Generally youthful appearance: rounded chin and prominent lips.
Obverse 2: Somewhat aged facial features: double chin and repressed upper lip.
Obverse 3: Even more aged features: double chin with a square front and depression over the eye.
Obverse 4: Smooth chin restored, but has repressed upper lip.

In addition to the portrait differences there are also several variations of lettering style, the most obvious of which occurs in association with Obv. 3. When the obverse was used in 1890, it had a normal (or nealy so) legend; however, the 1891-92 Obv. 3s *all* have a legend with more coarse style letters punched over the original.

Three major reverse varieties exist. The first (1876-82) is identical to the 1858-59 issues, except for some re-cutting of the leaf stems and vine stalk. The second has a new vine containing wider leaves with less venation. The third (1891-1901) has yet another vine containing narrow leaves with incuse venation. Each reverse was from a separate reducing machine model; the first two were by L.C. Wyon and the third is thought to be by G.W. De Saulles. There are numerous re-cuttings of the stems and stalks of the vines on the first and third reverses.

Date	Qty. Minted	G-4	VG-8	F-12	VF-20	EF-40	AU-50	UNC-60	BU-63
Provincial Leaves Reverse (1878-1882)									
1876H .. obv. 1 ... 4,000,000		1.50	2.75	4.00	6.50	10.00	25.00	70.00	300.00
1881H .. obv. 1 ... 2,000,000		2.00	3.50	6.00	9.00	15.00	35.00	85.00	275.00
1882H .. obv. 1, 2	4,000,000	1.00	2.50	3.50	5.50	10.00	20.00	45.00	175.00

Large Leaves Reverse 1884-1891   Small Leaves Reverse 1891-1901

Date	Qty. Minted	G-4	VG-8	F-12	VF-20	EF-40	AU-50	UNC-60	BU-63
Large Leaves Reverse (1884-1891)									
1884 .... obv. 1, 2	2,500,000	2.00	3.00	4.50	7.50	25.00	20.00	65.00	250.00
1886 .... obv. 1, 2	1,500,000	3.00	5.00	7.00	12.00	18.00	40.00	90.00	300.00
1887 .... obv. 2 ...	1,500,000	2.25	4.00	5.50	8.50	15.00	25.00	65.00	225.00
1888 .... obv. 2 ...	4,000,000	1.25	2.00	3.50	5.00	9.00	20.00	45.00	175.00
1890H .. obv. 3 ...	1,000,000	3.50	7.00	12.00	18.00	30.00	60.00	150.00	500.00
1891 .... obv. 2, 3									
large date	1,452,500	4.00	6.00	10.00	16.00	30.00	60.00	160.00	450.00
small date	inc. above	40.00	70.00	90.00	125.00	175.00	250.00	450.00	1,400

Large date   Small Date

Small Leaves Reverse (1891-1901)

Note: All large cents with small leaves reverse, including those dates 1891, have a small date.

Date	Qty. Minted	G-4	VG-8	F-12	VF-20	EF-40	AU-50	UNC-60	BU-63
1891 .... obv. 2, 3 incl. above		30.00	50.00	65.00	90.00	130.00	150.00	300.00	900.00
1892 .... obv. 2,3,4	1,200,000	2.00	4.00	7.00	11.00	17.00	30.00	70.00	200.00
1893 .... obv. 4 ...	2,000,000	1.75	2.50	4.00	7.00	12.00	25.00	45.00	160.00
1894 .... obv. 4 ...	1,000,000	5.00	8.00	12.00	18.00	30.00	65.00	150.00	350.00
1895 .... obv. 4 ...	1,200,000	2.50	5.00	8.00	12.00	18.00	40.00	90.00	275.00
1896 .... obv. 4 ...	2,000,000	1.50	2.00	3.50	5.50	8.00	20.00	45.00	160.00
1897 .... obv. 4 ...	1,500,000	1.50	2.50	4.50	6.50	10.00	25.00	55.00	180.00
1898H .. obv. 4 ...	1,000,000	3.00	5.00	8.00	12.00	20.00	35.00	90.00	350.00
1899 .... obv. 4 ...	2,400,000	1.50	2.50	4.50	6.00	8.00	18.00	45.00	160.00
1900 .... obv. 4 ...	1,000,000	5.00	8.00	12.00	18.00	30.00	45.00	100.00	300.00
1900H .. obv. 4 ...	2,600,000	1.50	2.00	3.50	5.50	7.00	18.00	40.00	150.00
1901 .... obv. 4 .'..	4,100,000	1.25	2.00	3.00	5.00	7.00	15.00	35.00	125.00

On the 1898 and 1900 Heaton
issues, the H mark is below the
bottom leaf in the wreath.

Edward VII, Large Cents, 1902-1910

Diameter: 25.40mm; weight 5.67 grams; composition; .955 copper, .030 tin, .015 zinc; edge: plain

G: *Band of crown worn through*
VG: *Band of crown worn through at*
    highest point
F: *Jewels in band of crown will be blurred*
VF: *Band of crown is still clear;*
    no longer sharp
EF: *Band of crown is slightly worn but*
    generally sharp and clear

A single obverse, designed and engraved by G.W. De Saulles (DES below bust),
was employed for the entire series.

The reverse was a continuation of the small leaves Victorian variety.

Date	Qty. Minted	G-4	VG-8	F-12	VF-20	EF-40	AU-50	UNC-60	BU-63
1902 3,000,000		1.00	1.50	3.00	43.00	6.50	10.00	25.00	65.00
1903 4,000,000		1.00	1.75	3.00	4.00	6.50	12.00	35.00	85.00
1904 2,500,000		1.25	2.50	4.00	6.00	8.00	15.00	45.00	120.00
1905 2,000,000		3.50	4.75	6.50	9.00	12.00	22.50	55.00	175.00
1906 4,100,000		1.00	1.75	3.00	4.00	6.50	12.00	35.00	80.00
1907 2,400,000		1.50	3.00	4.50	6.50	9.00	15.00	60.00	150.00

On the 1907 Heaton issue the mint mark is below the date.

Date	Qty. Minted	G-4	VG-8	F-12	VF-20	EF-40	AU-50	UNC-60	BU-63
1907H 800,000		7.00	12.00	17.50	25.00	37.50	60.00	130.00	400.00
1908 2,401,506		2.00	3.50	5.00	6.50	9.50	15.00	40.00	120.00
1909 3,973,339		1.00	1.75	5.00	4.00	6.00	12.00	30.00	85.00
1910 5,146,487		1.00	1.50	2.50	3.50	5.50	10.00	30.00	85.00

George V, Large Cents, 1911-1920

Diameter: 25.40 mm; weight 5.67 grams; composition: .955 copper, .030 tin, .015 zinc; edge: plain

G: *Band of crown worn through*
VG: *Band of crown worn through at highest point*
F: *Jewels in band of crown will be blurred*
VF: *Band of crown is still clear; no longer sharp*
EF: *Band of crown is slightly worn but generally sharp and clear*

The original obverse, used for the 1911 issues of the 1¢ to 50¢, bore a legend lacking the words DEI GRATIA ("by the grace of God") or some abbreviation for them. The public complained, calling these coins "Godless," and in 1912 a modified legend containing DEI GRA: was introduced. Both varieties were derived from a portrait model of the King by Sir E.B. MacKennal (initials B.M on truncation).

The reverse, although resembling previous designs, is completely new. The engraver was W.H.J. Blakemore.

Godless Obverse (1911)

1911 4,663,486		1.00	1.75	2.50	3.50	5.50	15.00	30.00	100.00

Modified Obverse Legend (1912-1920)

1912 5,107,642		.60	1.25	2.00	3.00	5.50	12.00	30.00	80.00
1913 5,735,405		.60	1.25	2.00	3.00	5.50	12.00	30.00	75.00
1914 3,405,958		.90	1.75	2.50	3.50	7.00	18.00	45.00	160.00

Date	Qty. Minted	G-4	VG-8	F-12	VF-20	EF-40	AU-50	UNC-60	BU-63
1915	4,932,134	.75	1.25	2.00	3.00	5.00	16.00	30.00	100.00
1916	11,022,367	.60	1.00	1.25	1.75	3.50	10.00	25.00	80.00
1917	11,899,254	.50	.75	1.00	1.50	2.50	7.50	16.00	55.00
1918	12,970,798	.50	.75	1.00	1.50	2.50	7.50	16.00	55.00
1919	11,279,634	.50	.75	1.00	1.50	2.50	7.50	16.00	55.00
1920	6,762,247	.50	.75	1.00	1.75	3.00	8.50	19.00	65.00

SMALL CENTS
George V, Small Cents, 1920-1936

Diameter: 19.05 mm; weight: 3.24 grams; thickness: 1.65 mm;
composition: .955 copper, .030 tin, .015 zinc; edge: plain

G: Band of crown worn through
VG: Band of crown worn through at highest point
F: Jewels in band of crown will be blurred
VF: Band of crown is still clear; no longer sharp
EF: Band of crown is slightly worn but generally
sharp and clear

In order to conserve copper, the large cent was replaced in 1920 with one of smaller size, like that of the United States. The obverse bust was MacKennal's familiar design and the reverse was a new design by Fred Lewis. The master matrices were prepared in London by W.H.J. Blakemore.

Date	Qty. Minted	G-4	VG-8	F-12	VF-20	EF-40	AU-50	UNC-60	BU-63
1920	15,483,923	.20	.30	.75	2.00	4.00	8.00	15.00	65.00
1921	7,601,627	.50	1.00	2.00	4.00	8.50	12.50	25.00	90.00
1922	1,243,635	8.00	14.50	17.00	25.00	40.00	80.00	175.00	450.00
1923	1,019,002	15.00	23.00	28.00	40.00	60.00	125.00	300.00	900.00
1924	1,593,195	4.50	6.50	8.50	12.00	20.00	40.00	140.00	350.00
1925	1,000,622	13.50	20.00	25.00	35.00	50.00	90.00	225.00	750.00
1926	2,143,372	1.75	3.50	5.00	8.00	15.00	40.00	100.00	300.00
1927	3,553,928	.90	1.50	2.00	3.75	8.00	17.50	40.00	175.00
1928	9,144,860	.25	.30	.50	2.00	3.00	7.00	18.00	70.00
1929	12,159,840	.25	.30	.50	2.00	3.00	7.00	18.00	70.00
1930	2,538,613	1.50	2.50	3.00	4.50	8.50	17.50	45.00	165.00
1931	3,842,776	1.00	1.50	2.00	3.50	5.50	12.50	35.00	125.00
1932	21,316,190	.25	.30	.60	1.00	2.75	7.00	18.00	70.00
1933	12,079,310	.25	.30	.60	1.00	2.75	7.00	18.00	70.00
1934	7,042,358	.25	.30	.60	2.00	3.00	7.00	18.00	70.00
1935	7,526,400	.25	.30	.60	2.00	3.00	7.00	18.00	70.00
1936	8,768,769	.25	.30	.60	2.00	3.00	7.00	18.00	70.00

George VI Issue Struck in Name of George V

King George V died early in 1936 and was succeeded by his son Edward VIII, whose portrait was planned for introduction on 1937 coinage. Edward abdicated late in 1936 and his younger brother was crowned as George VI. The Royal Mint in London did not have time to prepare new Canadian George VI obverse matrices and punches for shipment to Ottawa by the beginning of 1937. This led to an emergency situation because of a pressing demand for 1-, 10- and 25-cent coins, and in order to meet the emergency, these were struck using George V dies dated 1936. To denote that the coins were actually struck in 1937 a small round depression was punched into each die, causing a raised dot to appear in that position on the coins. On the cent the dot is centered below the date.

Of the three denominations thus made, only the 25¢ is readily available (in circulated condition), while the two others are known only in mint state and are very rare. Obviously if all had been released they would be known in greater quantity today; therefore it seems reasonable to explain the situation in one of two ways: (a) the 1¢ and 10¢ were not struck with the dots (it has often been suggested that the depression in these dies filled with extraneous matter or that they were never punched into the dies in the first place), or (b) they were made with dotes but not issued. The first explanation is quite doubtful because (1) a former mint employee who worked in the press room in early 1937 maintains that all three denominations were struck with dots, (2) the known 10¢ specimens have a dot larger than that on the 25¢, yet the "clogging" theory would require that the 25¢ dies did not fill up while all the rest did, and (3) one of the dot cents was found in the Pyx box, a container where coins taken at random from production runs are reserved for assay.

In view of the above, these authors suggest serious consideration of the possibility that the dot 1¢ and 10¢ pieces were struck but never issued (i.e., melted).

The physical specifications are as on the George V issues.

Date	Quantity Minted		
1936 raised dot below date .... (originally: 678,823)		Rare	5 known

George VI, Small Cents, 1937-1952

Diameter: 19.05 mm; weight: 3.24 grams; thickness: 1.65 mm; composition: (1937-41) .955 copper, .030 tin, .015 zinc; (1942-52) .980 copper, .005 tin, .015 zinc; edge: plain

VG: *No detail in hair above ear*
F: *Only slight detail in hair above ear*
VF: *Where not worn, hair is clear but not sharp*
EF: *Slight wear in hair over ear*

The obverses of the George VI issues are unique in that the monarch is bareheaded. The original obverse legend contains the phrase ET IND:IMP: (for *Et Indiae Imperator*, meaning "and Emperor of India"). Beginning with coins dated 1948, the phrase was omitted from the King's titles, India having gained independence from England during the previous year. Both varieties were derived from a portrait model by T.H. Paget (H.P. under bust).

In keeping with a government decision to modernize the designs, the simple but compelling "maple twig" design by G.E. Kruger-Gray (K•G under the right leaf) was adopted for the cent.

1947 maple leaf. Some specimens of all denominations dated 1947 have a tiny maple leaf after the date, to denote that they were actually struck in 1948. Later that year, while the Royal Canadian Mint was awaiting arrival of the new obverse matrices and punches bearing the modified legend from the Royal Mint in London, a pressing demand for all denom inations arose. In order to meet the demand, coins were struck with 1947 obverse and reverse dies, with the leaf added to indicate the incorrect date. After the new obverse punches and matrices arrived later in the year, normal 1948 coins were put into production.

Date	Qty. Minted	VG-8	F-12	VF-20	EF-40	AU-50	Unc-60	BU-63
"ET IND : IMP :" Obverse (1937-1947)								
1937	10,090,231	.40	.60	1.50	3.00	3.50	4.00	10.00
1938	18,365,608	.25	.35	1.50	1.00	2.75	5.00	12.00
1939	21,600,319	.25	.35	1.50	1.00	2.75	4.00	10.00
1940	85,740,532	.15	.20	.50	.75	2.00	3.50	9.00
1941	56,336,011	.15	.25	1.00	1.00	4.50	20.00	60.00
1942	76,113,708	.15	.25	1.00	1.00	4.50	15.00	45.00
1943	89,111,969	.15	.25	1.00	1.00	3.00	7.00	20.00
1944	44,131,216	.30	.40	.75	1.25	5.00	20.00	60.00
1945	77,268,591	.15	.20	.55	.75	1.00	3.00	8.00
1946	56,662,071	.15	.20	.55	.75	1.00	3.00	8.00
1947	31,093,901	.15	.20	.55	.75	1.25	3.50	9.50
1947 maple leaf	43,855,448	.15	.20	.55	.75	1.00	3.00	8.00

Modified Obverse Legend (1948-1952)

Date	Qty. Minted	VG-8	F-12	VF-20	EF-40	AU-50	Unc-60	BU-63
1948	25,767,779	.15	.35	.65	1.00	3.00	5.00	15.00
1949	33,128,933	.10	.20	.50	1.00	1.75	3.00	7.00
1950	60,444,992	.10	.20	.50	1.00	1.75	3.00	7.00
1951	80,430,379	.10	.20	.50	1.00	1.75	3.00	7.00
1952	67,631,736	.10	.20	.50	1.00	1.75	3.00	6.00

Elizabeth II, Laureate Bust Cents, 1953-1964

Diameter: 19.05 mm; weight: 3.24 grams; thickness: 1.65 mm;
composition: .980 copper, .005 tin, .015 zinc; edge: plain

F: *Leaves worn almost through;
shoulder fold indistinct*
VF: *Leaves considerably worn;
shoulder fold must be clear*
EF: *Laurel leaves somewhat worn*

No shoulder fold
1953-55

Note style of letters, relation to denticles.
The 'I' points between two denticles.

The initial obverse for the 1953 issue had a high relief, laureate portrait of the Queen by Mrs. Mary Gillick (M.G. on truncation) which did not strike up well on the coins. Later in the year, the relief was lowered and the hair and shoulder detail re-engraved by Thomas Shingles, chief engraver of the Royal Canadian Mint. Two lines at the shoulder, representing a fold in the gown, are clear on the second variety but almost missing on the first. (There has been a tendency to erroneously term them "shoulder strap" and "no shoulder strap," respectively, but even on the original portrait the ridge representing the top of the gown can be seen high above the shoulder). The two varieties also differ in the positioning of the legend relative to the rim denticles and in the styles of some of the letters.

The reverse throughout the 1953-64 period remained basically the same as that for George VI.

1954-55 No shoulder fold. Through an oversight, a small number of 1954 proof-like sets included cents struck from the rejected no shoulder fold obverse. An even smaller number of regular 1955 cents were also struck with this obverse.

With shoulder fold
1953-64

Note style of letters, relation to denticles
The 'I' points to a denticle.

Date	Qty. Minted	F-12	VF-20	EF-40	AU-50	UNC-60	BU-63
1953 no shoulder fold 67,806,016		.25	.35	.50	.75	1.00	3.00
with shoulder fold ... included above		2.00	3.00	5.00	10.00	20.00	45.00
1954 no shoulder fold 22,181,760		(proof-like only)				175.00	350.00
1954 with shoulder fold ... included above		.35	.50	1.00	2.00	4.00	9.00
1955 no shoulder fold 56,403,193		100.00	225.00	350.00	450.00	750.00	1,500
with shoulder fold ... included above		.15	.25	.35	.50	.75	2.00
1956 78,685,535		.15	.25	.35	.50	.75	1.25
1957 100,601,792		.15	.25	.35	.50	.75	1.25
1958 59,385,679		.15	.25	.35	.50	.75	1.25
1959 83,615,343		.10	.15	.25	.30	.50	1.00
1960 75,772,775		.10	.15	.25	.30	.40	1.00
1961 139,598,404		.10	.15	.25	.30	.40	.75
1962 227,244,069		.10	.15	.20	.25	.30	.50
1963 279,076,334		.10	.15	.20	.25	.30	.50
1964 484,655,322		.10	.15	.20	.25	.30	.50

Elizabeth II, Tiara Obverse, 1965-1978

In 1965 an obverse with a new style portrait by Arnold Machin was introduced. The Queen has more mature facial features and is wearing a tiara. Two obverse varieties exist for 1965: the first has a flat field and small rim beads, while the second has a concave field (sloping up toward the rim) and large rim beads. The second obverse was instituted because of the unacceptably short die life with the first. The large beads obverse was replaced because of the tendency for the rim detail in the dies to wear too rapidly. So, starting in 1966, the obverse has a less concave field and small rim beads. As with the 1953 issues, the 1965-66 varieties can be distinguished by the positioning of the legend relative to the rim beads.

Small beads   Large beads
Detail at 'A' in 'REGINA'

Pointed 5 (at top)   Blunt 5

1965 date and combinational varieties. Coupled with the two 1965 obverses in all combinations were two reverses, having trivially different 5s in the dates. The varieties of 5 have become popular, but the authors of this catalogue do not consider them significant.

Date	Qty. Minted	UNC-60	BU-63
1965 small beads, pointed 5 (Variety 1) 304,441,082		.75	3.00
small beads, blunt 5 (Variety 2) .... incl. above		.15	.35
large beads, blunt 5 (Variety 3) .... incl. above		.30	.60
large beads, pointed 5 (Variety 4) .... incl. above		25.00	65.00
1966 183,644,388		.10	.25

Confederation Centenary, 1967

All denominations for 1967 bore special reverses to commemorate the 1867 confederation of the provinces of Canada, Nova Scotia and New Brunswick to form the Dominion of Canada. The designer was Alex Colville, the device for the 1-cent being a rock dove in flight.

Date	Qty. Minted	UNC-60	BU-60
1967 Confederation commemorative 345,140,645		.15	.30

Maple Twig Reverse Resumed, 1968 -

	Qty. Minted	UNC-60	BU-60
1968 329,695,772		.10	.25
1969 335,240,929		.10	.25
1970 311,145,010		.10	.25
1971 298,228,936		.10	.25
1972 451,304,591		.10	.25
1973 457,059,852		.10	.25
1974 692,058,489		.10	.25
1975 642,318,000		.10	.25
1976 701,122,890		.10	.25
1977 453,050,666		.10	.25

Reduced Thickness, 1978-1979

Diameter: 19.05 mm; weight: 3.24 grams; thickness: 1.52 mm;
composition: .980 copper, .0175 zinc, .0025 other; edge: plain

	Qty. Minted	UNC-60	BU-60
1978 911,170,647		.10	.25

Elizabeth II, Modified Tiara Obverse, 1979-1989

Beginning with 1979, the portrait of the Queen was made smaller. This was done to standardize our coinage, making the size of the portrait proportional to the diameter of the coin, regardless of denomination.

Date	Qty. Minted	UNC-60	BU-60
1979	754,394,064	.10	.20

Reduced Weight, 1980-1981

Diameter: 19.00 mm; weight 2.80 grams; thickness: 1.45 mm;
composition: .980 copper, .0175 zinc, .0025 other; edge: plain

Pattern pieces dated 1979 were struck in 1978 with a reduced weight and a diameter of 16 mm. This action was in response to the rising cost of copper which was causing the 1-cent coin to be produced at a loss. However, the 16 mm cent was cancelled when it was found that this was the same diameter used for tokens by the Toronto Transit Commission. The 1979 cent was of the old weight and diameter. In 1980, a new decreased diameter coin was introduced with a decreased thickness and weight.

1980	912,052,318	.10	.15
1981	1,209,468,500	.10	.15

Elizabeth II, 12-Sided Cent, 1982 -

Diameter: 19.1 mm; weight: 2.50 grams; thickness: 1.45 mm;
composition: .980 copper, .0175 zinc, .0025 other; edge: plain

Beginning in 1982 the shape of the 1-cent coin was changed from round to 12-sided to make it easier for the blind to indentify. The new size also meant a reduction in weight.

Date	Qty. Minted	UNC-60	BU-60
1982	911,011,000	.10	.15
1983	975,510,000	.10	.15
1984	838,225,000	.10	.15
1985	782,752,500	.10	.15
1986	740,335,000	.10	.15
1987	774,549,000	.10	.15
1988	482,676,752	.10	.15
1989	1,077,347,200	.10	.15

Elizabeth II, Diadem Obverse, 1990 -

The first effigy designed by a Canadian for use on Canadian coins was introduced on the obverse of all Canadian issues for 1990. The design depicts a more contemporary portrait of the Queen wearing a necklace and earrings. The elaborate crown, last seen on Victorian issues, replaced the tiara used on previous issues. The obverse was designed by Dora dePédery-HUNT.

Date	Qty. Minted	Unc-60	BU-60
1990	218,035,000	.10	.15
1991	696,629,000	.10	.15

125th Anniversary of Confederation, 1992

To celebrate the 125th anniversary of Confederation, all circulation coins issued in 1992 bear the date "1867-1992."

1992	N/A	.10	.15
1993	N/A	.10	.15
1994	N/A	.10	.15

5 CENTS
Victoria, 5 Cents Silver, 1858-1901
Diameter: 15.494 mm; weight: 1.167 grams;
composition: .925 silver, .075 copper; edge: reeded

G: *Braid around ear worn through*
VG: *No detail in braid around ear*
F: *Segments of braid begin to merge into one another*
VF: *Braid is clear but not sharp*
EF: *Braid is slightly worn but generally sharp and clear*

Five different portraits of Victoria were employed for this denomination, each differing from the others in some facial features and in certain other respects. Except for the initial portrait, all varieties were designed and engraved by L.C. Wyon. None of these was a serious attempt to accurately portray the Queen as she looked at the time.

In some years two busts were coupled with a given date reverse. These are most easily distinguished as follows:

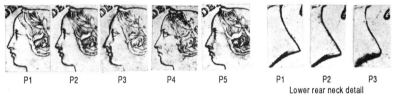

P1   P2   P3   P4   P5   P1   P2   P3
                                               Lower rear neck detail

P1 vs P2: P1 has a convex lower rear neck profile and an incuse hairline above the eye, while P2 has a straight lower rear neck profile and lacks the incuse hairline.

P2 vs P3: P2 has a prominent forehead, a smooth chin and a slightly rounded point at the lower right corner of the neck, while P3 has a recessed forehead, a slight double chin and a very blunted lower right neck corner.

P2 vs P5: P2 has a prominent upper lip and a smooth chin, while P5 has a repressed upper lip, generally "droopy" mouth and an irregular chin.

The basic reverse device consists of crossed maple boughs, tied at the bottom by a ribbon, and separated at the top by St. Edward's crown. Three major reverse varieties exist. The first (1858, 1870) has an unusually wide rim, long denticles and a crown with both bottom corners protruding. The second (1870-81, 1890-1901), derived from the first, has somewhat altered leaves, a narrow rim, short rim denticles and a crown on which only the left lower corner protrudes. The third variety (1882-89) is like the second, with an additional (22nd) maple leaf added to the lower right of the wreath. Sub varieties of all three reverses are known; for example, the 22nd leaf on the 1882 issue differs from and was added independently of that on the 1883-89 issues. The major, and most of the minor, varieties were designed and engraved by L.C. Wyon.

Wide rim,
long denticles

Small date

Large date over small date

5 Cents

Date	Qty. Minted	G-4	VG-8	F-12	VF-20	EF-40	AU-50	MS-60	MS-63

Wide Rim Reverse (1858, 1870)

Date	Qty. Minted	G-4	VG-8	F-12	VF-20	EF-40	AU-50	MS-60	MS-63
1858 small date P1	 500,000	9.00	18.00	30.00	50.00	75.00	125.00	300.00	750.00
lg. over sm. date .. P1	... incl. above	90.00	160.00	275.00	450.00	625.00	700.00	1,450	3,000
1870 .... P1	 2,800,000	8.00	15.00	25.00	50.00	80.00	140.00	325.00	850.00

Narrow rim,
short denticles

21 leaves
1870-81, 1890-1901

Narrow Rim, 21-Leaf Reverse (1870-1881)

Date	Qty. Minted	G-4	VG-8	F-12	VF-20	EF-40	AU-50	MS-60	MS-63
1870 .... P2	...incl. above	8.00	15.00	25.00	45.00	75.00	125.00	300.00	750.00
1871 .... P2	 1,400,000	8.00	15.00	25.00	45.00	75.00	125.00	300.00	800.00
1872H P2	 2,000,000	6.00	11.00	20.00	40.00	75.00	140.00	325.00	950.00

Plain 4, small date

Crosslet 4, large date

Small date

Large date

Date	Qty. Minted	G-4	VG-8	F-12	VF-20	EF-40	AU-50	MS-60	MS-63
1874H plain 4 ..... P2	.... 1.800.000	12.00	25.00	50.00	90.00	150.00	250.00	650.00	1,300
crosslet 4 ... P2	... incl. above	9.00	18.00	35.00	65.00	100.00	200.00	500.00	1,200
1875H small date .. P2	... incl. above	75.00	125.00	200.00	350.00	600.00	850.00	2,000	4,500
large date .. P2	... incl. above	85.00	160.00	250.00	450.00	700.00	1,000	2,500	5,500
1880H .... P2, 3 ..	3,000,000	3.00	5.00	12.00	25.00	50.00	90.00	225.00	700.00
1881H .... P 3	... 1,500,000	3.50	6.00	14.00	28.00	55.00	100.00	250.00	750.00

Note: 1874H and 1875H mintage figures were combined through a mint error.

22nd leaf added
1882-1889

Narrow Rim, 22-Leaf Reverse (1882-1889)

Date	Qty. Minted	G-4	VG-8	F-12	VF-20	EF-40	AU-50	MS-60	MS-63
1882H P4	 1,000,000	4.00	8.00	16.00	32.00	65.00	125.00	300.00	1,000
1883H P5	 600,000	12.00	22.00	45.00	75.00	125.00	250.00	700.00	1,700
1884 .... P5	 200,000	75.00	125.00	175.00	275.00	650.00	1,350	3,000	6,000

Large tail 5   Small tail 5   Small 6   Large 6

Date	Qty. Minted	G-4	VG-8	F-12	VF-20	EF-40	AU-50	MS-60	MS-63
1885 Large tail 5 ... P5	 1,000,000	7.00	12.00	24.00	50.00	90.00	200.00	600.00	1,750
small tail 5 ... P5	... incl. above	7.00	12.00	24.00	50.00	90.00	200.00	600.00	1,750
1886 small 6 ...... P5	... 1,700,000	3.50	6.00	13.00	25.00	60.00	150.00	350.00	750.00
large 6 .... P5	... incl. above	3.50	6.00	13.00	25.00	60.00	150.00	350.00	750.00
1887 .... P5	 500,000	11.00	20.50	35.00	65.00	120.00	225.00	450.00	1,000
1888 .... P5	.. 2,200,000	3.00	5.00	11.00	22.00	45.00	80.00	225.00	450.00
1889 .... P5	... incl. above	12.50	25.00	45.00	80.00	150.00	275.00	650.00	1,400

21-Leaf Reverse Resumed (1890-1901)

Date	Qty. Minted	G-4	VG-8	F-12	VF-20	EF-40	AU-50	MS-60	MS-63
1890H P5	 1,000,000	4.00	7.00	14.00	30.00	65.00	125.00	300.00	750.00
1891 .... P5, 2 ..	1,800,000	2.50	4.00	7.00	15.00	35.00	70.00	150.00	400.00

Date		Qty. Minted	G-4	VG-8	F-12	VF-20	EF-40	AU-50	MS-60	MS-63
1892	P5, 2	860,000	3.75	6.50	13.00	27.00	65.00	150.00	325.00	750.00
1893	P2	1,700,000	2.50	4.00	7.00	15.00	35.00	70.00	150.00	400.00
1894	P2	500,000	10.00	18.00	35.00	65.00	120.00	225.00	450.00	1,100
1896	P2	1,500,000	3.00	5.00	10.00	20.00	40.00	80.00	200.00	450.00
1897	P2	1,319,283	3.00	5.00	10.00	20.00	40.00	75.00	175.00	400.00
1898	P2	580,717	6.00	12.00	22.00	45.00	85.00	175.00	300.00	750.00
1899	P2	3,000,000	2.50	4.00	7.00	12.00	35.00	60.00	140.00	350.00

Large date, wide 0s   Small date, narrow 0s

Date		Qty. Minted	G-4	VG-8	F-12	VF-20	EF-40	AU-50	MS-60	MS-63
1900 large date	P2	1,800,000	12.00	25.00	45.00	75.00	150.00	250.00	500.00	1,250
small date	P2	incl. above	3.00	5.00	8.00	14.00	35.00	70.00	150.00	400.00
1901	P2	2,000,000	2.50	4.00	7.00	12.00	30.00	60.00	140.00	350.00

Edward VII, 5 Cents Silver, 1902-1910

Diameter: 15.494 mm; weight: 1.167 grams; composition: .925 silver, .075 copper; edge: reeded

G: *Band of crown worn through*
VG: *Band of crown worn through at highest point*
F: *Jewels in band of crown will be blurred*
VF: *Band of crown is still clear but no longer sharp*
EF: *Band of crown slightly worn but generally sharp and clear*

A single obverse, designed and engraved by G.W. De Saulles (DES. below bust), was used for the entire reign.

With the initiation of a new series, two basic changes were to be made in the reverse designs. First, the word CANADA was to be transferred from the obverse to the reverse legend. Second, the heraldic St. Edward's crown (depressed arches), used on English coinages throughout most of the 19th century and on the Victorian Canadian issues, was to be replaced with the Imperial State crown (raised arches). These objectives were realized on all silver denominations except the five cents, where a shortage of time at the Royal Mint forced a compromise. The 1902 design (London and Heaton) utilized the unaltered crown and wreath from the second variety Victorian reverse, with the date and modified legend added. The presence of the outmoded St. Edward's crown caused the public to surmise that an error had been made and the 1902 coinage was consequently hoarded.

Beginning with the 1903 Heaton issue, the Imperial State crown was incorporated into the five cent reverse design. Again the wreath was derived from the second variety of the Victorian reverse, in this instance with slight retouching of some of the leaves. The designer and engraver for the 1902 and probably the 1903H reverses was G.W. De Saulles.

A third major reverse variety, introduced for the 1903 London issue, is from a new reducing machine model, and as such represents the first completely new reverse since 1858. The designer is presumably W.H.J. Blakemore. This design, with 22 leaves, was used every year from 1903 through the conclusion of the reign. However, in 1909-10 a major variety derived therefrom was also used. This modification is characterized by the presence of a "+" cross cut over the original "bow tie" cross atop the crown, and by sharp points along the leaf edges. The fourth variety is presumably by Blakemore, modifying his previous design.

Large H   Small H

Date	Qty. Minted	G-4	VG-8	F-12	VF-20	EF-40	AU-50	MS-60	MS-63
St. Edward's Crown Reverse (1902)									
1902	2,120,000	1.25	2.50	3.50	7.00	13.00	27.00	60.00	100.00
1902H large H	2,200,000	1.50	3.00	5.00	9.00	17.00	35.00	75.00	125.00
small H	incl. above	5.50	12.00	20.00	40.00	70.00	100.00	200.00	300.00

Imperial crown
21 leaves
1903H only

Imperial Crown, 21-Leaf Reverse (1903 Heaton)

1903H	2,640,000	1.50	3.50	5.00	11.00	25.00	60.00	125.00	300.00

Imperial crown,   Leaves with rounded edges   Leaves with pointed edges
1903-1910   1903-1910   1909-1910

Rounded Leaves Reverse (1903-1910)

1903	1,000,000	3.00	7.00	13.00	25.00	50.00	125.00	300.00	450.00
1904	2,400,000	4.00	8.00	5.00	12.00	25.00	55.00	165.00	650.00
1905	2,600,000	3.50	3.00	5.00	11.00	22.00	50.00	135.00	325.00
1906	3,100,000	3.00	4.00	3.50	7.00	15.00	35.00	100.00	225.00
1907	5,200,000	3.00	4.00	3.50	7.00	14.00	35.00	90.00	200.00

Large 8   Small 8   'Bow tie' cross   '+' cross
Note shape of inner circles   Cross at top of crown

1908 varieties: The normal reverse (bow tie cross atop crown) for 1908 has a large 8; a second variety has a "+" cross cut over the bow tie, as on the 1909-1910 reverse, with sharp leaf points and a small date.

1908 large 8	1,197,780	3.50	7.00	11.00	25.00	45.00	75.00	175.00	350.00
small 8	incl. above	3.50	7.00	11.00	25.00	45.00	75.00	175.00	350.00
Pointed Leaves Reverse (1909-1910)									
1909 round leaves	1,890,865	2.25	3.50	5.50	14.00	30.00	75.00	250.00	550.00
pointed leaves	incl. above	2.25	3.50	5.50	14.00	30.00	75.00	250.00	550.00
1910 round leaves	5,850,325	1.50	2.50	3.50	6.50	13.00	30.00	70.00	145.00
pointed leaves	incl. above	1.50	2.50	3.50	6.50	13.00	30.00	70.00	145.00

George V, 5 Cents Silver, 1911-1921

Diameter: 15.494 mm; weight: 1.167 grams;
composition: (1911-19) .925 silver, .075 copper, (1920-21) .800 silver, .200 copper; edge: reeded

Two obverse varieties exist; the first (1911) lacks the phrase DEI GRATIA or an abbreviation thereof, while the second (1912-21) has DEI GRA : incorporated into

> G: *Band of crown worn through*
> VG: *Band of crown worn through at highest point*
> F: *Jewels in band of crown will be blurred*
> VF: *Band of crown is still clear but no longer sharp*
> EF: *Band of crown slightly worn but generally sharp and clear*

the legend. Both obverses were derived from a portrait model by Sir E.B. Mac-Kennal (B.M. on truncation). See text on the 1-cent issue for more details.

The reverse is identical to Blakemore's rounded leaves design introduced in the Edward VII series. On May 3, 1921, the Canadian government passed an act authorizing the substitution of a larger nickel 5-cent piece to replace the small silver coin. Consequently, almost the entire coinage of the silver 5-cent pieces dated 1921 was melted. About 400 specimens of this date are known, most or all of which were (a) regular strikes sold by the mint in 1921 to visitors, or (b) specimen strikes sold or given to individuals as part of 1921 specimen sets.

Date	Qty. Minted	G-4	VG-8	F-12	VF-20	EF-40	AU-50	MS-60	MS-63
"Godless" Obverse (1911)									
1911	3,692,350	1.50	3.00	5.00	10.00	20.00	55.00	135.00	250.00

Date	Qty. Minted	G-4	VG-8	F-12	VF-20	EF-40	AU-50	MS-60	MS-63
Modified Obverse Legend (1912-1921)									
1912	5,863,170	1.50	2.50	4.00	6.00	12.00	30.00	75.00	175.00
1913	5,588,048	1.50	2.50	3.50	6.00	10.00	20.00	50.00	80.00
1914	4,202,179	1.75	3.00	4.00	6.50	13.00	35.00	90.00	220.00
1915	1,172,258	6.00	12.00	20.00	35.00	75.00	175.00	375.00	750.00
1916	2,481,675	2.50	4.50	8.00	12.50	35.00	80.00	150.00	350.00
1917	5,521,373	1.50	2.50	3.50	5.00	9.00	25.00	65.00	125.00
1918	6,052,289	1.50	2.50	3.50	4.50	8.00	20.00	50.00	100.00
1919	(Orig.: 7,835,400)	1.50	2.50	3.50	4.50	8.00	20.00	50.00	100.00
1920	(Orig.: 10,649,851)	1.50	2.50	3.50	4.50	8.00	20.00	50.00	100.00
1921	(Orig.: 2,582,495)	1,600	2,000	2,700	3,750	6,000	9,500	17,000	30,000

George V, 5 Cents Nickel, 1922-1936

Diameter: 21.21 mm; weight: 4.54 grams; thickness: 1.70 mm; composition: .99 nickel; edge: plain

> G: *Band of crown worn through*
> VG: *Band of crown worn through at highest point*
> F: *Jewels in band of crown will be blurred*
> VF: *Band of crown is still clear but no longer sharp*
> EF: *Band of crown slightly worn but generally sharp and clear*

In order to provide a 5-cent piece of more manageable size, and "because nickel is essentially a Canadian metal" the Canadian government introduced a coin of pure nickel in 1922, similar in size to the 5-cent coins of the United States.

The obverse was derived from the MacKennal portrait model (initials B.M. on truncation); the reverse was engraved by W.H.J. Blakemore. Mint records do not clearly specify the designer; it was either W.H.J. Blakemore or Fred Lewis.

Date	Qty. Minted	G-4	VG-8	F-12	VF-20	EF-40	AU-50	MS-60	MS-63
1922	4,763,186	.30	.50	1.50	4.50	10.50	25.00	65.00	135.00
1923	2,475,201	.40	.75	2.50	6.50	15.00	50.00	150.00	350.00
1924	3,066,658	.30	.60	1.50	5.00	12.00	35.00	125.00	275.00
1925	200,050	27.50	40.00	55.00	105.00	250.00	700.00	1,500	2,500

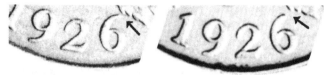

'Near 6' tip near leaf   'Far 6' tip far from leaf

1926 date varieties. Most of the 1926 issue was derived from a matrix in which the tip of the 6 is very close to the right-hand maple leaf. A second matrix (or perhaps individual die) had the 6 punched in a lower position, so that it appeared farther from the leaf. Such digit spacing and position differences are considered trivial by these cataloguers, and these 1926 varieties are included only because their listing in previous catalogues has led to their widespread acceptance by collectors.

Date	Qty. Minted	G-4	VG-8	F-12	VF-20	EF-40	AU-50	MS-60	MS-63
1926 near 6	933,577	2.50	4.00	10.00	25.00	75.00	175.00	400.00	1,200
1926 far 6	incl. above	75.00	110.00	150.00	250.00	450.00	1,000	2,500	4,000
1927	5,285,627	.30	.50	1.50	4.50	12.00	30.00	80.00	200.00
1928	4,588,725	.30	.50	1.50	4.50	12.00	30.00	70.00	150.00
1929	5,562,262	.30	.50	1.50	4.50	12.00	30.00	80.00	200.00
1930	3,685,991	.30	.50	1.50	4.50	12.00	35.00	125.00	300.00
1931	5,100,830	.30	.50	1.50	4.50	12.00	35.00	125.00	300.00
1932	3,198,566	.30	.50	1.50	5.00	13.50	45.00	140.00	300.00
1933	2,597,867	.40	.75	1.75	6.00	15.00	70.00	250.00	600.00
1934	3,827,303	.30	.50	1.50	4.50	12.50	40.00	150.00	350.00
1935	3,900,000	.30	.50	1.50	4.50	12.50	40.00	125.00	325.00
1936	4,400,450	.30	.50	1.50	4.50	12.50	25.00	75.00	150.00

George VI, Beaver Reverse, 1937-1942
Diameter: 21.21 mm, weight: 4.54 grams; thickness: 1.70 mm; composition: .99 nickel, edge: plain

VG: *No detail in hair above the ear*
F: *Only slight detail in hair above the ear*
VF: *Where not worn, hair is clear but not sharp*
EF: *Slight wear in hair over the ear*

Both obverses (for the round and 12-sided issues) display a bare-headed portrait of the King designed by T.H. Paget (H.P. below bust).

In keeping with the decision to modernize the new George VI reverses, the now-familiar beaver motif was chosen for the 5-cent piece (after first being considered for the 10-cent piece). The 1937 issue has a period after the date to balance the design, but after 1937 the period was omitted. The original design was by G.E. Kruger-Gray (K•G to the left of the log).

Period after date, 1937 only   No period after date, 1938-1942

Date	Qty. Minted	VG-8	F-12	VF-20	EF-40	AU-50	MS-60	MS-63
Nickel Issues (1937-1942)								
1937 (period after date)	4,593,263	.50	.75	2.75	5.00	8.00	20.00	35.00
1938	3,898,974	.50	1.75	4.00	12.00	40.00	120.00	225.00
1939	5,661,123	.40	1.00	3.00	8.50	30.00	75.00	135.00
1940	13,920,197	.30	.75	2.00	4.50	10.00	25.00	70.00
1941	8,681,785	.30	.75	2.00	5.00	12.00	30.00	75.00
1942	6,847,544	.30	.75	2.00	4.50	10.00	25.00	70.00

12-Sided Coinage, 1942-1962

George VI, Tombac (Brass), 1942-1943

Diameter: 21.23-21.29 mm (opposite corners), 20.88-20.93 mm (opposite sides); weight: 4.54 grams; thickness: 1.70 mm; composition: .880 copper, .120 zinc; edge: plain

Because nickel was needed for World War II, its use for coinage was suspended late in 1942. The substitute first used was a brass alloy commonly called "tombac." This alloy quickly tarnished to the brownish hue acquired by bronze, so the new coins were made 12-sided to avoid their confusion with the cents. Due to lack of time, the new matrices (obverse and reverse) were made without the conventional rim denticles.

1942 (12 sided)	3,396,234	.75	1.00	2.00	3.00	4.00	5.00	15.00

Victory Reverse, 1943-1945

Composition (1944-45): steel, coated with .0127 mm layer of nickel and .0003 mm plating of chromium. Other specifications as for 1942 tombac issue

This design was introduced with the aim of furthering the war efforts. The obverse used was as the 1942 tombac issue, except that rim denticles were added.

The torch and 'V' on the reverse symbolize sacrifice and victory (the V also indicates the denomination, the idea coming from the U.S. Liberty 5-cent pieces of 1883-1912). Instead of rim denticles, a Morse code (dot-dash) pattern reading WE WIN WHEN WE WORK WILLINGLY was used. The designer was the chief engraver of the Royal Canadian Mint, Thomas Shingles (T.S. at right of torch), who cut the master matrix entirely by hand – a feat few present-day engravers can accomplish.

The 1943 issue was struck in tombac. This alloy, however, was replaced with chromium-plated steel in 1944-45 because copper and zinc were needed for the war effort.

Date	Qty. Minted	VG-8	F-12	VF-20	EF-40	AU-50	MS-60	MS-63
Tombac Issue (1943)								
1943 24,760,256		.40	.50	1.00	2.00	3.00	4.00	12.00
Chromium-Plated Steel Issue (1944-1945)								
1944 11,532,784		.25	.40	1.00	2.00	3.00	4.00	8.50
1945 18,893,216		.25	.40	1.00	2.00	3.00	4.00	8.50

Beaver Reverse Resumed, 1946-1950

Diameter: 21.234 mm (opposite corners), 20.878 mm (opposite sides); weight: 4.54 grams;
thickness: 1.70 mm; composition: .999 nickel, edge: plain

After the conclusion of World War II the 5-cent piece was again struck in nickel, but the 12-sided shape had become popular and was retained. The initial obverse was identical to the 1943-45 issues. A second variety, introduced in 1948, incorporates the modified titles of the King (see 1-cent text). This second obverse was used for the 1948-50, 1951 commemorative, and a portion of the 1951 beaver issues. A third variety was coupled with most of the 1951 beaver and all of the 1952 issues. This variety is distinguishable by the lower relief of the portrait and the different positioning of the legend relative to the rim denticles.

Two major reverse varieties are known. The first (1946-50) differs from the 1942 tombac issue only in having rim denticles. The second variety (1951-52), introduced simultaneously with the change to steel composition, has a slightly larger beaver and is perhaps slightly lower in relief.

1947 'dot'
(deterioriated die)

1947 maple leaf
(official issue)

1947 "dot." This item is apparently the product of a deterioriated die and hence is not a true die variety. Some have suggested that this was an official issue because of the fact that the 25-cent and dollar (pointed 7) issues dated 1947 are also known with a "dot" after the date. The alternative explanation, currently favoured by most students of decimal coins, is that the "dots" resulted from small pieces chipping out of the chromium plating and leaving pits in individual dies. These pits would appear as raised "dots" on struck coins. It is conceded, however, that if the latter were true it would be a remarkable coincidence. In any case, the 1947 "dot" coins are probably not official because (a) the dots are irregular and of poor quality, and (b) the engravers who would have prepared such dies are quite certain that they did not do so.

1947 maple leaf variety. This was an official issue struck in 1948, which is explained in the text for the 1-cent issue.

Date	Qty. Minted	VG-8	F-12	VF-20	EF-40	AU-50	MS-60	MS-63
Small Beaver Reverse (1946-1950)								
1946 6,952,684		.30	.50	1.00	3.75	7.00	20.00	45.00
1947 normal date 7,603,724		.25	.35	.75	3.00	6.00	14.00	30.00
1947 "dot" .... incl. above		17.50	22.50	35.00	75.00	250.00	400.00	700.00
1947 maple leaf 9,595,124		.25	.35	.75	3.00	5.00	12.00	25.00
Modified Legend (1948-1952)								
1948 1,810,789		.75	1.00	2.00	5.00	12.50	25.00	40.00
1949 13,736,276		.20	.25	.50	1.00	2.50	6.50	13.00
1950 11,950,520		.20	.25	.50	1.00	2.50	6.50	13.00

Modified legend,
high relief portrait
1948-1951

High relief portrait
Last 'A' of 'GRATIA'
points to denticle

Isolation of Nickel Bicentennial, 1951

Physical specifications remain the same as 1946-1950 issues.

As Canada is the world's largest single producer of nickel, it seemed appropriate
to issue a commemorative piece on the 200th anniversary of the isolation and
naming of the element by the Swedish chemist A.F. Cronstedt. The obverse was
as on the 1948-50 issues; the reverse, showing a nickel refinery, was designed by
Stephen Trenka (ST monogram at lower right).

Date	Qty. Minted	VG-8	F-12	VF-20	EF-40	AU-50	MS-60	MS-63
1951 commemorative	8,329,231	.20	.25	.50	.75	1.00	3.00	6.00

Beaver Reverse Resumed, Steel Coinage, 1951-1952

Physical specifications are the same as the 1943-1945 issues.

Low relief,
last 'A' of 'GRATIA'
points between denticles

Low relief portrait   Large beaver reverse
1951-1952

Because nickel was needed for the Korean War, the use of nickel was suspended
near the end of 1951. The beaver reverse was resumed for the balance of 1951
5-cent pieces with the composition changed to steel. New lower relief dies had
to be prepared for both the obverse and reverse since the harder steel surface did
not strike well with the higher relief dies the mint had been using. By error, a
small quantity of 1951 pieces were struck with a high relief obverse die, creating
two varieties for 1951. As mentioned above, the two dies are distinguishable by
the difference in relief of the portraits and the different positioning of the legend
relative to the rim denticles.

Large Beaver Reverse (1951-1952)

		VG-8	F-12	VF-20	EF-40	AU-50	MS-60	MS-63
1951 high relief obverse	4,313,410	300.00	450.00	750.00	1,000	1,500	2,000	3,500
low relief obverse	incl. above	.25	.50	1.00	2.00	3.00	5.00	12.00
1952 (low relief obverse)	10,891,148	.20	.40	.75	1.75	2.75	4.50	7.50

Elizabeth II, Laureate Bust, 1953-1964

Physical specifications for 1953-1954 remain the same as the previous issue;
composition (1955-64): .999 nickel

VF: Laurel leaves considerably worn
EF: Laurel leaves somewhat worn

No shoulder
fold, 1953

Large beaver,
1953-1954

The initial obverse for the 1953 issue, a laureate portrait of the Queen by Mrs. Mary Gillick (M.G. on truncation) was engraved in high relief and did not strike up well on the coins. Later in the year the relief was lowered and the hair and shoulder detail re-engraved. The re-engraving included sharpening two lines which represent a fold in, not a shoulder strap on, the Queen's gown. The two varieties also differ in the positioning of the legend relative to the rim denticles and the styles of some of the letters. (See 1-cent text for more details.) The second portrait was not modified when the shape of the 5-cent piece was changed back to round in 1963.

No
shoulder
fold
1953

Note style of
letters, relation
to denticles

Date	Qty. Minted	F-12	VF-20	EF-40	AU-50	MS-60	MS-63
"No Shoulder Fold" Obverse (1953)							
1953 no shoulder fold 16,635,552		.40	.85	1.75	2.75	5.00	8.00

With
shoulder
fold
1953-1962

Note style of
letters, relation
to denticles

"Shoulder Fold" Obverse (1953- 1964)							
1953 shoulder fold .... incl. above		.40	.85	1.75	3.50	6.50	12.00
1954 6,998,662		.50	1.00	2.00	4.50	8.50	14.00

Four noteworthy reverse varieties appeared during the 1953-64 period. The first is associated with the 1953 "no shoulder fold" obverse and is identical to the 1951-52 George VI beaver design. The second reverse variety has the design elements placed closer to the rim denticles than before, and was used for the 1953 "shoulder fold" and 1954 issues. The third variety was introduced with the resumption of nickel composition in 1955 when the smaller beaver, last used in 1950, was restored. The fourth variety occurred when the beaver was re-adapted with the change in shape of the 5-cent piece to round in 1963 because of continuing difficulties with the 12-sided collars.

Design far
from rim, 1953

Design near rim,
1953-1954

Small beaver
1955-1962

Date	Qty. Minted	F-12	VF-20	EF-40	AU-50	MS-60	MS-63
Small Beaver Reverse, 12-sided (1955-1962)							
1955 5,355,028		.35	.65	1.50	2.50	4.50	8.00
1956 9,399,854		.25	.50	.85	1.50	2.75	6.00
1957 7,387,703		.25	.35	.75	1.50	2.75	5.00
1958 7,607,521		.25	.35	.75	1.50	2.75	5.00
1959 11,552,523		—	.25	.40	.65	1.00	2.00
1960 37,157,433		—	—	—	.40	.65	2.00
1961 47,889,051		—	—	—	—	.25	1.00
1962 46,307,305		—	—	—	—	.25	1.00

Round Coinage Resumed (1963-1964)

1964
'Extra
waterline'

Date	Qty. Minted	EF-40	AU-50	MS-60	MS-63
1963 43,970,320		—	—	.25	1.00
1964 78,075,068		—	—	.25	1.00
1964 (extra waterline) .... incl. above		20.00	30.00	40.00	50.00

Elizabeth II, Tiara Obverse, 1965-1978

Diameter: 21.21 mm; weight: 4.54 grams; thickness: 1.70 mm;
composition: (1965-1981) .999 nickel; edge: plain

In 1965 an obverse with a new style portrait by Arnold Machin was introduced. The Queen has more mature facial features and is wearing a tiara.

The reverses and physical specifications during 1965-66 are the same as for the 1963-64 issues.

Date	Qty. Minted	MS-60	MS-63
1965 84,876,018		.20	.35
1966 27,976,648		.20	.35

Confederation Centennial, 1967

All denominations for 1967 bore special reverses to commemorate the 1967 confederation of the province of Canada, Nova Scotia and New Brunswick to the Dominion of Canada. The 5 cents reverse device depicts a hopping rabbit. Designer: Alex Colville. The obverse and physical specifications are as for the 1956-66 issues.

Date	Qty. Minted	MS-60	MS-63
1967 Confederation commemorative 36,876,574		.25	.40

Beaver Reverse Resumed, 1968 -
The obverse, reverse and physical specifications are as or the issues of 1965-66.

Date	Qty. Minted	MS-63
1968	99,253,330	.20
1969	27,830,229	.20
1970	5,726,010	.75
1971	27,312,609	.20
1972	62,417,387	.20
1973	53,507,435	.20
1974	94,704,645	.20
1975	138,882,000	.20
1976	55,140,213	.20
1977	89,120,791	.20
1978	137,079,273	.20

Modified Obverse, 1979-1989

Beginning with the 1979 issue, the portrait of the Queen was made smaller. This was done to standardize our coinage, making the size of the portrait proportional to the diameter of the coin, regardless of denomination.

Date	Qty. Minted	MS-63
1979	186,706,667	.20
1980	135,247,457	.20
1981	99,107,900	.20

Cupro-nickel alloy, 1982 -

Diameter: 21.20 mm; weight: 4.6 grams; thickness: 1.76 mm;
composition: .75 copper, .25 nickel; edge: plain

In 1982, the five-cent piece was first coined in cupro-nickel, an alloy of 75% copper and 25% nickel. This is the same alloy used in United States coinage.

Date	Qty. Minted	MS-63
1982	64,924,400	.20
1983	72,596,000	.20
1984	84,088,000	.20
1985	126,618,000	.20
1986	156,104,000	.20
1987	106,299,000	.20
1988	75,025,000	.20
1989	141,570,538	.20

Elizabeth II, Diadem Obverse, 1990 -

The first effigy designed by a Canadian for use on Canadian coins was introduced on the obverse of all Canadian issues for 1990. The design depicts a more contemporary portrait of the Queen wearing a necklace and earrings. The elaborate crown, last seen on Victorian issues, replaced the tiara used on previous issues. The obverse was designed by Dora dePédery-HUNT.

Date	Qty. Minted	MS-63
1990	42,537,000	.20
1991	10,931,000	.20

125th Anniversary of Confederation, 1992

To celebrate the 125th anniversary of Confederation, all circulation coins issued in 1992 bear the date "1867-1992."

1992	N/A	.20
1993	N/A	.20
1994	N/A	.20

10 CENTS
Victoria, 10 Cents Silver, 1858-1901

Diameter: 18.034 mm; weight: 2.32 grams;
composition: .925 silver, .075 copper; edge: reeded

G: *Braid near ear worn through*
VG: *No details in braid around ear*
F: *Segments of braid begin to merge into one another*
VF: *Braid is clear but not sharp*
EF: *Braid is slightly worn but generally sharp and clear*

In all, six different portrait varieties of Victoria were used for this denomination. Each differs from the others in some of the facial features and in certain other respects. Except for the initial portrait, all subsequent varieties were created by re-engraving a previous design; these modifications were probably the work of the original designer, L.C. Wyon. None of them represent a serious attempt to accurately portray Victoria as she looked at the time.

In some years two busts were coupled with a given date reverse. Such varieties are most easily distinguished as follows:

P1   P2   P3   P4   P5   P6

P1 vs P2: P1 has a smooth chin and a narrow truncation, extending almost the entire length of the lower neck, while P2 has a slightly "double" chin and a wide truncation, restricted to the rear half of the lower neck.

P4 vs P5: P4 has a rounded forehead, smooth chin and much hairline detail above the eye, while P5 has a flat forehead, slightly double chin and very little hair detail above the eye.

P5 vs P6: P5 is as described above, P6 has the general characteristics of P4.

The basic reverse device consists of crossed maple boughs tied at the bottom by a ribbon. At the top is St. Edward's crown. Two major device varieties exist; the first has a wreath with 21 leaves and the second, derived from the first, has a 22nd leaf added to the lower rigbt. Numerous sub-varieties of both reverses are known; for example, the 22nd leaf on the 1882 issue differs from, and was added independently to that on the 1883-1901 issues. Both of the major and most of the minor varieties were designed and engraved by L.C. Wyon.

1871H Newfoundland / Canada mule. See page 133.

21 leaves
1858-1881, 1891

22 leaves
1882-1901

Date	Qty. Minted	G-4	VG-8	F-12	VF-20	EF-40	AU-50	MS-60	MS-63
12-Leaf Reverse (1858-1881, 1891)									
1858 .... P1 1,250,000		10.00	18.00	35.00	70.00	125.00	180.00	425.00	1,200
1870 .... P1 1,600,000		10.00	18.00	35.00	70.00	130.00	200.00	450.00	1,250

Date	Qty. Minted	G-4	VG-8	F-12	VF-20	EF-40	AU-50	MS-60	MS-63
1871 .... P1 800,000		10.00	20.00	40.00	80.00	165.00	250.00	550.00	1,500
1871H P1 1,870,000		12.00	23.00	45.00	100.00	200.00	350.00	650.00	1,600
1872H P1 1,000,000		45.00	80.00	150.00	300.00	600.00	1,000	1,500	4,000
1874H P1 1,600,000		6.00	10.00	20.00	50.00	100.00	175.00	450.00	1,500
1875H .... P1 .... incl. above		135.00	250.00	450.00	800.00	1,750	2,500	5,000	10,000
1880H .... P1, 2 .. 1,500,000		5.00	9.00	18.00	40.00	85.00	150.00	400.00	1,250
1881H .... P1, 2 ... 950,000		6.00	12.00	28.00	60.00	125.00	210.00	500.00	1,350

22-Leaf Reverse (1882-1901)

Date	Qty. Minted	G-4	VG-8	F-12	VF-20	EF-40	AU-50	MS-60	MS-63
1882H P3 1,000,000		6.00	13.00	30.00	60.00	125.00	225.00	475.00	1,400
1883H P3 300,000		15.00	35.00	70.00	150.00	300.00	500.00	1,400	3,500
1884 .... P4 150,000		100.00	175.00	400.00	850.00	2,000	2,700	7,000	15,000
1885 .... P4, 5 ... 400,000		12.50	28.00	55.00	125.00	275.00	450.00	1,600	4,500

Small 6   Large over small 6   Large knobbed 6

Date	Qty. Minted	G-4	VG-8	F-12	VF-20	EF-40	AU-50	MS-60	MS-63
1886 small 6 ...... P4, 5 800,000		8.00	15.00	30.00	70.00	140.00	250.00	600.00	1,700
large over small 6 . P5 ... incl. above		10.00	20.00	40.00	90.00	180.00	325.00	750.00	2,000
large pointed 6 ... P5 ... incl. above		10.00	20.00	40.00	90.00	180.00	325.00	750.00	2,000
large knobbed 6 .. P5 ... incl. above		10.00	20.00	40.00	90.00	180.00	325.00	750.00	2,000
1887 .... P5 350,000		15.00	30.00	60.00	150.00	400.00	800.00	2,500	7,000
1888 .... P5 1,100,000		5.00	9.00	18.00	45.00	90.00	160.00	425.00	1,250
1889 .... P5 ... incl. above		300.00	500.00	1,000	2,000	3,200	4,500	10,000	17,500
1890H P5 450,000		8.00	15.00	30.00	65.00	150.00	250.00	550.00	1,500

Small date   Large date

2 over 1,
large 9

Normal date,
small 9

Date	Qty. Minted	G-4	VG-8	F-12	VF-20	EF-40	AU-50	MS-60	MS-63
1891 21 lvs., sm. dt. P5 800,000		7.50	15.00	30.00	70.00	160.00	275.00	650.00	1,500
22 lvs., lg. date ... P5 ... incl. above		7.00	15.00	30.00	70.00	160.00	275.00	650.00	1,500
1892 2 over 1, lg. 9 . P5 520,000		6.00	12.00	25.00	60.00	130.00	225.00	550.00	1,500
norm. date, sm. 9 . P5, 6 . incl. above		6.00	12.00	25.00	60.00	130.00	225.00	550.00	1,500

Flat top 3   Round top 3

Date	Qty. Minted	G-4	VG-8	F-12	VF-20	EF-40	AU-50	MS-60	MS-63
1893 flat top 3 ...... P5, 6 ... 500,000		10.00	20.00	45.00	100.00	200.00	350.00	800.00	2,500
round top 3 ... P5, 6 . incl. above		325.00	550.00	1,200	2,500	5,000	6,500	10,000	18,000
1894 .... P5, 6 ... 500,000		10.00	20.00	40.00	85.00	175.00	250.00	600.00	2,000
1896 .... P5, 6 ... 650,000		4.50	8.00	18.00	40.00	85.00	150.00	400.00	1,000
1898 .... P6 720,000		4.50	8.00	20.00	40.00	90.00	160.00	425.00	1,200

Small 9s   Large 9s

Date	Qty. Minted	G-4	VG-8	F-12	VF-20	EF-40	AU-50	MS-60	MS-63
1899 small 9s P6 1,200,000		4.00	7.00	15.00	40.00	85.00	130.00	325.00	900.00
large 9s ...... P6 ... incl. above		7.00	14.00	25.00	60.00	145.00	250.00	550.00	1,600
1900 .... P6 1,100,000		3.50	6.00	14.00	30.00	70.00	110.00	250.00	700.00
1901 .... P6 1,200,000		3.50	6.00	14.00	30.00	70.00	110.00	250.00	700.00

Edward VII, 10 Cents Silver, 1902-1910

Diameter: 18.034 mm; weight: 2.32 grams; composition: .925 silver, .075 copper; edge: reeded

G: Band of crown worn through
VG: Band of crown worn through at highest point
F: Jewels in band of crown will be blurred
VF: Band of crown is still clear but no longer sharp
EF: Band of crown slightly worn but generally
sharp and clear

Only a single obverse, designed and engraved by G.W. De Saulles (initials DES. below bust), was employed. The initial reverse was partially by De Saulles; the wreath was taken unaltered from Wyon's 22-leaf Victorian variety and a new legend and the Imperial State crown added. The leaves of the wreath have moderate venation, with all of the veins raised. A second variety, from a new reducing machine model, has broader leaves with extensive, incuse venation. It was designed and engraved by W.H.J. Blakemore (copying the previous design).

Victorian leaves, 1902-1909   Broad leaves, 1909-1910

Date	Qty. Minted	G-4	VG-8	F-12	VF-20	EF-40	AU-50	MS-60	MS-63
Victorian Leaves Reverse (1902-1909)									
1902	720,000	2.50	5.00	12.00	28.00	65.00	100.00	275.00	750.00
1902H	1,100,000	1.50	3.00	8.00	18.00	45.00	75.00	175.00	400.00
1903	500,000	6.00	12.00	25.00	70.00	175.00	400.00	1,500	3,500
1903H	1,320,000	2.50	5.00	11.00	28.00	65.00	115.00	300.00	750.00
1904	1,000,000	4.00	8.00	14.00	40.00	100.00	175.00	400.00	850.00
1905	1,000,000	3.50	7.00	13.00	40.00	100.00	175.00	425.00	650.00
1906	1,700,000	2.00	4.00	10.00	25.00	60.00	100.00	300.00	650.00
1907	2,620,000	2.00	4.00	10.00	22.00	50.00	85.00	275.00	650.00
1908	776,666	4.00	8.00	16.00	40.00	100.00	160.00	400.00	800.00
1909 Victorian leaves	1,697,200	2.50	5.00	14.00	35.00	80.00	150.00	500.00	1,200
Broad Leaves Reverse (1909-1910)									
1909 broad leaves	incl. above	4.00	8.00	18.00	45.00	100.00	225.00	600.00	1,700
1910	4,468,331	1.50	3.00	8.00	15.00	45.00	75.00	175.00	475.00

George V, 10 Cents Silver, 1911-1936

Diameter: 18.034 mm; weight: 2.33 grams; composition: (1910-19) .925 silver, .075 copper;
(1920-36) .800 silver, .200 copper; edge: reeded

G: Band of crown worn through
VG: Band of crown worn through at highest point
F: Jewels in band of crown will be blurred
VF: Band of crown is still clear but no longer sharp
EF: Band of crown slightly worn but generally
sharp and clear

Two obverse varieties exist; the first (1911) lacks the phrase DEI GRATIA or an abbreviation for it and the second (1912-36) has DEI GRA: incorporated into the legend. Both obverses were derived from a portrait model by Sir. E.B. MacKennal (B.M. on truncation). See the 1-cent text for more details.

The series began with the broad leaves design introduced late in the Edward

VII series. However, this was replaced in 1913 with another Blakemore design (from a new model) in which the maple leaves are distinctly smaller and have less venation.

Obverse
1912-1936

Broad leaves, 1911-1913

Date	Qty. Minted	G-4	VG-8	F-12	VF-20	EF-40	AU-50	MS-60	MS-63
Broad Leaves Reverse (1911-1913)									
1911 (no DEI GRA:)	2,737,584	4.00	8.00	20.00	30.00	75.00	110.00	250.00	650.00
1912	2,235,557	1.75	3.00	4.00	11.00	30.00	85.00	275.00	750.00
1913 broad leaves	3,613,937	75.00	125.00	200.00	450.00	900.00	3,500	6,500	12,500

Small leaves, 1913-1936

Small Leaves Reverse (1913-1936)									
1913 (small leaves)	incl. above	1.25	2.25	4.00	10.00	25.00	90.00	250.00	750.00
1914	2,549,811	1.25	2.50	4.00	9.50	25.00	90.00	250.00	800.00
1915	688,057	4.75	8.00	15.00	45.00	150.00	300.00	650.00	1,400
1916	4,218,114	1.25	2.00	3.00	5.00	15.00	60.00	150.00	425.00
1917	5,011,988	1.25	2.00	3.00	5.00	11.00	50.00	90.00	200.00
1918	5,133,602	1.25	2.00	3.00	5.00	11.00	45.00	75.00	140.00
1919	7,877,722	1.25	2.00	3.00	5.00	11.00	45.00	75.00	125.00
1920	6,305,345	1.25	2.00	3.00	5.00	11.00	50.00	90.00	200.00
1921	2,469,562	1.50	2.75	4.00	7.00	17.00	60.00	100.00	250.00
1928	2,458,602	1.25	2.00	3.75	7.00	15.00	50.00	95.00	225.00
1929	3,253,888	1.25	2.00	3.75	7.00	15.00	50.00	95.00	225.00
1930	1,831,043	1.50	2.75	4.00	7.50	17.00	60.00	100.00	250.00
1931	2,067,421	1.25	2.00	4.00	7.00	15.00	50.00	95.00	225.00
1932	1,154,317	1.75	3.00	5.00	8.50	25.00	75.00	145.00	325.00
1933	672,368	2.25	4.00	6.00	12.00	45.00	100.00	300.00	750.00
1934	409,067	3.50	6.00	10.00	30.00	90.00	200.00	600.00	1,500
1935	384,056	3.50	6.50	10.00	22.50	100.00	175.00	450.00	1,000
1936	2,460,871	1.25	2.00	3.00	5.00	13.00	45.00	80.00	125.00

George VI Issue Struck in the Name of George V

A portion of the 1-, 10- and 25-cent pieces dated 1936 have a small raised dot on the reverse, denoting that they were actually struck in 1937 for George VI. On the 10-cent coins, the dot is below the bow in the wreath. There is some question whether all of the dot 1- and 10-cent pieces reported to have been struck exist today (see the 1-cent text for more details). The grading and physical specifications are as for the George V issues.

Date	Qty. Minted	
1936 raised dot below wreath	(originally: 191,237)	4 known

George VI, 10 Cents Silver, 1937-1952

Diameter: 18.034 mm; weight: 2.33 grams; composition: .800 silver, .200 copper; edge: reeded

VG: *No detail in hair above ear*
 F: *Only slight detail in hair above ear*
VF: *Where not worn, hair is clear but not sharp*
EF: *Slight wear in hair over ear*

The first obverse for this series has a legend containing the phrase ET IND: IMP: for *Et Indiae Imperator* (and Emperor of India). Beginning with coins dated 1948 the phrase was omitted from the King's titles, as India had gained independence from England the previous year. Both varieties were derived from a portrait model by T.H. Paget (initials H.P. under bust). The obverses of this series are unique in that the monarch is bare-headed.

A Government decision was made to modernize the reverse designs for the George VI series, and the popular fishing schooner motif was selected for this denomination. The design was first considered for the 25 cents, with the beaver design to be used for the 10 cents. Although the Government proclamation stated that a "fishing schooner under sail" is shown, it is clear that the designer, Emanuel Hahn, in fact used the famous Canadian racing yacht *Bluenose* as the source for his model. Hahn's initial H appears above the waves to the left. The small date on the 1937 issue proved to wear badly in circulation, so beginning in 1938, the date was enlarged and placed higher in the field. Some of the coins dated 1947 have a tiny maple leaf after the date. This denotes that they were actually struck in 1948. For more information see text on the 1-cent.

Small low date
1937 only

Large high date,
1938-1952

Date	Qty. Minted	VG-8	F-12	VF-20	EF-40	AU-50	MS-60	MS-63
"ET IND : IMP :" Obverse (1937-1947)								
1937 (small date)	2,500,095	2.50	4.00	5.00	7.00	10.00	25.00	40.00
1938	4,197,323	2.00	4.00	5.00	15.00	40.00	80.00	150.00
1939	5,501,748	2.00	4.00	5.00	12.50	35.00	70.00	140.00
1940	16,526,470	1.00	2.00	3.00	6.00	12.00	30.00	50.00
1941	8,716,386	1.00	2.00	5.00	1250	30.00	70.00	150.00
1942	10,214,011	1.00	2.00	3.00	8.50	20.00	55.00	80.00
1943	21,143,229	1.00	2.00	3.00	7.50	12.00	25.00	50.00
1944	9,383,582	1.00	2.00	3.00	9.50	20.00	45.00	80.00
1945	10,979,570	1.00	2.00	3.00	7.00	12.00	20.00	40.00
1946	6,300,066	2.00	3.00	4.00	9.00	20.00	45.00	80.00
1947	4,431,926	2.00	3.00	5.00	12.00	25.00	60.00	90.00
1947 maple leaf	9,638,793	1.00	2.00	3.00	5.50	10.00	20.00	35.00

Obverse
1948-1952

Date	Qty. Minted	VG-8	F-12	VF-20	EF-40	AU-50	MS-60	MS-63
Modified Obverse Legend (1948-1952)								
1948	422,741	5.00	7.50	14.00	30.00	45.00	75.00	130.00
1949	11,336,172	1.00	2.00	3.00	5.00	7.00	15.00	25.00
1950	17,823,075	1.00	2.00	2.50	3.25	5.00	12.00	20.00
1951	15,079,265	1.00	2.00	2.50	3.25	4.00	12.00	18.00
1952	10,474,455	1.00	2.00	2.50	3.25	4.00	10.00	15.00

Elizabeth II, Laureate Bust, 1953-1964

Diameter: 18.034 mm; weight: 2.33 grams; composition: .800 silver, .200 copper; edge: reeded

F: Leaves almost worn through; shoulder fold indistinct
VF: Leaves worn considerably; shoulder fold must
be clear
EF: Laurel leaves on head somewhat worn

The initial obverse for the 1953 issue had a high relief, laureate portrait of the Queen by Mrs. Mary Gillick (M.G. on truncation) which did not strike up well on the coins. Later in the year, the relief was lowered and the hair and shoulder detail re-engraved. The re-engraving included sharpening two lines which represented a fold in the Queen's gown. The two varieties also differ in the positioning of the legend relative to the rim denticles and the styles of some of the letters. See the text on the 1-cent for more details.

The reverse used during this period remained basically the same as that introduced in the previous series.

With
shoulder fold
1953-1964

Note style of
letters, relation
of 'I' to
denticles

No
shoulder fold,
1953

"No Shoulder Fold" Obverse (1953)								
1953 (no fold)	17,706,395	*	1.00	2.00	2.50	3.50	8.00	12.00
"Shoulder Fold" Obverse (1953-1964)								
1953 (with fold)	incl. above	*	1.00	2.00	3.00	4.50	10.00	15.00
1954	4,493,150	*	1.00	2.00	3.50	6.00	13.00	25.00
1955	12,237,294	*	*	1.00	2.25	3.25	7.00	10.00
1956	16,732,844	*	*	1.00	2.25	3.25	6.00	8.00
1956 dot	(incl. above)	2.50	4.00	6.00	8.00	12.00	20.00	30.00
1957	16,110,229	*	*	*	1.00	2.00	3.00	4.00
1958	10,621,236	*	*	*	1.00	1.50	3.00	4.00
1959	19,691,433	*	*	*	*	*	3.00	4.00
1960	45,446,835	*	*	*	*	*	2.00	3.00
1961	26,850,859	*	*	*	*	*	1.75	2.00
1962	41,864,335	*	*	*	*	*	1.75	2.00
1963	41,916,208	*	*	*	*	*	1.75	2.00
1964	49,518,549	*	*	*	*	*	1.75	2.00

Elizabeth II, Tiara Obverse, 1965-1978

In 1965 an obverse with a new style portrait by Arnold Machin was introduced. The Queen has more mature facial features and is wearing a tiara. The reverse and physical specifications for the 1965-66 period remain as before.

Date	Qty. Minted	VG-8	F-12	VF-20	EF-40	AU-50	MS-60	MS-63
1965	56,965,392	*	*	*	*	*	1.50	2.00
1966	34,330,199	*	*	*	*	*	1.50	2.00

Confederation Centennial, 1967

All denominations for 1967 bore special reverses to commemorate the 1867 confederation of Nova Scotia, New Brunswick and the Province of Canada, to form the Dominion of Canada. The design for this denomination, by Alex Colville, shows a mackerel. During the issue, the alloy was changed to .500 silver, .500 copper. The alloy varieties are not distinguishable by eye, so only a single catalogue value is given below.

Date	Qty. Minted	MS-60	MS-63
1967 .800 silver	32,309,135	1.75	2.00
.500 silver	30,689,080	1.75	2.00

*Note: Common silver coins (marked with *) are worth a premium only for their silver content. This price may vary according to prevailing market value of silver bullion.*

Schooner Reverse Resumed, 1968 -

Diameter: 18.034 mm; weight: (silver) 2.33 grams, (nickel) 2.07 grams; thickness: (nickel) 1.16 mm; composition: (1968) .500 silver, .500 copper, (1968-1977) .999 nickel, edge: reeded

Two major reverse varieties have appeared since the 1968 resumption of the fishing schooner design. The first is as the previous issue; the second, by Myron Cook (but still bearing Emanuel Hahn's initial H), has the size of the device reduced and a smaller date placed lower in the field.

1968 varieties. The earlier portion of the 1968 issue was in silver. Later, the composition was changed to nickel. The nickel specimens are slightly darker in color and are attracted to a magnet. Due to lack of time, the Royal Canadian Mint made arrangements with the United States Mint at Philadelphia to strike many of the nickel 10-cent pieces for 1968. The Ottawa and Philadelphia strikings differ only in the number of reeds on the edge and shape of the slots between them.

Large high date, 1968-1969

Ottawa Mint
V-shaped grooves

Philadelphia Mint
flat-bottomed grooves

Date	Qty. Minted	EF-40	MS-60	MS-63
Large Schooner Reverse (1968-1969)				
1968 .500 silver	70,460,000			2.00
nickel, Ottawa	87,412,930			.35
nickel, Philadelphia	85,170,000			.35
1969 large date (rarity not yet known)	incl. below	12,000	16,000	

Small schooner, small low date, 1969 -

Small Schooner Reverse (1969-)				
1969 (small date)	55,833,929			.35
1970	5,249,296			1.25
1971	41,016,968			.35
1972	60,169,387			.35
1973	167,715,435			.35
1974	210,566,565			.35
1975	207,680,000			.35
1976	95,018,533			.35
1977	128,452,206			.35

Increased Thickness, 1978

Diameter: 18.03 mm; weight: 2.07 grams; thickness: 1.19 mm; composition: .99 nickel; edge: reeded

1978	170,366,431			.35

Modified Tiara Obverse, 1979-1989

Diameter: 18.03 mm; weight: 2.07 grams; thickness: 1.22 mm; composition: .99 nickel; edge: reeded

Beginning with 1979, the portrait of the Queen was made smaller. This was done to standardize our coinage, making the size of the portrait porportional to the diameter of the coin, regardless of denomination.

1979	237,321,321			.25
1980	170,111,533			.25
1981	123,912,900			.25
1982	93,475,000			.25

Date	Qty. Minted	MS-63
1983	111,065,000	.25
1984	121,690,000	.25
1985	143,025,000	.25
1986	168,620,000	.25
1987	147,309,000	.25
1988	162,998,558	.25
1989	199,104,414	.25

Elizabeth II, Diadem Obverse, 1990 -

The first effigy designed by a Canadian for use on Canadian coins was introduced on the obverse of all Canadian issues for 1990. The design depicts a more
contemporary portrait of the Queen wearing a necklace and earrings. The elaborate crown, last seen on Victorian issues, replaced the tiara used on previous
issues. The obverse was designed by Dora de Pédery-HUNT.

1990	75,023,000	.25
1991	46,693,000	.25

125th Anniversary of Confederation, 1992

To celebrate the 125th anniversary of Confederation, all circulation coins issued
in 1992 bear the date "1867-1992."

1992	N/A	.25
1993	N/A	.25
1994	N/A	.25

20 CENTS
Victoria, 20 Cents Silver, 1858
Diameter: 23.27 mm; weight: 4.67 grams; composition: .925 silver, .075 copper; edge: reeded

G: *Braid around ear worn through*
VG: *No details in braid around ear*
F: *Segments of braid begin to merge into one another*
VF: *Braid is clear but not sharp*
EF: *Braid is slightly worn but generally sharp and clear*

The English shilling being valued at slightly over 24 cents and the Halifax currency shilling valued at 20 cents (there was no actual coin in the latter instance), the Province of Canada decided to issue a 20-cent instead of a 25-cent coin.

This move proved unpopular because of the ease of confusion of the coin with U.S. and later Canadian 25-cent pieces. Consequently, the 20-cent coin was never again issued for circulation.

In 1870, when the Dominion of Canada issued its first coins, the 25-cent piece was selected and by a proclamation dated 9 September, 1870, the old 20-cent pieces were withdrawn. More than half the issue was returned to the Royal Mint at various times between 1885 and 1906, melted and the silver recoined into 25-cent pieces.

Date	Qty. Minted	G-4	VG-8	F-12	VF-20	EF-40	AU-50	MS-60	MS-63
1858	(Originally 750,000)	50.00	70.00	100.00	150.00	300.00	575.00	1,500	5,000

25 CENTS
Victoria, 25 Cents Silver, 1870-1901
Diameter: 23.62 mm; weight: 5.81 grams; composition: .925 silver, .075 copper; edge: reeded

G: *Hair over ear worn through*
VG: *No details in hair over the ear; jewels in diadem are partly worn away*
F: *Strands of hair over the ear begin to merge together; jewels slightly blurred*
VF: *Hair and jewels are clear but not sharp*
EF: *Hair over ear and jewels in diadem are slightly worn but generally sharp and clear*

A total of five minor varieties of the Queen's portrait were used for this denomination, each differing in some of the facial features and in certain other respects. Each successive variety was created by re-engraving one of those used previously. The initial and probably all later portraits were designed and engraved by L.C. Wyon and only on the final variety was he probably attempting to portray Victoria as she appeared in real life.

In some instances two portraits are coupled with a given date reverse. Such portraits are most easily differentiated as follows:

P1 vs P2: The ribbon end extending toward the rear has a relatively constant width on P1 but gradually narrows on P2.

P4 vs P5: The P5 face has much more aged features and a larger nose.

The reverse device shows crossed boughs of maple, tied at the bottom with a

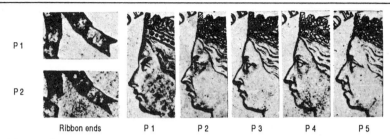

| P 1 | Ribbon ends | P 1 | P 2 | P 3 | P 4 | P 5 |

ribbon and separated at the top by St. Edward's crown. Although there were several modifications of the design, the most noteworthy came in 1886. This second design, derived from the first, has longer cut ends to the maple boughs, slight re-cutting of other portions of the wreath and the design elements generally closer to the rim denticles. Both of these reverses were by L.C. Wyon.

Short bough ends
1870-1886

1 8 7 0 7 0

Narrow 0   Wide 0

Date		Qty. Minted	G-4	VG-8	F-12	VF-20	EF-40	AU-50	MS-60	MS-63
Short Bough Ends Reverse (1870-1886)										
1870 narrow 0	P1	900,000	7.50	13.50	25.00	70.00	150.00	300.00	900.00	2,300
wide 0	P2	incl. above	7.50	13.50	25.00	70.00	150.00	300.00	900.00	2,300
1871	P1, 2	400,000	8.50	16.50	30.00	95.00	250.00	525.00	1,100	3,000
1871H	P1, 2	748,000	9.50	20.00	35.00	110.00	300.00	500.00	1,000	2,750
1872H	P1, 2	2,240,000	5.00	8.50	15.00	35.00	100.00	225.00	600.00	1,500
1874H	P2	2,600,000	5.00	8.50	15.00	35.00	110.00	225.00	650.00	1,600

Wide 0   Narrow 0 over wide 0   Narrow 0

1875H	P2	incl. above	175.00	275.00	600.00	1,600	3,250	5,000	8,500	17,500
1880H wide 0	P2	400,000	70.00	120.00	225.00	500.00	1,000	1,650	3,250	7,000
narrow over wide 0	P2	incl. above	30.00	45.00	100.00	250.00	500.00	1,050	2,750	5,000
narrow 0	P2	incl. above	22.50	45.00	90.00	250.00	500.00	750.00	1,450	3,500
1881H	P2	820,000	8.00	13.50	30.00	80.00	200.00	425.00	1,000	2,500
1882H	P3	600,000	9.00	17.50	35.00	100.00	250.00	475.00	1,100	2,750
1883H	P4	960,000	7.00	12.00	25.00	65.00	175.00	450.00	1,000	2,750
1885	P2	192,000	60.00	110.00	200.00	500.00	1,100	2,000	5,000	10,000

Long bough ends
1886-1901

1886 short b. ends	P2, 4, 5	540,000	7.50	15.00	25.00	85.00	275.00	550.00	1,500	3,250
Long Bough Ends Reverse (1886-1901)										
1886 long b. ends	P5	incl. above	7.50	15.00	25.00	85.00	275.00	550.00	1,500	3,250
1887	P5	400,000	55.00	100.00	200.00	450.00	1,000	2,000	5,000	10,000

Narrow 8s   Wide 8s

Date	Qty. Minted	G-4	VG-8	F-12	VF-20	EF-40	AU-50	MS-60	MS-63
1888 narrow 8s P5 400,000		6.50	12.50	25.00	70.00	185.00	375.00	9,000	2,000
wide 8s ...... P5 ... incl. above		7.50	15.00	35.00	70.00	200.00	450.00	1,250	2,250
1889 .... P5 66,324		70.00	125.00	225.00	500.00	1,200	2,500	6,000	12,500
1890H P5 200,000		10.00	20.00	35.00	100.00	300.00	575.00	1,750	3,750
1891 .... P5 120,000		35.00	60.00	110.00	275.00	600.00	850.00	2,000	4,500
1892 .... P5 510,000		6.00	12.00	20.00	60.00	200.00	400.00	900.00	2,750
1893 .... P5 100,000		45.00	85.00	175.00	400.00	800.00	1,100	2,750	5,500
1894 .... P5 220,000		9.00	17.50	32.50	75.00	225.00	550.00	1,500	3,000
1899 .... P5 415,580		4.00	7.50	12.00	40.00	110.00	250.00	700.00	1,750
1900 .... P5 1,320,000		4.00	6.00	10.00	35.00	90.00	200.00	600.00	1,500
1901 .... P5 640,000		4.00	6.00	10.00	35.00	90.00	200.00	600.00	1,500

Edward VII, 25 Cents Silver, 1902-1910

Diameter: 23.62 mm; weight: 5.81 grams; composition: .925 silver, .075 copper; edge: reeded

G: *Band of crown worn through*
VG: *Band of crown worn through at highest point*
F: *Jewels in band of crown will be blurred*
VF: *Band of crown still clear but no longer sharp*
EF: *Band of crown slightly worn but generally sharp and clear*

A single obverse, designed and engraved by G.W. De Saulles (DES. below bust), was used for the entire series.

For the first reverse, De Saulles used the almost unaltered wreath from the second Victorian reverse and coupled it with the Imperial State crown and a new legend. A major modification, presumably by W.H.J. Blakemore, appeared in 1906. It has a larger crown and many of the leaves are re-engraved. A specimen dated 1906 with the small crown reverse has been documented. The issues of 1908-10 to have thickened stems.

Small Crown Reverse (1902-1906)

1902 464,000		4.00	7.00	14.00	45.00	130.00	250.00	800.00	2,250
1902H 800,000		3.00	5.00	10.00	35.00	80.00	140.00	350.00	750.00
1903 846,000		4.00	7.00	14.00	45.00	140.00	300.00	750.00	1,500
1904 400,000		6.50	15.00	35.00	110.00	335.00	600.00	1,500	4,000
1905 800,000		4.50	8.00	16.00	55.00	200.00	450.00	1,350	3,500
1906 .... incl. below		3.00	6.00	11.00	35.00	100.00	200.00	600.00	1,400

Large Crown Reverse (1906-1910)

1906 1,237,843		3.00	6.00	11.00	35.00	100.00	200.00	600.00	1,600
1907 2,088,000		3.00	6.00	11.00	35.00	100.00	200.00	550.00	1,400
1908 495,016		5.00	8.50	22.50	55.00	200.00	300.00	700.00	1,500
1909 1,335,929		3.50	7.00	14.00	40.00	140.00	300.00	800.00	2,500
1910 3,577,569		3.00	5.00	10.00	35.00	80.00	130.00	350.00	750.00

George V, 25 Cents Silver, 1911-1936
Diameter: 23.62 mm; weight: 5.83 grams; composition: (1911-19) .925 silver, .075 copper,
(1920-36) .800 silver, .200 copper; edge: reeded

G: *Band of crwon worn through*
VG: *Band of crown worn through at highest point*
F: *Jewels in band of crown will be blurred; (CAN of CANADA worn but readable on 1936 dot.)*
VF: *Band of crown still clear but no longer sharp*
EF: *Band of crown slightly worn but generally sharp and clear*

As in the case of all other Canadian denominations, the 1911 legend did not include the phrase DEI GRATIA (by the grace of God). Public objection to this break with tradition resulted in the addition of the abbreviation DEI GRA: the following year. Both varieties were based on the design of Sir E.B. MacKennal, whose initials B.M. appear on the truncation of the bust. The reverse is identical to that used for 1908-10 issues.

Date	Qty. Minted	G-4	VG-8	F-12	VF-20	EF-40	AU-50	MS-60	MS-63
"Godless" Obverse (1911)									
1911	1,721,341	5.00	10.00	25.00	50.00	130.00	225.00	600.00	1,350

Modified Obverse Legend (1912-1936)									
1912	2,544,199	2.50	5.00	8.50	18.00	45.00	125.00	500.00	1,750
1913	2,213,595	2.50	5.00	8.50	18.00	45.00	110.00	475.00	1,750
1914	1,215,397	3.00	5.50	9.00	22.00	50.00	200.00	750.00	2,500
1915	242,382	10.00	20.00	40.00	150.00	450.00	1,300	3,000	7,500
1916	1,462,566	2.00	5.00	8.00	17.00	35.00	80.00	325.00	800.00
1917	3,365,644	2.00	4.00	6.50	17.00	30.00	50.00	125.00	350.00
1918	4,175,649	2.00	4.00	6.50	17.00	30.00	50.00	125.00	300.00
1919	(Orig. 5,852,262)	2.00	4.00	6.50	17.00	30.00	50.00	125.00	300.00
1920	1,975,278	2.00	4.00	6.50	17.00	40.00	65.00	200.00	700.00
1921	597,337	7.50	15.00	35.00	100.00	250.00	700.00	1,700	3,500
1927	468,096	17.50	35.00	60.00	125.00	300.00	725.00	1,500	3,000
1928	2,114,178	2.00	4.00	6.00	14.50	40.00	65.00	175.00	500.00
1929	2,690,562	2.00	4.00	5.50	14.50	35.00	60.00	175.00	500.00
1930	968,748	2.50	5.50	8.00	20.00	45.00	70.00	325.00	800.00
1931	537,815	2.50	5.50	8.00	22.50	45.00	100.00	400.00	1,000
1932	537,994	2.50	5.50	8.50	22.50	60.00	120.00	350.00	800.00
1933	421,282	3.00	6.00	9.50	25.00	65.00	125.00	325.00	700.00
1934	384,350	4.00	7.50	12.50	33.00	85.00	175.00	325.00	625.00
1935	537,772	4.00	7.50	10.50	30.00	70.00	150.00	350.00	750.00
1936	972,094	2.00	4.00	5.50	14.00	35.00	55.00	150.00	375.00

George VI Issue, Struck in the Name of George V
A portion of the 1-, 10- and 25-cent pieces dated 1936 have a small raised dot on the reverse, denoting that they were actually struck in 1937 for George VI. On the 25-cent pieces the dot is below the ribbon of the wreath. See text on the 1-cent piece for more details.

This issue seems to be particularly liable to "ghosting," thus the CAN of CA-NADA often will be much weaker than the rest of the legend. Nevertheless, the entire CANADA must still be readable for any specimen to grade at least Very Good. Otherwise, the grading and physical specifications are exactly as for the regular George V issues.

Date	Qty. Minted	G-4	VG-8	F-12	VF-20	EF-40	AU-50	MS-60	MS-63
1936 raised dot under wreath	153,685	20.00	40.00	90.00	225.00	450.00	725.00	1,500	3,500

George VI, 25 Cents Silver, 1937-1952
Diameter: 23.62 mm; weight: 5.83 grams; composition: .800 silver, .200 copper; edge: reeded

VG: *No detail in hair above the ear*
F: *Only slight detail in hair above the ear*
VF: *Hair above ear and side of head is clear but not sharp*
EF: *Slight wear in the hair over the ear*

Three obverse varieties are known for this series. The first two have in common a high relief bust of the King by T.H. Paget (H.P. below bust); the second variety has the ET IND : IMP : omitted from the legend (see the 1-cent text). The third has a low relief modification of the original portrait. The latter variety, the work of Thomas Shingles, was made to improve the overall appearance and the clarity with which the design could be struck up. In addition to the relief of the portraits, the second and third varieties can be differentiated by the position of the legend relative to the rim denticles and by the style of some of the letters.

In keeping with the government decision to modernize the reverse designs, the caribou motif was selected for the 25-cent piece. At one time the fishing schooner had been considered for this denomination. The designer was Emanuel Hahn (H under caribou's neck).

'Dot' after date (deteriorated die)   1947 maple leaf (official issue)

1947 "dot." This item is apparently the product of a deteriorated die. See text on the 5-cent piece for more details.

1947 maple leaf variety. This is an official issue struck in 1948. See text on the 1-cent piece for details.

Date	Qty. Minted	VG-8	F-12	VF-20	EF-40	AU-50	MS-60	MS-63
"ET IND : IMP :" Obverse (1937-1947)								
1937	2,689,813	*	5.00	6.50	10.00	14.00	25.00	60.00
1938	3,149,245	*	5.00	7.50	15.00	50.00	125.00	250.00
1939	3,532,495	*	5.00	7.50	12.00	40.00	110.00	225.00
1940	9,583,650	*	4.00	5.00	7.50	12.00	25.00	55.00
1941	6,654,672	*	4.00	5.00	7.50	12.00	30.00	60.00
1942	6,935,871	*	4.00	5.00	7.50	12.00	30.00	60.00
1943	13,559,575	*	4.00	5.00	7.50	12.00	30.00	60.00
1944	7,216,237	*	4.00	5.00	9.50	20.00	50.00	125.00
1945	5,296,495	*	4.00	5.00	7.50	10.00	25.00	55.00
1946	2,210,810	*	4.00	6.50	12.50	30.00	75.00	125.00
1947 normal date	1,524,544	*	4.00	7.00	15.00	40.00	90.00	175.00
1947 dot	incl. above	32.50	70.00	110.00	200.00	300.00	500.00	1,100
1947 maple leaf	4,393,938	*	4.00	5.00	6.00	12.50	30.00	50.00

High relief 1948-1952	Low relief 1951-1952	High relief Low relief
		Note style of letters, relation of 'A' to denticles

Modified Legend, High Relief Bust (1948-1952), Low Relief Bust (1951-1952)

Date	Qty. Minted	VG-8	F-12	VF-20	EF-40	AU-50	MS-60	MS-63
1948	2,564,424	*	4.00	6.50	12.50	35.00	90.00	200.00
1949	7,988,830	*	*	4.00	5.00	8.50	20.00	40.00
1950	9,673,335	*	*	4.00	5.00	7.00	15.00	30.00
1951 high relief bust	8,290,719	*	*	4.00	5.00	6.50	12.00	25.00
1951 low relief bust	incl. above	*	*	4.00	5.00	6.50	12.00	25.00
1952 high relief bust	8,859,642	*	*	4.00	5.00	6.50	12.00	25.00
1952 low relief bust	incl. above	*	*	4.00	5.00	6.50	12.00	25.00

Elizabeth II, Laureate Bust, 1953-1964

Diameter: (1953 large date) 23.62 mm, (1953 small date to 1964) 23.88 mm; weight: 5.83 grams; composition: .800 silver, .200 copper; edge: reeded

F: Leaves worn almost through; shoulder fold indistinct
VF: Leaves considerably worn; shoulder fold must be clear
EF: Laurel leaves on the head are somewhat worn

The initial obverse for the 1953 issue had a high relief, laureate portrait of the Queen by Mrs. Mary Gillick (M.G. on truncation) which did not strike up well on the coins. Later in the year, the rim width and coin diameter were increased, the obverse relieve lowered and the hair and shoulder detail re-engraved. The re-engraving included sharpening two lines which represented the fold in (not a shoulder strap on) the Queen's gown. The two varieties also differ in the positioning of the legend relative to the rim denticles and the style of some of the letters.

The reverse coupled with the "no shoulder fold" obverse in 1953 is exactly as that for the George VI issues. Together with the obverse change, however, came a new reverse with a smaller date, wider rim and modified caribou (note the change in the contour of the lower neck). After 1953, the reverse design was not significantly altered until 1967.

No shoulder fold, high relief,
narrow rim, 1953

Large date, narrow rim
1953

Date	Qty. Minted	F-12	VF-20	EF-40	AU-50	MS-60	MS-63
Large Date, No Shoulder Fold (1953)							
1953 large date 10,456,769			3.50	4.50	6.00	9.50	12.50

Shoulder fold, low relief,
wide rim, 1953-1964

Small date, wide rim,
modified caribou, 1953-1964

Date	Qty. Minted	F-12	VF-20	EF-40	AU-50	MS-60	MS-63
Small Date, Shoulder Fold (1953-1964)							
1953 small date .... incl. above		*	3.50	4.50	6.50	15.00	25.00
1954 2,318,891		*	6.50	13.50	22.50	45.00	65.00
1955 9,552,505		*	*	*	4.00	8.00	12.00
1956 11,269,353		*	*	*	4.00	6.00	8.00
1957 12,770,190		*	*	*	4.00	5.00	7.00
1958 9,336,910		*	*	*	*	5.00	6.00
1959 13,503,461		*	*	*	*	5.00	6.00
1960 22,835,327		*	*	*	*	5.00	6.00
1961 18,164,368		*	*	*	*	5.00	6.00
1962 29,559,266		*	*	*	*	4.00	5.00
1963 21,180,642		*	*	*	*	4.00	5.00
1964 36,479,343		*	*	*	*	4.00	5.00

*NOTE: Common silver coins (marked with *) are worth a premium only for their silver content. This price may vary according to prevailing market value of silver bullion.*

Elizabeth II, Tiara Obverse, 1965-1978

In 1965 an obverse with a new style portrait by Arnold Machin was introduced. The Queen has more mature facial features and is wearing a tiara. The reverse was continued as before, and physical specifications are as on the previous issues.

Date	Qty. Minted	MS-60	MS-63
1965 44,708,869		4.00	5.00
1966 25,388,892		4.00	5.00

Confederation Centennial, 1967

All denominations for 1967 bore special reverses to commemorate the 1867 confederation of Nova Scotia, New Brunswick and the Province of Canada, to form the Dominion of Canada. The design for this denomination, by Alex Colville, shows a bobcat as its device. During 1967 the alloy was changed to .500 silver, .500 copper.

Date	Qty. Minted	MS-60	MS-63
1967 .800 silver 48,855,500		3.00	4.00
.500 silver .... incl. above		3.00	4.00

Elizabeth II, 25 Cents Nickel, 1968 -

Diameter: 23.88 mm; weight: (silver) 5.83 grams (nickel) 5.05 grams; thickness (nickel): 1.60 mm; composition: (1968 silver) .500 silver, .500 copper, (nickel) .999 nickel; edge: reeded

During 1968, the composition was changed to pure nickel. The nickel specimens are slightly darker in color and are attracted to a magnet.

Date	Qty. Minted	MS-60	MS-63
1968 .500 silver 71,464,000		*	2.00
pure nickel 88,686,931		—	1.00
1969 133,037,929		—	1.00
1970 10,302,010		—	4.00
1971 48,170,428		—	1.00
1972 43,743,387		—	1.00

Royal Canadian Mounted Police Centennial, 1973

Large bust   Small bust

The 25-cent pieces for 1973 bore a special reverse designed by Paul Cedarberg (PC behind horse) marking the centenary of the founding of the Royal Canadian Mounted Police. The initial circulation strikes were made with an obverse bearing a small portrait engraved from Patrick Brindley's modification of the Machin bust of Queen Elizabeth. Aside from having a smaller portrait with more hair detail, Brindley's obverse has fewer beads, pulled in farther from the edge. To date the Brindley obverse has been used only in 1973.

Date	Qty. Minted	F-12	VF-20	EF-40	AU-50	MS-60	MS-63
1973 small bust	134,958,589	—	—	—	—	—	1.00
large bust	incl. above	50.00	75.00	100.00	125.00	150.00	200.00

Caribou Reverse Resumed, 1974 -

Date	Qty. Minted	MS-63
1974	192,360,598	1.00
1975	141,486,838	1.00
1976	86,898,261	1.00
1977	99,634,555	1.00

Increased Thickness, 1978 -

Diameter: 23.88 mm; weight: 5.10 grams; thickness: 1.58 mm; composition: .999 nickel; edge: reeded

1978	176,475,408	1.00

Modified Obverse, 1979-1989

Beginning with 1979, the portrait of the Queen was made smaller. This was done to standardize our coinage, making the size of the portrait proportional to the diameter of the coin, regardless of denomination.

1979	231,453,747	.75
1980	77,547,645	.75
1981	131,583,900	.75
1982	171,926,000	.75
1983	13,162,000	.75
1984	121,668,000	.75
1985	158,734,000	.75
1986	132,220,000	.75
1987	53,408,000	.75
1988	80,368,473	.75
1989	119,796,307	.75

Elizabeth II, Diadem Obverse, 1990 -

The first effigy designed by a Canadian for use on Canadian coins was introduced on the obverse of all Canadian issues for 1990. The design depicts a more contemporary portrait of the Queen wearing a necklace and earrings. The elaborate crown, last seen on Victorian issues, replaced the tiara used on previous issues. The obverse was designed by Dora de Pédery-HUNT.

Date	Qty. Minted	MS-63
1990	31,258,000	.75
1991	459,000	.75

125th Anniversary of Confederation, 1992

To celebrate the 125th anniversary of Confederation, all circulation 25-cent pieces issued in 1992 bear the date "1867-1992" on the obverse, below the Dora de Pédery-HUNT effigy of the queen. Ten million pieces each of twelve different reverse designs were issued, one for each province and territory, with a different reverse design released each month during 1992. The sequence of the release dates was determined by random draw.

The "CANADA 125" program of special commemorative issues for 1992 includes the 12 different 25-cent pieces and a commemorative aureate dollar released on July 1st. The 25-cent pieces will also be struck in sterling silver and released as individually cased proof coins.

A cased proof set consisting of the commemorative aureate dollar and the twelve sterling silver 25-cent pieces was also issued.

New Brunswick   Northwest Territories   Newfoundland   Manitoba

Yukon   Alberta   Prince Edward Island   Ontario

Nova Scotia   Quebec   Saskatchewan   British Columbia

Prov. / Territory	Release Date	Design	Artist	MS-65
New Brunswick	January 9	Covered Bridge, Newton, N.B.	Ronald Lambert	.75
Northwest Territories	February 6	Pre-historic Inuit "inukshuk"	Ms. Beth McEachen	.75
Newfoundland	March 5	Fisherman in Grandy Dory	Christopher Newhook	.75
Manitoba	April 7	Lower Fort Garry	Murriel E. Hope	.75
Yukon	May 7	Kaskawalsh Glacier	Elizabeth (Libby) Dulac	.75
Alberta	June 4	Hoodoos	Melvin (Mel) Heath	.75
Prince Edward Island	July 7	Cousins Shore	Nigel Graham Roe	.75
Ontario	August 6	Jack Pines	Greg Salmela	.75
Nova Scotia	September 9	Lighthouse at Peggy's Cove	Bruce Wood	.75
Quebec	October 1	Percé Rock	Romualdus Bukauskas	.75
Saskatchewan	November 5	Prairie symbols	Brian E. Cobb	.75
British Columbia	November 9	Natural Beauty of B.C.	Carla Herrera Egan	.75

Date	Qty. Minted	MS-63
1993	.... N/A	.75
1994	.... N/A	.75

50 CENTS
Victoria, 50 Cents Silver, 1870-1901
Diameter: 29.72 mm; weight: 11.62 grams; composition: .925 silver, .075 copper; edge: reeded

G: *Hair over ear worn through*
VG: *No details in hair over ear; jewels in diadem are partly worn away*
F: *Strands of hair over ear begin to merge together; jewels slightly blurred*
VF: *Hair and jewels clear but not sharp*
EF: *Hair over ear and jewels of diadem slightly worn but generally sharp and clear*

In all, four portraits were used for this denomination. Except for the first two varieties, which have the same face, the portraits differ in the facial features as well as certain other respects. Each variety after the first was created by re-engraving an earlier one. The first and probably all later portraits were designed and engraved by L.C. Wyon but only on the final one or two varieties could he have been attempting to portray Queen Victoria as she appeared at the time. In some instances two portraits were coupled with a given date reverse. These are most easily differentiated as follows:

 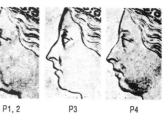

P1   P2   P1, 2   P3   P4

P1 vs P2: P1 has no initials on the truncation, a blank space immediately behind the front cross in the crown and a break in the left-hand ribbon end; P2 has L.C.W. on the truncation, a shamrock behind the front cross in the crown and no breaks in the ribbon ends.

P3 vs P4: P3 has a rounded chin front, and the lower front corner of the crown is in front of the forehead; P4 has a flat chin front and the lower front corner of the crown is even with the forehead.

The reverse device consists of crossed maple boughs, tied at the bottom by a ribbon and separated at the top by St. Edward's crown. Although there were several slight modifications, the most noteworthy occurred in 1871. This variety (1871-1901), derived from the first, has parts of both the crown and the wreath re-engraved. Both reverse varieties were by L.C. Wyon.

Date	Qty. Minted	G-4	VG-8	F-12	VF-20	EF-40	AU-50	MS-60	MS-63
First Reverse Design (1870)									
1870 no LCW P1	450,000	450.00	800.00	1,600	3,200	5,500	9,000	17,500	40,000
1870 LCW on obv. .. P2 ... incl. above		30.00	55.00	110.00	255.00	500.00	1,300	6,500	20,000
Modified Reverse Design (1871-1901) (See next page for illustration .)									
1871 .... P2	200,000	40.00	75.00	150.00	350.00	750.00	1,700	8,000	22,500
1871H P2	45,000	60.00	110.00	225.00	550.00	1,200	2,400	10,000	27,500

Normal 2   Short base 2

Specimens of the 1872H often have part or all of the
reverse legend repunched.

1872H, inverted A over V

Date		Qty. Minted	G-4	VG-8	F-12	VF-20	EF-40	AU-50	MS-60	MS-63
1872H normal 2	...P2	80,000	30.00	50.00	110.00	250.00	500.00	1,300	7,500	22,500
short base 2	.....P2 ...	incl. above	30.00	50.00	110.00	250.00	500.00	1,300	7,500	22,500
inv. A over V	....P2 ...	incl. above	60.00	125.00	250.00	600.00	1,300	3,000	9,000	25,000
1881H	...........P3	150,000	30.00	60.00	125.00	275.00	600.00	1,400	6,500	20,000
1888	...........P3	60,000	85.00	150.00	300.00	650.00	1,500	2,500	10,000	30,000
1890H	...........P3, 4 ...	20,000	550.00	1,000	2,000	3,500	6,500	11,000	20,000	45,000
1892	...........P4	151,000	35.00	65.00	140.00	325.00	650.00	1,500	9,000	25,000
1894	...........P4	29,036	175.00	350.00	650.00	1,500	3,000	5,000	15,000	35,000
1898	...........P4	100,000	35.00	65.00	140.00	325.00	625.00	1,500	8,000	22,500
1899	...........P4	50,000	65.00	125.00	275.00	650.00	1,600	2,700	11,000	30,000
1900	...........P4	118,000	20.00	50.00	90.00	225.00	500.00	1,250	7,500	20,000
1901	...........P4	80,000	25.00	50.00	90.00	225.00	500.00	1,250	7,000	20,000

Edward VII, 50 Cents Silver, 1902-1910

Diameter: 29.72 mm; weight: 11.62 grams; composition: .925 silver, .075 copper; edge: reeded

G: Band of crown worn through
VG: Band of crown worn through at
highest point
F: Jewels blurred in band of crown
VF: Band of crown still clear but no
longer sharp
EF: Band of crown slightly worn;
generally sharp and clear

A single obverse, designed and engraved by G.W. De Saulles (DES below bust), was used for the entire series.

For the initial reverse (1902-10) De Saulles utilized the unmodified wreath from the later Victorian reverse with a new legend and the Imperial State crown. A modification of the first variety (probably by W.H.J. Blakemore) appeared in 1910; several leaves and the cross atop the crown differ. The most noticeable change is in the two leaves at the far right opposite CANADA. On the first variety the leaves have long, pointed corners, whereas they are much shorter on the second.

Victorian Leaves Reverse (1902-1910) (Illustration on following page.)

1902	....	120,000	8.00	15.00	35.00	125.00	275.00	650.00	1,800	5,500
1903H	....	140,000	15.00	32.50	65.00	200.00	400.00	800.00	2,500	7,500
1904	....	60,000	60.00	125.00	250.00	500.00	1,100	2,250	6,000	15,000
1905	....	40,000	75.00	150.00	350.00	700.00	1,500	3,000	9,500	25,000

Victorian leaves
1902-1910

Edwardian leaves
1910.

Note 3 leaf tips near rim

Date	Qty. Minted	G-4	VG-8	F-12	VF-20	EF-40	AU-50	MS-60	MS-63
1906	350,000	10.00	20.00	40.00	110.00	275.00	650.00	2,000	6,500
1907	300,000	8.00	15.00	35.00	90.00	240.00	600.00	2,000	6,500
1908	128,119	17.50	40.00	80.00	225.00	550.00	1,000	2,250	6,500
1909	203,118	11.00	25.00	60.00	160.00	450.00	950.00	2,500	10,000
1910 (Victorian leaves)	649,521	8.00	16.00	35.00	90.00	235.00	550.00	1,800	6,500
Edwardian Leaves Reverse (1910)									
1910 (Edwardian leaves)	incl. above	8.00	15.00	35.00	90.00	235.00	550.00	1,800	5,500

George V, 50 Cents Silver, 1911-1936

Diameter: 29.72 mm; weight: (1911-1919) 11.62 grams, (1920-1936) 11.66 grams;
composition: (1911-19) .925 silver, .075 copper, (1920-36) .800 silver, .200 copper; edge: reeded

G: Band of crown worn through
VG: Band of crown worn through at
highest point
F: Jewels blurred in band of crown
VF: Band of crown clear but no longer
sharp
EF: Band of crown slightly worn;
generally sharp and clear

Two obverse varieties exist. The first (1911) lacks the phrase DEI GRATIA or an abbreviation for it and the second (1912-36) has DEI GRA incorporated into the legend. Both obverses were derived from a portrait model by Sir E.B. MacKennal (B.M. on truncation). See the 1-cent text for more details. The reverse is identical to the Edwardian leaves variety, introduced in the previous series.

1921. During the late teens and early 1920s far more 50-cent pieces were struck than were needed. Many of them remained in the Mint with only about 24,000 pieces being issued in 1921-28. In 1929 a sizable demand for this denomination arose. The Mint, however, fearing the public would doubt the authenticity of new coins bearing "old" dates, melted the 500,000 50-cent pieces in stock and struck new ones with the current date (1929). It seems very likely that most of the original 1921 mintage of 206,398 was included in this melt. Only about 100 of the 1921 issue survive today; most of these are business strikes, but a few specimen strikes (originally issued as part of specimen sets) are known.

"Godless" Obverse (1911)

Date	Qty. Minted	G-4	VG-8	F-12	VF-20	EF-40	AU-50	MS-60	MS-63
1911	209,972	12.00	20.00	100.00	400.00	850.00	1,200	2,200	4,500
Modified Obverse Legend (1912-1936)									
1912	285,867	5.00	8.50	30.00	120.00	300.00	800.00	2,000	4,500
1913	265,889	5.00	8.50	30.00	120.00	300.00	800.00	2,000	5,500
1914	160,128	10.00	20.00	80.00	275.00	700.00	1,500	3,000	10,000
1916	459,070	4.00	6.00	25.00	90.00	225.00	500.00	1,300	3,500
1917	752,213	3.50	5.50	20.00	60.00	180.00	350.00	900.00	2,500
1918	854,989	3.00	5.00	15.00	40.00	140.00	275.00	700.00	2,000
1919	1,113,429	3.00	5.00	15.00	40.00	140.00	275.00	700.00	1,800
1920	(Originally: 584,691)	3.00	5.00	18.00	60.00	225.00	450.00	1,000	2,500

Date	Qty. Minted	G-4	VG-8	F-12	VF-20	EF-40	AU-50	MS-60	MS-63
1921	.... (Originally: 206,328)	7,500	13,000	17,500	22,500	30,000	35,500	40,000	60,000
1929	 228,328	3.00	5.00	20.00	60.00	175.00	400.00	900.00	2,500
1931	 57,581	6.50	12.50	35.00	110.00	300.00	850.00	1,800	4,000
1932	 19,213	30.00	50.00	150.00	375.00	775.00	1,700	3,500	8,000
1934	 39,539	9.00	16.00	45.00	125.00	325.00	900.00	1,600	3,500
1936	 38,550	8.00	13.50	35.00	100.00	300.00	650.00	1,200	2,000

George VI, 50 Cents Silver, 1937-1952

Diameter: 29.72 mm; weight: 11.66 grams; composition: .800 silver, .200 copper, edge: reeded

VG: *No detail in hair above the ear*
F: *Only slight detail in hair above ear*
VF: *Where not worn, hair is clear but not sharp*
EF: *Slight wear in hair over ear*

There are two obverses, both of which have the bare-headed portrait of the King by T.H. Paget (H.P. below). The varieties differ in that the second (1948-52) incorporated the change in the King's titles which ensued when India was granted independence from England. See text on the 1-cent series for details.

In keeping with a Government decision to modernize all reverses, a simplified Canadian coat of arms was chosen for this denomination. The simplification involved omission of the crest, helmet and mantling, motto and floral emblems; in addition, no attempt was made to heraldically colour the shield and banners. The shield consists of the arms of England (three lions), Scotland (rearing lion), royalist France (three fleurs-de-lis) and Ireland (a harp) and is surmounted by a stylized Imperial crown. At the left is the English lion holding a lance with the Union flag; on the right is a Scottish unicorn holding a lance with the flag of royalist France. The whole is resting upon a layer of serried clouds. The initials KG flanking the crown indicate the designer, George Kruger-Gray.

The position of the final digit in the date varies because, during most of the 1940s, it was punched separately into each die. Such varieties are too minor to include in a catalogue of this kind.

Date	Qty. Minted	VG-8	F-12	VF-20	EF-40	AU-50	MS-60	MS-63
"ET IND : IMP :" Obverse (1937-1947)								
1937	 192,016	5.00	7.00	12.00	20.00	30.00	55.00	150.00
1938	 192,018	5.00	15.00	25.00	55.00	90.00	250.00	650.00
1939	 287,976	5.00	9.00	20.00	35.00	80.00	200.00	500.00
1940	 1,996,566	4.00	5.50	6.50	9.00	18.00	40.00	150.00
1941	 1,714,874	4.00	5.50	6.50	9.00	18.00	40.00	150.00

Date	Qty. Minted	VG-8	F-12	VF-20	EF-40	AU-50	MS-60	MS-63
1942	1,974,165	4.00	5.50	6.50	9.00	16.00	40.00	150.00
1943	3,109,583	4.00	5.50	6.50	9.00	16.00	40.00	150.00
1944	2,460,205	4.00	6.00	7.50	10.00	17.50	40.00	150.00
1945	1,959,528	4.00	5.50	6.50	9.00	16.00	40.00	150.00

'Hoof' in 6   Tall 7   Short 7   Tall 7   Short 7
(deteriorated die)   Without maple leaf   With maple leaf after date

1946 and 1949 "hoof." These items are apparently the products of damaged dies and as such are not true die varieties. (See *Introduction* for further comments on such items.)

1947 maple leaf and 7 varieties. The 1947 (no maple leaf) issue comes with two styles of 7 in the date. One is a rather tall figure, the bottom of which points to the left and the other is a shorter 7 with the bottom curving back to the right. Both 7s were also used for the maple leaf issue struck in 1948. See text for the l-cent series.

Date	Qty. Minted	VG-8	F-12	VF-20	EF-40	AU-50	MS-60	MS-63
1946 normal 6	950,235	4.50	6.00	8.00	13.50	30.00	90.00	250.00
'hoof' in 6	incl. above	25.00	35.00	75.00	200.00	600.00	1,600	3,000
1947 tall 7	424,885	5.00	7.50	10.50	25.00	70.00	150.00	300.00
1947 short 7	incl. above	5.00	7.50	10.50	25.00	70.00	150.00	325.00
1947 maple leaf, tall 7	38,433	20.00	30.00	55.00	90.00	150.00	325.00	550.00
1947 maple leaf, short 7	incl. above	1,800	2,400	3,000	3,500	5,000	6,500	8,500

Obverse, 1948-1952   'Hoof' over 9
                               (deteriorated die)

Modified Obverse Legend (1948-1952)

Date	Qty. Minted	VG-8	F-12	VF-20	EF-40	AU-50	MS-60	MS-63
1948	37,784	60.00	80.00	110.00	150.00	225.00	325.00	500.00
1949 normal 9	858,991	5.00	8.00	11.00	18.00	27.50	75.00	200.00
'hoof' over 9	incl. above	10.00	20.00	40.00	100.00	265.00	675.00	1,500

Lines in 0   No lines in 0
                 (overpolished die)

1950 no lines in 0. In 1950, the 50-cent dies were derived from a single, fully dated matrix in which the 0 of the date had 4 horizontal lines in its centre. Depending upon the amount of polishing or repolishing of each individual die, the lines in the 0 ranged from completely present to partially missing to entirely absent. Previous cataloguers have chosen to list as a separate entry those pieces that lack the lines. For futher comments on such items see *Introduction*.

Date	Qty. Minted	VG-8	F-12	VF-20	EF-40	AU-50	MS-60	MS-63
1950 lines in 0	2,384,179	*	5.00	7.50	9.50	12.00	20.00	40.00
1950 no lines in 0	incl. above	8.50	12.50	18.50	30.00	125.00	300.00	550.00
1951	2,421,730	*	5.00	6.00	7.00	10.00	15.00	35.00
1952	2,596,465	*	5.00	6.00	7.00	10.00	15.00	35.00

Elizabeth II, Laureate Bust, 1953-1964

Diameter: 29.72 mm; weight: 11.66 grams; composition: .800 silver, .200 copper; edge: reeded

VF: *Leaves considerably worn, shoulder fold must show*
EF: *Laurel leaves on head somewhat worn*
AU: *Trace of wear on laurel leaves*

The initial obverse for the 1953 issue had a high relief portrait by Mrs. Mary Gillick (M.G. on truncation) which did not strike up well on the coins. Later in the year the relief was lowered and the hair and shoulder detail re-engraved. On the second variety two lines at the shoulder, representing a fold in the Queen's gown, are clear, while on the first variety they are almost missing. The obverses also differ in the shape of some letters and in positioning of the legend relative to the rim denticles. See the 1-cent series for more details.

The first reverse for the 1953 issue, used only on the high relief "no shoulder fold" obverse, is identical to that used for the 1950-52 George VI coinages, both in the device and the style and size of the date. Later in the year a new reverse with a larger date and with design elements positioned closer to the rim denticles was introduced. The second reverse is associated with both the high and low relief obverses, the former combination being a mule.

In an attempt to reduce the "ghosting" that had been so common in the past, a third modification was introduced in 1955. It is characterized by smaller design elements.

	No shoulder fold, 1953			Small date, 1953			
Date	Qty. Minted	F-12	VF-20	EF-40	AU-50	MS-60	MS-63
Small Date Reverse (1953)							
1953 no shoulder fold	1,630,429	*	5.00	5.50	6.00	12.00	20.00

	With shoulder fold, 1953-1964			Large date, 1953-1964		

Date	Qty. Minted	F-12	VF-20	EF-40	AU-50	MS-60	MS-63
Large Date Reverse (1953-1954)							
1953 no shoulder fold .... incl. above		10.00	20.00	30.00	65.00	150.00	250.00
with shoulder fold .... incl. above		*	5.50	6.50	9.00	35.00	60.00
1954 506,305		6.00	9.00	15.00	25.00	40.00	60.00

Modified Reverse, 1955-1958

Date	Qty. Minted	F-12	VF-20	EF-40	AU-50	MS-60	MS-63
Smaller Coat of Arms (1955-1958)							
1955 753,511		5.00	7.00	10.00	18.50	30.00	45.00
1956 1,379,499		*	5.00	7.00	8.00	10.00	15.00
1957 2,171,689		*	*	5.00	6.00	9.00	12.00
1958 2,957,266		*	*	5.00	6.00	8.00	10.00

Complete Coat of Arms Reverse, 1959-1964

Physical specifications remain the same as previous issues.

The obverse for the 1959-64 issues continued to be the shoulder fold variety.

In 1957 the Canadian coat of arms, as described by the Royal proclamation of 21 November, 1921, was approved for all government purposes (except for the replacement of the Imperial crown with the St. Edward's crown, which Queen Elizabeth preferred). A representation of the complete coat of arms was consequently modelled and engraved for this denomination by Thomas Shingles (TS flanking lower part of the shield). As far as was practical, considering the size of the coins, heraldic colouring of the arms and flags was attempted: blue being represented by horizontal lines, while white or silver was left unshaded. On the 1959 issue, the background of the lower section of the shield (the Canadian emblem) was inadvertently coloured blue, instead of the correct white or silver. The lines were removed beginning with the 1960 issue and no further changes were made in the reverse until 1967.

Horizontal lines in
lower shield, 1959

No lines in lower
shield, 1960-1966

Date	Qty. Minted	EF-40	AU-50	MS-60	MS-63
"Blue" Lower Panel Reverse (1959)					
1959 3,095,535		*	5.50	6.50	10.00
"White" Lower Panel Reverse (1960-1966)					
1960 3,488,897		*	5.00	6.00	8.00
1961 3,584,417		*	*	6.00	8.00
1962 5,208,030		*	*	6.00	8.00
1963 8,348,871		*	*	5.50	7.00
1964 9,377,676		*	*	5.50	7.00

Elizabeth II, Tiara Obverse, 1965-1989

In 1965 an obverse with a new style portrait by Arnold Machin was introduced. The Queen has more mature facial features and is wearing a tiara.

The reverse and physical specifications continued as previously.

Date	Qty. Minted	AU-50	MS-60	MS-63
1965 12,629,974		*	5.50	7.00
1966 7,683,228		*	5.50	7.00

*Note: Common silver coins (marked with *) are worth a premium only for their silver content. This price may vary according to prevailing market value of silver bullion.

Confederation Centennial, 1967

All denominations for 1967 bore special reverses to commemorate the 1867 confederation of Nova Scotia, New Brunswick and the Province of Canada, to form the Dominion of Canada. The design, by Alex Colville, shows a howling wolf.

Date	Qty. Minted	AU-50	MS-60	MS-63
1967 Confederation commemorative 4,211,395		*	5.50	7.50

Elizabeth II, 50 Cents Nickel, 1968 -

Diameter: 27.13 mm; weight 8.10 grams; thickness: (1968-1979) 1.93 mm, (1980 -) 2.00 mm; composition: .99 nickel (min.); edge: reeded

With the resumption of the regular reverse design in 1968, two significant changes were made. The diameter and weight were reduced, and the composition was changed to nickel.

Date	Qty. Minted	MS-63
1968	3,966,932	$1.00
1969	7,113,929	1.00
1970	2,429,516	1.50
1971	2,166,144	1.00
1972	2,515,632	1.00
1973	2,546,096	1.00
1974	3,436,650	1.00
1975	3,710,000	1.00
1976	2,940,719	1.00

Modified Obverse and Reverse, 1977

1977 709,939   3.00

Modified Obverse and Reverse, 1978-1989

Square beads   Round beads

Date	Qty. Minted	MS-63
1978 square beads in crown 3,341,892		1.00
round beads in crown .... included above		5.00
1979 3,835,842		1.00
1980 1,943,155		1.00
1981 2,588,900		1.00
1982 2,236,674		1.00
1983 1,177,000		1.00
1984 1,502,989		1.00
1985 2,188,374		1.00
1986 781,400		1.00
1987 373,000		1.00
1988 220,000		1.00
1989 266,419		1.00

Elizabeth II, Diadem Obverse, 1990 -

The first effigy designed by a Canadian for use on Canadian coins was introduced on the obverse of all Canadian issues for 1990. The design depicts a more contemporary portrait of the Queen wearing a necklace and earrings. The elaborate crown, last seen on Victorian issues, replaced the tiara used on previous issues. The obverse was designed by Dora de Pédery-HUNT.

Date	Qty. Minted	MS-63
1990	207,000	1.00
1991	490,000	1.00

125th Anniversary of Confederation, 1992

To celebrate the 125th anniversary of Confederation, all circulation coins issued in 1992 bear the date "1867-1992."

	Qty. Minted	MS-63
1992	N/A	1.00
1993	N/A	1.00
1994	N/A	1.00

1 DOLLAR
George V, Silver Jubilee Dollar, 1935
Diameter: 36.06 mm; weight: 23.3 grams; thickness: 2.84 mm;
composition: .800 silver, .200 copper; edge: reeded

F: *Jewels in band of crown will be blurred*
V.F.: *Band of crown still clear but no longer sharp*
EF: *Band of crown slightly worn but generally sharp and clear*
AU: *Trace of wear in band of crown*

The first Canadian dollar issued for circulation had a special obverse to mark the 25th anniversary of the accession of George V. The portrait was from a model by Percy Metcalfe, used previously for the obverses of certain Australian and New Zealand coinages of 1933-35. The Latin legend is translated: "George V, King, Emperor; Regnal year 25."

The reverse device consists of a canoe manned by an Indian and a voyageur (travelling agent of a fur company), behind which is an islet with two trees. In the sky are lines representing the northern lights. On the front bundle in the canoe are the incuse initials HB; these signify Hudson's Bay Co., which played an important role in Canada's early history. The designer was Emanuel Hahn (EH at left under canoe).

Date	Qty. Minted	F-12	VF-20	EF-40	AU-50	MS-60	MS-63	MS-64	MS-65
1935	428,707	30.00	50.00	75.00	85.00	100.00	150.00	200.00	400.00

George V, Silver Dollar, 1936

The obverse for 1936 had the regular design for George V, first seen on the 1-cent through 50-cent business strikes in 1912. The designer was Sir E.B. MacKennal (B.M. on truncation). The master matrix from which the 1936 obverse dies were prepared was that made in 1911 for the dollar proposed at that time.

The reverse design, physical specifications and grading are as for the 1935 issue.

Date	Qty. Minted	F-12	VF-20	EF-40	AU-50	MS-60	MS-63	MS-64	MS-65
1936	306,100	15.00	20.00	25.00	35.00	60.00	150.00	350.00	950.00

George VI, Silver Dollar, 1937-1952

Diameter: 36.06 mm; weight: 23.3 grams; thickness: 2.84 mm;
composition: .800 silver, .200 copper; edge: reeded

F: *Only slight detail in hair above ear*
VF: *Where not worn, hair is clear but not sharp*
EF: *Slight wear in hair over ear*
AU: *Trace of wear in hair*

The obverse has the conventional bare-headed portrait of the King by T.H. Paget (H.P. under rear of neck), as used for the lower denominations.

The reverse remains unchanged from the George V issues.

Date	Qty. Minted	F-12	VF-20	EF-40	AU-50	MS-60	MS-63	MS-64	MS-65
1937	241,002	15.00	20.00	25.00	40.00	60.00	125.00	200.00	750.00
1938	90,304	35.00	50.00	70.00	80.00	130.00	400.00	1,000	2,500

Royal Visit Commemorative, 1939

In 1939 a special reverse was used on the dollar to mark the visit of George VI and Queen Elizabeth to Canada. The design shows the centre block of the Parliament buildings in Ottawa. Above is the Latin phrase *Fide Suorum Regnat*, meaning "he reigns by the faith of his people." The designer was Emanuel Hahn; his initials EH flanked the building on the original model, but were removed by government decision prior to the manufacture of the dies. Because of lack of demand, about 150,000 specimens were returned to the Mint and melted in 1940.

The obverse design and physical specifications are as for the 1937-38 issues.

1939	1,363,816	10.00	15.00	20.00	25.00	30.00	60.00	150.00	500.00

Voyageur Reverse Resumed, 1945-1948

During 1945-48 two major obverse varieties appeared on this and all lower denominations. The first has the usual legend containing ET IND : IMP : ("and Emperor of India") and the second has this phrase deleted. (See text on the 1-cent for more details).

The reverse design and physical specifications are as for the 1937-38 issues.

1947 varieties. The 1947 issue of the dollar has two styles of 7 in the date, which differ mainly in the lower tip of the 7. The 1947 maple leaf coins of 1948 have only one of these 7s. See the 1-cent text for details.

Pointed 7	Blunt 7	Maple leaf (blunt 7 only)

Date	Qty. Minted	F-12	VF-20	EF-40	AU-50	MS-60	MS-63	MS-64	MS-65
"ET IND : IMP :" Obverse (1945-1947)									
1945	38,391	95.00	140.00	175.00	250.00	400.00	900.00	1,650	2,750
1946	93,055	25.00	35.00	45.00	75.00	150.00	600.00	1,200	2,250
1947 pointed 7	65,595	110.00	140.00	175.00	350.00	700.00	1,800	3,500	7,500
blunt 7	included above	50.00	80.00	100.00	125.00	250.00	600.00	1,100	2,250
1947 maple leaf	21,135	150.00	200.00	250.00	375.00	600.00	1,200	2,000	3,250

Modified Obverse Legend, 1948-1952

1948	18,780	750.00	825.00	925.00	1,000	1,200	2,000	3,500	5,500

Newfoundland Commemorative, 1949

On December 31, 1949, Newfoundland became a province of the Dominion of Canada. To mark this event a special reverse appeared on the dollar for that year. The *Matthew*, the ship in which John Cabot is thought to have discovered Newfoundland, is depicted. Below is the Latin phrase FLOREAT TERRA NOVA. "May the new found land flourish." Thomas Shingles was the designer and engraver, engraving the master matrix entirely by hand. (T.S. above horizon at right) The obverse is as the 1948 issue, and the physical specifications remain unchanged.

Date	Qty. Minted	F-12	VF-20	EF-40	AU-50	MS-60	MS-63	MS-64	MS-65
1949	672,218	18.00	25.00	30.00	35.00	45.00	60.00	80.00	100.00

Voyageur Reverse Resumed, 1950-1952

The obverse for the final George VI Voyageurs is as on the 1948-49 issues. There are two noteworthy reverse varieties. The first is the usual "water lines" variety, used for all Voyageurs prior to 1950. The second is the so-called "no water lines" reverse of 1952. On this interesting variety the water lines on both sides of the canoe have been removed and the right-hand tip of the islet re-engraved so that it is both wider and longer than before. There can be no question that the "no water lines" was a deliberate issue; furthermore, unlike the "Arnpriors," it was created by the alteration of a matrix — not simply an individual die or dies. For some reason the modification was apparently not acceptable because it was used only during the one year.

"Arnprior" dollars of 1950 and 1955. In 1955 a firm in Arnprior, Ontario order-ed and received 2,000 silver dollars for use as Christmas bonuses. It was later discovered that these coins had only 1½ water lines (instead of the normal 3) to the right of the canoe. This difference became popular and was collected sep-arately from the "normal" counterpart. Further study revealed that some dollars of 1950, 1951 and perhaps 1952-53 have a similar water line configuration. Only the 1950 and 1955s are currently included in the major listings. These items are the result of inadvertent overpolishing of individual dies and as such are *not* true die varieties. In fact, for 1950, 1955 and certain other years there is a whole gamut of water line differences, ranging from 3 full lines to parts of all 3 to 1½. Collectors and cataloguers have tended to deem all partial water lines greater than 1½ as normal. Whether items like this have any place in a more general catalogue is very questionable; they are included here only because of their cur-rent popularity. For further comments on such issues, see *Introduction*. Physical specifications are as for the previous issues.

3 water lines, small islet tip (normal, 1935-1952)	1½ water lines 1950	No water lines 1952

Date	Qty. Minted	F-12	VF-20	EF-40	AU-50	MS-60	MS-63	MS-64	MS-65
"Water Lines" Reverse (1950-1952)									
1950 normal water lines	261,002	10.00	13.00	17.50	22.00	35.00	65.00	125.00	225.00
1½ lines "Arnprior"	incl. above	15.00	18.00	25.00	50.00	80.00	250.00	400.00	500.00
1951 normal water lines	416,395	10.00	13.00	16.00	20.00	35.00	70.00	125.00	175.00
1½ lines "Arnprior"	incl. above	40.00	80.00	100.00	150.00	300.00	450.00	700.00	1,100
1952	406,148	10.00	13.00	17.50	20.00	30.00	70.00	125.00	200.00
"No Water Lines" Reverse (1952)									
1952	incl. above	14.00	18.00	20.00	25.00	35.00	65.00	120.00	225.00

Elizabeth II, Laureate Bust, 1953-1964

Diameter: 36.06 mm; weight: 23:3 grams; thickness: 2.84 mm
composition: .800 silver, .200 copper; edge: reeded

VF: *Leaves considerably worn, shoulder fold must show*
EF: *Laurel leaves on head somewhat worn*
AU: *Trace of wear on laurel leaves*

The first obverse for 1953 had a high relief, laureate portrait of the Queen by Mrs. Mary Gillick (M.G. on truncation) which did not strike up well on the coins. Later in the year the rim width and coin diameter were increased, the relief lowered, and the hair and shoulder detail re-engraved. The re-engraving included sharpening two lines representing a fold in the Queen's gown. The two varieties also differ in the positioning of the legend relative to the rim denticles and the styles of some letters.

The reverse used with the 1953 "no shoulder fold" obverse was the "water lines" George VI variety. This has a very narrow rim and the triangular islet tip, extending to the canoe's right, ends about half way to the rim denticles. Together with the obverse change came a slightly modified reverse, the most distinctive features of which are a wider rim and a right-hand islet tip extending almost to the rim denticles.

1955 Arnprior. See previous series.

1957, 1 water line. This item had the same cause as the "Arnpriors" (see previous series) and is therefore not a true die variety.

Date	Qty. Minted	VF-20	EF-40	AU-50	MS-60	MS-63	MS-64	MS-65
Narrow Rim Reverse (1953)								
1953 no shoulder fold	1,074,578	12.00	14.00	16.00	20.00	40.00	80.00	175.00

No shoulder fold, 1953

Narrow rim, short islet tip, 1953

With shoulder fold

Wide rim, longer islet tip

Date	Qty. Minted	F-12	VF-20	EF-40	AU-50	MS-60	MS-63	MS-64	MS-65
Wide Rim Reverse (1953-1957)									
1953 with shoulder fold .... incl. above		7.00	12.00	14.00	16.00	20.00	40.00	80.00	125.00
1954	246,606	8.00	11.00	15.00	20.00	30.00	65.00	110.00	200.00
1955 normal water lines	268,105	8.00	11.00	15.00	20.00	30.00	65.00	110.00	200.00
"Arnprior"	incl. above	100.00	150.00	175.00	210.00	250.00	350.00	450.00	650.00
1956	209,092	12.00	17.00	20.00	25.00	40.00	85.00	160.00	275.00
1957 normal water lines	496,389	6.50	10.00	12.00	14.00	15.00	30.00	60.00	100.00
one water line	incl. above	10.00	17.00	20.00	25.00	30.00	60.00	125.00	225.00

'Arnprior' water lines (overpolished die) 1955

1 water line (overpolished die) 1957

British Columbia Commemorative, 1958

To commemorate the gold rush centenary and the establishment of British Columbia as an English Crown colony, a special reverse by Stephen Trenka was employed. (ST at right bottom of totem) British Columbia is the only area in Canada where the Indians constructed totem poles, so the design is very appropriate. It was rumored that this issue was unpopular with the coastal Indians because it contained an element which to them signified death.

The physical specifications for the coin remained unchanged.

Date	Qty. Minted	VF-20	EF-40	AU-50	MS-60	MS-63	MS-64	MS-65
1958 3,039,630		8.00	10.00	11.00	25.00	30.00	50.00	80.00

Voyageur Reverse Resumed, 1959-1963

There are two major varieties of the Voyageur reverse during this period. The first is the wide rim design, introduced in late 1953. The second has re-engraved water lines and northern lights.

Date	Qty. Minted	VF-20	EF-40	AU-50	MS-60	MS-63	MS-64	MS-65
Reverse of 1953-1957 (1959)								
1959 1,443,502		6.00	7.00	8.00	10.00	20.00	30.00	50.00
Recut Water Lines and Northern Lights (1960-1963)								
1960 1,420,486		6.00	7.00	8.00	10.00	20.00	30.00	50.00
1961 1,262,231		6.00	7.00	8.00	10.00	20.00	30.00	50.00
1962 1,884,789		6.00	7.00	8.00	10.00	20.00	30.00	50.00
1963 4,179,981		6.00	7.00	8.00	10.00	20.00	30.00	50.00

Confederation Meetings Commemorative, 1964

To mark the 100th anniversary of the meetings at Charlottetown, Prince Edward Island and Quebec, P.Q. which paved the way for Confederation, a special reverse was used for the 1964 dollar coin. The device is a circle within which are the conjoined French fleur-de-lis, Irish shamrock, Scottish thistle and English rose. The model was prepared by Thomas Shingles (chief engraver at the Royal Canadian Mint) from a sketch by designer Dinko Vodanovic. The initials of both men (D.V. and T.S.) appear along the inner circle.

The portrait on the obverse of this issue was re-engraved by Myron Cook, modifying Thomas Shingles' alteration of the original Gillick design. The revised features consist mostly of sharpened gown details.

The physical specifications for the coin remained unchanged.

Date	Qty. Minted	EF-40	AU-50	MS-60	MS-63	MS-64	MS-65
1964 7,296,832		7.00	8.00	10.00	20.00	30.00	50.00

Elizabeth II, Tiara Obverse, 1965-1989

In 1965 a new obverse portrait by Arnold Machin was introduced. The Queen has more mature features and is depicted wearing a tiara. Three obverse varieties exist for 1965. The first has a flat field and small rim beads, and was replaced because of unacceptably short die life. The second variety has a slighlty concave field, medium sized rim beads and slight changes in the portrait. Most distinctive is a very thin support to the rearmost jewel on the tiara. This variety was struck from a single "test die," made to determine whether a concave field would give better die life. The experiment was successful and a new matrix, punches and dies were prepared. Coins from these dies have the concave field and rim beads even larger than on the "test" variety. In addition, the medium and large beads varieties differ in the positioning of the legend relative to the rim beads.

The 1965-66 reverse is similar but not identical to the earlier Voyageurs. Physical specifications remain unchanged.

Small beads   Medium beads   Large beads
Details of NA in REGINA; note bead size and position
relative to apex of A

Pointed   Blunt   Detail of rear jewel in tiara
5   5   Small and large   Medium bead
                                      bead obverses   obverse

1965 date and combinational varieties. Coupled with the small and large beads obverses were two reverses, having trivially different 5s in the dates. The medium beads obverse is coupled with only one of the 5s.

Date	Qty. Minted	EF-40	AU-50	MS-60	MS-63	MS-64	MS-65
1965 small beads, pointed 5 .. Variety 1 ..	10,768,569	7.00	8.00	10.00	20.00	30.00	50.00
small beads, blunt 5 .... Variety 2 ..	incl. above	7.00	8.00	10.00	20.00	30.00	50.00
large beads, blunt 5 .. Variety 3 ..	incl. above	7.00	8.00	10.00	20.00	30.00	50.00
large beads, pointed 5 .. Variety 4 ..	incl. above	8.00	13.00	20.00	25.00	40.00	60.00
medium beads, pointed 5. Variety 5 ..	incl. above	15.00	20.00	30.00	70.00	125.00	250.00
1966 large beads obverse	9,912,178	10.00	11.00	12.00	20.00	30.00	50.00
1966 small beads obverse	incl. above		1,800	2,100	2,400	2,800	4,000

Confederation Centennial, 1967

All denominations of 1967 coins bore Confederation commemorative reverses designed by Alex Colville. During 1966, trial production runs were made with dies of the new designs. Those for the dollar had flat fields and the coins did not strike up well, so new dies with convex fields (giving concave or dished fields to the coins) were prepared. Almost all of the flat field dollars were apparently melted. Apart from the fields, the initial designs can be distinguished from the adopted ones by the positioning of the legends relative to the rim beads.

Flat fields

Concave fields

Note size and spacing of beads

Date	Qty. Minted	AU-50	MS-60	MS-63	MS-64	MS-65
1967 flat fields*	6,767,496**		Rare			
concave fields	incl. above	17.00	10.00	20.00	30.00	50.00

*Rarity not yet known.   **Note: Originally 6,909,237, but 141,741 pieces were re-coined in 1967.

Elizabeth II, Nickel Dollars, 1968-1986

Diameter: 32.13 mm; weight: 15.62 grams; thickness: 2.62 mm; composition: .99 nickel; edge: reeded

With the decision to eliminate silver from all circulating coins in 1968, the circulating dollar was reduced in size to achieve better striking on the hard nickel blanks. The obverse bearing Machin's effigy of the Queen was used throughout this series, with Hahn's voyageur reverse appearing on all issues except special commemoratives.

Voyageur Reverse, 1968-1976

Typical obverse 1968-1971	Voyageur reverse 1968, 1969, 1972, 1975, 1976	Typical obverse 1972-1976

Date	Qty. Minted	MS-63	Date	Qty. Minted	MS-63
1968	 5,579,714	2.25	1975	 3,685,615	2.50
1969	 4,809,313	2.25	1976	 3,256,000	4.00
1972	 2,193,000	2.75			

Manitoba Centennial, 1970

The reverse device depicts the prairie crocus and celebrates the centennial of Manitoba's entry into Confederation. The reverse design was by Raymond Taylor (RT to the right of the centre stem). The obverse was the same as for 1968-69.

Date	Qty. Minted	MS-63
1970 Manitoba	 4,140,058	3.50

British Columbia Centennial, 1971

The circulating dollar for 1971 uses a reverse de signed by Thomas Shingles (TS below shield), in corporating both the B.C. provincial arms and the flowering dogwood, official flower of British Col umbia, The obverse remained the same as for the previous issues.

Date	Qty. Minted	MS-63
1971 British Columbia	 4,260,781	3.50

Note:
In 1971 the mint began issuing collectors' dollars struck in .500 silver. These are not considered circulating coinage and are sold by the mint at a premium over the face value. All .500 silver dollars from 1971 to the present are listed in the section titled *Collectors' Issues.*

Prince Edward Island Centennial, 1973

The obverse of the 1973 circulating dollar features Patrick Brindley's modification of the Machin effigy of Elizabeth II (as used on the collectors' silver dollar in 1971). The reverse design depicts the PEI Provincial Legislature building and was modelled by Walter Ott (WO at right) from a sketch by Terry Manning (TM at left).

Date	Qty. Minted	MS-63
1973 Prince Edward Island	3,196,452	3.50

Winnipeg Centennial, 1974

The reverse design was modelled by Patrick Brindley (B at top) from a sketch by Paul Pederson (PP at bottom) and features a large "100" with an 1874 scene of Winnipeg's main street in the first "0" and the corresponding 1974 scene in the second "0."

The same design was used for the 1974 collectors' silver dollar.

Date	Qty. Minted	MS-63
1974 Winnipeg (nickel)	2,799,363	4.00

Modified Voyageur Reverse, 1977

In 1977 Emanuel Hahn's voyageur reverse was altered. The device was made smaller and the legend reduced in size and placed farther from the rim of the coin. The rim denticles were replaced by beads.

Date	Qty. Minted	MS-63
1977	1,393,745	4.00

Modified Obverse and Reverse, 1978-1986

In 1978 both sides of the circulating dollar were modified to appear more like the issues prior to 1977. The unmodified Machin portrait was restored to the obverse and the reverse returned to the pre-1977 voyageur design with rim denticles restored.

Date	Qty. Minted	MS-63	Date	Qty. Minted	MS-63
1978	2,948,488	3.50	1983	2,267,525	3.50
1979	2,954,842	3.50	1984	1,223,486	3.50
1980	3,291,221	3.50	1985	3,104,592	3.50
1981	2,778,900	3.50	1986	3,089,225	3.50
1982	1,098,500	3.50			

Constitution Commemorative, 1982

1982 was the first year in which two circulating nickel dollars were issued: a voyageur dollar and the commemorative Constitution dollar. The obverse of the latter bears a reduced version of the Machin design, with the 1982 date incorporated into the legend. The reverse features the well known painting of the Fathers of Confederation. This dollar was also issued encapsulated and cased, in select uncirculated condition, for collectors.

Date	Qty. Minted	Issue Price	MS-63
1982 Constitution commemorative	9,709,422		3.50
Select uncirculated in maroon velvet case	107,353	9.75	10.00

Jacques Cartier, 1984

Issued to commemorate Cartier's landing at Gaspé in 1534, this dollar bears the same obverse as the 1982 commemorative dollar with the date changed. The reverse design is by Hector Greville. An encapsulated, cased collectors' version of this dollar was also issued in proof quality only.

Date	Qty. Minted	Issue Price	MS-63
1984 Jacques Cartier commemorative	7,009,323		3.50
Encapsulated proof in green velvet case	87,776	9.75	Proof 10.00

Modified Design, 1987 -

Diameter: 26.72 mm (11-sided); weight: 7.0 grams; thickness: 1.95 mm; composition: aureate bronze plated on pure nickel; edge: plain

To overcome the high production cost of the dollar note, a new circulating dollar coin was introduced in 1987. Significantly smaller than previous dollar and 50-cent coins which did not circulate well because of their large size and weight, the new circulating dollar is only slightly larger than the 25-cent piece. To simplify identification of the new coin by the visually handicapped and by machine, its shape was changed from round to 11-sided, and the colour changed from white nickel to yellow gold.

The obverse bears the Arnold Machin effigy of Queen Elizabeth II, while the reverse device, designed by Robert Carmichael, depicts a Canadian Loon.

Although the loon dollar was the only circulation dollar issued during 1987, the familiar Voyageur nickel dollar was used in lieu of the loon in all three numismatic sets issued in 1987. The loon dollar was also issued singly in proof quality in 1987.

The one dollar note was not issued after July 1st, 1988.

Date	Qty. Minted	MS-63
1987	205,405,000	2.50
1988	138,893,539	2.50
1989	184,773,902	2.50

Elizabeth II, Diadem Obverse, 1990 -

The first effigy designed by a Canadian for use on Canadian coins was introduced on the obverse of all Canadian issues for 1990. The design depicts a more contemporary portrait of the Queen wearing a necklace and earrings. The elaborate crown, last seen on Victorian issues, replaced the tiara used on previous issues. The obverse was designed by Dora de Pédery-HUNT.

Date	Qty. Minted	MS-63	Date	Qty. Minted	MS-63
1990 68,402,000		2.50	1993 .... N/A		2.00
1991 23,156,000		2.00	1994 .... N/A		2.00
1992 .... N/A		2.00			

125th Anniversary of Confederation, 1992

A commemorative aureate dollar coin was released on July 1 to celebrate the 125th anniversary of Confederation. The reverse, designed by Rita Swanson of Churchbridge, Saskatchewan, depicts three children with a Canadian flag, seated before the centre block of the Parliament Buildings. The obverse bears the dates 1867-1992 below the Dora de Pédery-HUNT effigy of the queen. The commemorative aureate dollar was also struck in proof finish and sold as part of the "CANADA 125" proof set. For more information see page 111.

Date	Qty. Minted	MS-63
1992 Commemorative dollar .... N/A		N/A

GOLD 5 DOLLARS
George V, 5 Dollars Gold, 1912-1914
Diameter: 21.59 mm; weight: 8.36 grams; thickness: 1.82 mm;
composition: .900 gold, .100 copper; edge: reeded

VF: Band of crown still clear but no longer sharp
EF: Band of crown slightly worn but generally
   sharp and clear
AU: Trace of wear on band of crown

The obverse of this brief series was derived from a portrait model of the King by Sir E.B. MacKennal (B.M. on truncation).

The design selected for the reverse is still considered one of the most beautiful on Canadian coins. The device consists of the shield from the Canadian coat of arms, as granted by Queen Victoria in a Royal Warrant of May 26, 1868, behind which are crossed boughs of maple. The quartered shield has the arms of the four provinces which originally formed the Dominion. The arms are as follows: St. George's Cross above, three maple leaves below (Ontario); two fleurs-de-lis above, lion in centre, three maple leaves below (Quebec); a lion above, ancient galley below (New Brunswick); two thistles above, salmon in centre, single thistle below (Nova Scotia).

Date	Qty. Minted	VF-20	EF-40	AU-50	MS-60	MS-63
1912	154,745	200.00	250.00	300.00	450.00	1,000
1913	93,791	200.00	250.00	300.00	475.00	1,000
1914	29,078	450.00	550.00	700.00	1,100	3,500

GOLD 10 DOLLARS
George V, 10 Dollars Gold, 1912-1914
Diameter: 26.92 mm; weight: 16.72 grams; thickness: 2.08 mm;
composition: .900 gold, .100 copper; edge: reeded

The obverse was derived from the well known portrait model of the King by Sir E.B. MacKennal (B.M. on truncation).

The reverse, designed and engraved by W.H.J. Blakemore, is very similar to that on the five dollars described above. It is worth noting that the Canadian government also wanted to have additional gold denominations for George V. This is evidenced by a letter dated November 10, 1910, from the Master of the Royal Canadian Mint to the Royal Mint in London requesting that matrices and punches be prepared for "... $20 gold, $10 gold, $5 gold, $2½ gold ...." Obviously, plans were altered and only the $5 and $10 denominations were actually issued.

Date	Qty. Minted	VF-20	EF-40	AU-50	MS-60	MS-63
1912	70,752	425.00	525.00	700.00	1,250	4,000
1913	141,994	425.00	525.00	700.00	1,250	4,500
1914	135,292	550.00	650.00	850.00	1,500	4,750

3
CANADIAN COLLECTORS' ISSUES

This section includes those items and sets produced by the mint as collectors' issues and not released as circulating coinage. These are of special quality or unique design and are sold directly to collectors at a premium over the face value of the coins. Some sets issued in proof-like, specimen or proof condition have been broken by dealers or collectors to acquire higher-quality samples of the year's circulating coinage, although these coins were never released individually in these conditions. In these instances, this catalogue lists only the value of the complete sets as issued. Where, however, a coin was released exclusively as part of a set, the coin has been listed as an individual collectors' item as well.

The quality of strike on collectors' issues varies from series to series and care must be exercised in determining the quality of the strike.

PROOF-LIKE: This term is commonly used to describe the select uncirculated coins produced by the mint for collectors. These coins have been struck more slowly than the regular circulating coinage, using well-polished dies and select ed blanks, to produce a superior finish. Sometimes mistaken for specimen or proof coins by collectors, these coins are not double struck and the edges in particular are not as sharp and crisp as the superior specimen and proof strikes.

SPECIMEN: Prior to 1973, the Royal Canadian Mint lacked the capability of producing true proof-quality coins. Specimen sets and singles were produced prior to 1973. These were double-struck under higher pressure than circulating coins and possess sharper details and squarer edges than the proof-like quality, but do not come up to the superlative quality of proof coins.

PROOF: This is the highest quality in which coins are minted. Struck on selected blanks, they are the result of multiple, slow strikes under extreme pressure, using specially-prepared dies. The first proof-quality coins struck by the Royal Canadian Mint were those of the Olympic series, beginning in 1973. Proof quality coins usually exhibit a frosted relief with polished mirror fields and have sharp crisp edges. A proof coin should have no marks or abrasions.

CASED SILVER DOLLARS, 1971 -
(1971-1978): Diameter: 36.06 mm; weight: 23.3 grams; thickness: 2.84 mm;
(1971-1991): composition: .500 silver, .500 copper; edge: reeded

In 1971 the mint began issuing a series of .500 silver dollars in specimen condition for collectors. These were packaged in black leather cases and the coins have been issued encapsulated since 1974. Except for 1977 and 1978, when obverses were designed specifically for the issues, the obverse, with minor revisions, remained the same from1971 to1989, and illustrates the Patrick Brindley modification of the Arnold Machin effigy of Queen Elizabeth II. A new obverse design by Dora de Pédery-HUNT was introduced in 1990.

Since 1981 the dollars have been issued in brilliant uncirculated and proof each year.

British Columbia Centennial, 1971

Commemorating the entry of British Columbia into Confederation in 1871, this was the first non-circulating collectors' dollar ever issued in Canada. The reverse design, based on the provincial arms of B.C., was designed and modelled by Patrick Brindley.

Voyageur Reverse, 1972

The traditional Emanuel Hahn voyageur reverse was revised by Patrick Brindley for the collectors' silver dollar in 1972. The revised reverse design used beads rather than rim denticles.

Date	Qty. Minted	Issue Price	Value
1971	555,564	3.00	19.00
1972	350,019	3.00	12.00

Royal Canadian Mounted Police Centennial, 1973

In addition to the commemorative 25-cent circulation pieces, a collectors' .500 silver RCMP commemorative dollar was struck in 1973. The reverse design was modelled and engraved by Paul Cederberg.

Winnipeg Centennial, 1974

The obverse and reverse designs of this .500 silver commemorative are the same as the 1974 dollar struck in nickel, except that the diameter was increased to 36 mm.

1973 Black case	709,670	3.00	19.00
1973 Blue case with metal coat of arms	included above		35.00
1974 silver	728,947	3.50	19.00

Calgary Centennial, 1975

The 100th anniversary of the founding of the city of Calgary, Alberta, is commemorated by this issue. Donald D. Paterson designed the reverse, which depicts a rider on a bucking horse with oil wells and the city skyline in the background.

Date	Qty. Minted	Issue Price	Value
1975 silver	833,095	3.50	11.00

Library of Parliament Centenary, 1976

The reverse design for the 1976 silver dollar commemorates the centenary of the completion of the Library of Parliament building and was modelled principally by Walter Ott.

Date	Qty. Minted	Issue Price	Value
1976 Black case	483,722	4.00	22.00
1976 Blue leather case ..	incl. above		35.00

Queen Elizabeth II, Silver Jubilee, 1977

The silver dollar issue for 1977 commemorates the 25th anniversary of Queen Elizabeth's accession to the throne. The reverse, designed by Raymond Lee depicts the throne of the Senate of Canada, used for ceremonial events.

11th Commonwealth Games, 1978

The 11th Commonwealth Games, held in Edmonton, Alberta, August 3-12, are commemorated by this silver dollar. Featured on the reverse, designed by Raymond Taylor, is the symbol of the Commonwealth Games, surrounded by symbols depicting the ten games involved.

Date	Qty. Minted	Issue Price	Value
1977 Black case	744,848	4.25	19.00
1977 Brown velvet case	included above		45.00
1978 silver	640,000	4.50	19.00

Griffon Commemorative, 1979

Diameter: 36.07 mm; weight: 23.33 grams; thickness: 2.66 mm

Recognition of the first voyage on the Great Lakes by a commercial ship was the intent of this commemorative issue. The reverse, which depicts the *Griffon*, was designed by Walter Schluep.

Arctic Territories, 1980

Diameter: 36.07 mm; weight: 23.33 grams; thickness: 2.74 mm

This issue commemorated the centenary of the transfer of the Arctic Islands to the government of the Dominion of Canada by the British government. The reverse features a polar bear and was designed by Donald D. Paterson.

Date	Qty. Minted	Issue Price	Value
1979 Silver	670,697	5.50	30.00
1980 Silver	389,564	22.00	80.00

Trans-Canada Railway, 1981

1981-1982: Diameter: 36.07 mm; weight: 23.33 grams; thickness: 2.95 mm

The centennial of the construction of the Trans-Canada Railway is commemorated by this issue. The reverse, designed by Christopher Gorey, depicts a steam locomotive with a map of Canada in the background.

Founding of Regina, 1982

The 100th anniversary of the founding of Regina is commemorated by the 1982 silver dollar. The reverse was designed by Huntley Brown.

1981 uncirculated	496,400	14.00	45.00
1981 proof .... included above		18.00	55.00
1982 uncirculated	722,980	10.95	16.00
1982 proof .... included above		15.25	30.00

World University Games, Edmonton, 1983

Diameter: 36.07 mm; weight: 23.33 grams; thickness: 2.86 mm

This silver dollar was issued to commemorate the World University Games, held in Edmonton in July, 1983. The reverse was designed by Carola Tietz.

Toronto Sesquicentennial, 1984

The 150th anniversary of the incorporation of the City of Toronto is commemorated by this issue. The reverse design by David Craig depicts a voyageur with the City of Toronto skyline in the background.

Date	Qty. Minted	Issue Price	Value
1983 uncirculated	159,450	10.85	20.00
1983 proof	340,068	16.15	20.00
1984 uncirculated	133,563	11.40	20.00
1984 proof	571,079	16.95	17.00

National Parks Centennial, 1985

The 100th anniversary of the establishment of Canada's National Parks is commemorated by this issue. The reverse design by Karel Rohlicek depicts a moose against a wilderness background.

Vancouver Centennial, 1986

This dollar was issued to commemorate the centenaries of the City of Vancouver and the first transcontinental train crossing in 1886. The reverse was designed by Elliot John Morrison.

Date	Qty. Minted	Issue Price	Value
1985 uncirculated	163,314	12.00	30.00
1985 proof	576,317	17.50	20.00
1986 uncirculated	124,574	12.25	30.00
1986 proof	496,418	18.00	25.00

John Davis Expeditions, 1987

This issue commemorates the 400th anniversary of the John Davis expedition in search of the North West Passage. The reverse was designed by Christopher Gorey and modelled by Ago Aarand.

Canada's Industrial Pioneers, 1988

The 1988 silver collectors' dollar celebrates the 250th anniversary of the Saint-Maurice Ironworks, Canada's first heavy industry. They reverse design was conceived by Robert Ralph Carmichael.

Date	Qty. Minted	Issue Price	Value
1987 uncirculated	118,722	14.00	30.00
1987 proof	408,098	19.00	30.00
1988 uncirculated	118,281	15.00	30.00
1988 proof	278,891	20.00	50.00

Mackenzie River Bicentennial, 1989

The 1989 silver dollar celebrates Mackenzie's 1789 canoe expedition to the Arctic. The reverse was designed by John Mardon.

1989 uncirculated	86,624	16.25	25.00
1989 proof	275,585	21.75	50.00

Henry Kelsey, 1990

The 1990 silver dollar commemorates the 300th anniversary of Henry Kelsey's 1690 expedition to make peace with remote native tribes and establish trade for the Hudson's Bay Company. The reverse was designed by David Craig.

A new obverse design by Dora de Pédery-HUNT, depicting a more contemporary portrait of the Queen wearing a necklace and earrings as well as an elaborate crown last used on Victorian issues, was introduced in 1990. This is the first effigy designed by a Canadian for use on Canadian coins.

Date	Qty. Minted	Issue Price	Value
1990 uncirculated	99,445	16.75	20.00
1990 proof	254,959	22.95	30.00

Steamship Frontenac, 1991

The 175th anniversary of the launching of the Steamer *Frontenac*, the first Canadian-built steamship to operate on Lake Ontario, is commemorated by the 1991 issue. The reverse depicting the *Frontenac* passing at Gibraltar Point Lighthouse on Toronto Island was designed by David J. Craig.

Date	Qty. Minted	Issue Price	Value
1991 uncirculated	23,843	16.75	
1991 proof	195,424	22.95	

Kingston-York Stagecoach, 1992

Diameter: 36.070 mm; weight: 25.175 grams; thickness: 2.77 mm;
composition: .925 silver, .075 copper; edge reeded

The 1992 cased silver dollar commemorates the inauguration of the stagecoach service between Kingston and York (now Toronto) in 1817. Because of road conditions the service was maintained through the winter months only. The reverse design by Vancouver artist Karsten Smith depicts a horse-drawn coach with runners in lieu of wagon wheels. The obverse again features the Dora de Pédery-HUNT effigy of the queen.

This is the first coin of the series to be issued in sterling (92.5% silver); all previous issues having been struck in 50% silver and 50% copper.

Date	Qty. Minted	Issue Price	Value
1992 uncirculated	N/A	17.50	
1992 proof	N/A	23.95	

Stanley Cup, 1993

The reverse of the 1993 cased silver dollar celebrating the 100th anniversary of the Stanley Cup was designed by Toronto artist Stewart Sherwood. The obverse bears the Dora de Pédery-HUNT effigy of the queen.

The physical properties remain the same as for the previous issue.

Date	Qty. Minted	Issue Price	Value
1993 Uncirculated	N/A	17.50	
1993 Proof	N/A	23.95	

GOLD 20 DOLLARS
Diameter: 27.05 mm; weight: 18.27 grams; composition: .900 gold, .100 copper; edge: reeded

Elizabeth II, Confederation Centennial, 1967

This denomination was struck only for the special specimen set of Confederation Centennial coins (in a black leather box), originally sold to collectors for $40. This is the only coin in the set which does not bear the commemorative dates: 1867-1967. The obverse bears Arnold Machin's design, introduced on regular denominations in 1965. The reverse is an adaptation of the Canadian coat of arms by Myron Cook, using Thomas Shingles' model for the 50¢ type of 1959.

Date	Qty. Minted	Specimen
1967 Confederation commemorative 337,688		280.00

GOLD 100 DOLLARS

Olympic Commemorative, 1976

Uncirculated (with beads): diameter: 27.00 mm; weight: 13.337 grams; thickness: 2.15 mm; composition: .583 gold, .313 copper; .064 zinc; edge: reeded
Proof (without beads): diameter: 25.00 mm; weight: 16.965 grams; thickness: 1.962 mm; composition: .9166 gold, .010 silver, .0734 copper; edge: reeded

Two coins were issued in 1976 to commemorate the XXI Olympiad. Both obverses bear the Arnold Machin effigy of Queen Elizabeth II and are similar to the silver $5 and $10 olympic issues. The reverse device was designed by Dora de Pedery-HUNT, and depicts an athlete of ancient Greece being crowned with a laurel wreath. The larger uncirculated edition, struck in 14k gold, has beads around the perimeter of both sides. The 22k version was struck in proof quality only and has no beads.

Date	Qty. Minted	Issue Price	Value
1976 Olympic, uncirculated, 14k, with beads 650,000		105.00	115.00
1976 Olympic, proof, 22k, without beads 350,000		150.00	220.00

Elizabeth II, Silver Jubilee Commemorative, 1977

1977-1980: Diameter: 27.00 mm; weight: 16.965 grams; thickness: 2.55 mm;
composition: .9167 gold, .0833 silver; edge: reeded

The reverse device for 1977 features a bouquet of the official flowers of the provinces and territories designed by Raymond Lee. The obverse bears the Arnold Machin effigy of Queen Elizabeth II.

Canadian Unity, 1978

The reverse design by Roger Savage depicts twelve Canada Geese flying in formation to represent the unity of the ten provinces and two territories of Canada. The obverse, once again, is by Arnold Machin.

Date	Qty. Minted	Issue Price	MS-65 Proof
1977 Silver Jubilee	182,838	140.00	235.00
1978 Unity	200,000	150.00	230.00

International Year of the Child, 1979

Designed by Carola Tietz, the reverse depicts children playing beside a globe and commemorates the International Year of the Child. The obverse bears the Machin effigy of Queen Elizabeth II.

Arctic Territories, 1980

Arnold Machin's obverse design was used again in 1980. The reverse device, by Arnaldo Marchetti. bears no legend. The issue commemorated the centenary of the transfer of the Arctic islands from Britain to Canada.

Date	Qty. Minted	Issue Price	MS-65 Proof
1979 Year of the Child	250,000	185.00	230.00
1980 Arctic Territories	130,275	430.00	230.00

"O Canada" Commemorative, 1981

1981-1982: Diameter: 27.0 mm; weight: 16.965 grams; thickness: 2.393 mm;
composition: .9167 gold, .0833 silver; edge: reeded

This proof issue commemorates the adoption of *O Canada* as the Canadian national anthem on July 1, 1980. The reverse design is by Roger Savage and the obverse by Arnold Machin.

Canadian Constitution, 1982

This issue celebrates the patriation of the Canadian Constitution. The reverse was designed by Friedrich Peter, obverse by Arnold Machin.

Date	Qty. Minted	Issue Price	MS-65 Proof
1981 "O Canada"	100,950	300.00	230.00
1982 Constitution	121,706	285.00	230.00

St. John's Newfoundland, 1983

1983-1986: Diameter: 27.0 mm; weight: 16.965 gramms; thickness: 2.25 mm;
composition: .9167 gold, .0833 silver; edge: reeded

The 400th anniversary of Sir Humphrey Gilbert's landing in Newfoundland is commemorated by the 1983 issue. The obverse is by Arnold Machin and the reverse by John Jaciw. The word CANADA appears on the edge.

Jacques Cartier, 1984

The 450th anniversary of Cartier's landing at Gaspe in 1534 is the subject of this issue. The reverse is by Carola Tietz and the obverse by Arnold Machin. The edge security lettering of 1983 was not repeated for 1984.

National Parks, 1985

The 100th anniversary of the establishment of Canada's National Parks is commemorated by this issue. The reverse was designed by Hector Greville.

Date	Qty. Minted	Issue Price	MS-65 Proof
1983 St. John's Nfld.	83,200	310.00	235.00
1984 Jacques Cartier	67,662	325.00	245.00
1985 National Parks	61,332	325.00	270.00

International Year of Peace, 1986

Celebrating the International Year of Peace, the reverse device was designed and modelled by Dora de Pédery-HUNT. The obverse bears the Arnold Machin effigy of Queen Elizabeth II.

Date	Qty. Minted	Issue Price	MS-65 Proof
1986 Peace	76,225	325.00	235.00

XVth Winter Olympic Games, 1987

1987-1990: Diameter: 27.00 mm; weight: 13.338 grams; thickness: 2.18 mm; composition: .5833 gold, .4167 silver; edge: (1987) lettered, (1988 -) reeded

Commemorating the winter olympic games held in Calgary in 1988, the reverse device was designed by Friedrich Peter. The obverse is once again by Arnold Machin. The legend XV OLYMPIC WINTER GAMES – XVES JEUX OLYMPIQUES D'HIVER appears on the edge of the coin.

Bowhead Whale, 1988

The 1988 issue was intended to bring public attention to environmental issues. The Bowhead whale is a protected species. The revers was designed by Robert Ralph Carmichael and the obverse, again, is by Arnold Machin.

Date	Qty. Minted	Issue Price	MS-65 Proof
1987 Olympics	145,175	255.00	150.00
1988 Bowhead whale	52,594	255.00	320.00

Sainte-Marie Among the Hurons, 1989

The reverse of this issue, which commemorates the 350th anniversary of the first european settlement in Ontario, was designed by David Craig. The Arnold Machin effigy of the Queen was again used on the obverse.

Date	Qty. Minted	Issue Price	MS-65 Proof
1989 Sainte-Marie Among the Hurons	63,642	245.00	235.00

International Literacy Year, 1990

The 1990 issue celebrates the United Nations Literacy Year, and bears a reverse design by John Mardon. The obverse bears the new effigy of the Queen by Dora de Pédery-HUNT.

Date	Qty. Minted	Issue Price	MS-65 Proof
1990 United Nations Literacy Year	49,940	245.00	245.00

Empress of India Centennial, 1991

Diameter: 26.09 mm; weight: 13.338 grams; thickness: 2 mm;
composition: .583 gold, .417 silver; edge: reeded

Commemorating the beginning of the era of the "Great White Empresses," three ships commissioned by the Canadian Pacific to provide passenger and cargo service across the Pacific at record speeds.

The reverse was designed by Karsten Smith and depicts the arrival of the *Empress of India* at the Port of Vancouver on her maiden voyage from Japan in 1891.

Date	Qty. Minted	Issue Price	MS-65 Proof
1991 Empress of India Centennial	33,966	245.00	260.00

350th Anniversary of Montreal, 1992

Issued to celebrate the 350th anniversary of the founding of Montreal (then Ville-Marie), the coin features a reverse designed by Ontario artist Stewart Sherwood. The date appears on the obverse, below the Dora de Pédery-HUNT effigy of the queen.

Date	Qty. Minted	Issue Price	MS-65 Proof
1992 Montreal .... N/A		239.85	250.00

The Featherstonhaugh, 1993

Diameter: 27.0 mm; weight: 13.338 grams; thickness: 2.15 mm;
composiyion: .583 gold, .417 silver; edge: reeded.

Celebrating the evolution of the automobile 100 years ago, the reverse features the Featherstonhaugh, Canada's first electric car, built in 1893. The reverse design is by John Mardon. The obverse again features the Dora de Pédery-HUNT effigy of the queen.

1993 Featherstonhaugh .... N/A	239.85	250.00

GOLD 200 DOLLARS, 1990 -

Diameter: 29 mm; weight: 17.106 grams; composition: .916 gold, .0833 silver; edge: reeded

Silver Jubilee of Canadian Flag, 1990

The first Canadian $200 gold coin was issued to commemorate the 25th anniversary of the Canadian flag, and honours the spirit and promise of Canadian youth. The issue was limited to 25,000 proof pieces worldwide.

The obverse bears the new effigy of the Queen by Dora de Pédery-HUNT. The reverse was designed by Stewart Sherwood and illustrates a multicultural group of Canadian children carrying the flag of Canada.

Date	Qty. Minted	Issue Price	MS-65 Proof
1990 Jubilee of Canadian Flag	20,980	395.00	405.00

Hockey, a National Passion, 1991

The 1991 issue pays tribute to the game of hockey. The reverse was designed by Stewart Sherwood. The obverse bears the Dora de Pédery-HUNT effigy of the queen.

Niagara Falls, 1992

The reverse of the third in a series of $200 gold coins celebrating the spirit and promise of Canadian youth features two children playing near the Niagara Falls and was designed by Ontario artist John Mardon.

The obverse bears the Dora de Pédery-HUNT effigy of the queem.

Date	Qty. Minted	Issue Price	MS-65 Proof
1991 Hockey, a National Passion	8,741	425.00	435.00
1992 Niagara Falls	N/A	389.65	

125th Anniversary of Confederation, 1992

(Aureate Dollar): Diameter: 26.50 mm; weight: 7.0 grams; edge: plain;
composition: aureate bronze plated on pure nickel
(25¢ sterling): Diameter: 23.88 mm; weight: 6.0 grams; edge: reeded;
composition: .925 silver, .075 copper

To celebrate the 125th anniversary of Confederation, the Royal Canadian Mint issued a different 25-cent piece each month during 1992 to represent the 10 provinces and 2 territories. On July 1st, a commemorative aureate dollar was issued, representing the country as a whole.

The CANADA 125 proof set consists of one each of the 25-cent pieces, struck in .925 sterling silver, housed together with the commemorateive aureate dollar in a flocked royal blue display case.

The commemorative sterling silver 25-cent pieces were also offered singly in individual display cases.

Description	Qty. Minted	Issue Price	Proof
1992 CANADA 125 proof set	N/A	129.45	135.00
1992 Commemorative 25¢ proof (each)	N/A	9.95	10.00

PROOF-LIKE MINT SETS AND DOLLARS

The Numismatic Section of the Royal Canadian Mint was established in 1949. Prior to this the Ottawa branch of the Bank of Canada had accepted orders for Uncirculated sets of the coinage for the current year (and sometimes the previous year) at face value plus postage. The sets were shipped in cellophane envelopes until 1953 and in white cardboard holders enclosed in cellophane envelopes from 1953 to 1960. Most of the coins in the year sets of this period were regular production strikes but some of the coins for at least the period 1951-53 possessed a markedly superior finish. In 1954 dealer J.E. Charlton coined the term "proof-like" to describe one such 1953 set. These coins represented the modest beginnings of attempts by the mint to produce superior quality coins for collectors.

From 1961 to the present, all "uncirculated" or "select uncirculated" year sets sold by the mint have been of proof-like quality (although difficulty was experienced in producing a good surface on the coins in 1965 and again in 1968-69) and sealed in pliofilm or polyester film.

Most years it was possible to order proof-like dollars separately. These were not officially issued in 1953 or 1965-67, but are available from broken sets. Proof-like dollars were issued separately in separate cases from 1970 to 1976 but have been available only as part of complete proof-like year sets since that time.

PROOF-LIKE SETS

Date		Qty. Minted	Issue Price	PL-65
1953	Shoulder fold .... *		2.20	1,500
1954	No shoulder fold 1¢ 7,426**		2.50	750.00
1954	Shoulder fold 1¢ .. incl. above		2.50	350.00
1955	.... 6,301**		2.50	260.00
1955	Arnprior .... incl. above		2.50	375.00
1956	.... 9,018**		2.50	150.00
1957	.... 11,862**		2.50	80.00
1958	 18,259		2.50	70.00
1959	 31,577		2.50	40.00
1960	 64,097		2.60	22.00
1961	 98,373		3.00	17.00
1962	 200,950		3.00	16.00
1963	 673,006		3.00	9.00
1964	 1,653,162		3.00	9.00
1965	Pointed 5 dollar 2,904,352		4.00	9.00
1965	Blunt 5 dollar ..... incl. above		4.00	9.00
1966	 672,514		4.00	9.00
1967	 963,714		4.00	15.00
1968	 521,641		4.00	4.00
1969	 326,203		4.00	4.00
1970	 349,120		4.00	5.00
1971	 253,311		4.00	4.00
1972	 224,275		4.00	4.00
1973	Small bust 25¢ ... 243,695		4.00	4.00
1973	Large bust 25¢ ... incl. above		4.00	175.00
1974	 213,589		5.00	5.00
1975	 197,372		5.00	4.00
1976	 171,737		5.25	6.00
1977	 225,307		5.25	5.00
1978	 260,000		5.25	4.00
1979	 187,624		6.25	6.00
1980	 169,390		8.00	8.00

PROOF-LIKE DOLLARS

Date		Qty. Minted	PL-65
1949	.... *		125.00
1950	.... *		275.00
1951	.... *		300.00
1952	No water lines ..... *		300.00
1953	Shoulder fold ...... *		850.00
1954	.... 1,268**		250.00
1955	.... 5,501**		175.00
1955	Arnprior incl. above		300.00
1956	.... 6,154**		100.00
1957	.... 4,379**		55.00
1958	 14,978		40.00
1959	 13,583		25.00
1960	 18,631		18.00
1961	 22,555		15.00
1961	 47,591		12.00
1962	 290,529		10.00
1964	 1,209,279		8.00
1965	Pointed 5 .... —		8.00
1965	Blunt 5 .... —		8.00
1966	.... —		8.00
1967	.... —		10.00
1968	 885,124		2.00
1969	 211,112		2.00
1970	 297,547		3.00
1971	 181,091		3.00
1972	 143,392		3.00
1973	 174,810		3.00
1974	 105,901		3.00
1975	 88,102		3.00
1976	 74,207		3.00
1977	.... —		3.00
1978	.... —		3.00
1979	.... —		3.00
1980	.... —		3.00

*Unknown   **Estimated

NOTE: Nickel dollars from 1970 to 1976 were cased individually and were also in proof-like sets. After 1976, all proof-like dollars have been available only in proof-like or uncirculated sets.

UNCIRCULATED SETS, 1981 -

In 1981 the Numismatic Products Section of the mint began issuing the year's decimal coinage in three distinct qualities (Proof, Specimen and Uncirculated) for collectors. The uncirculated sets replace the proof-like sets of previous years and are similarly packaged. Except in 1987, when a nickel voyageur dollar was substituted for the loon dollar, these sets contain one of each denomination of the year's circulation coinage.

Because of the continued popularity of the dollars contained in these sets, their value is also listed separately.

		UNCIRCULATED SETS				DOLLARS	
Date		**Qty. Minted**	**Issue Price**	**Value**	**Date**		**Value**
1981		186,250	5.00	7.00	1981		5.00
1982		203,287	5.00	6.00	1982		4.00
1983		190,838	5.40	10.00	1983		7.00
1984		181,249	6.65	9.00	1984		5.00
1985		173,924	6.95	11.00	1985		6.00
1986		167,338	6.95	16.00	1986		8.00
1987	Voyageur dollar*	212,136	6.95	10.00	1987	Voyageur	7.00
1988	Loon dollar	182,048	7.25	10.00	1988	Loon	7.00
1989		173,622	7.70	15.00	1989		7.00
1990		170,791	7.70	14.00	1990		—
1991		130,867	8.50	—	1991		—
1992		N/A	9.50	—	1992		—
1993		N/A		—	1993		—

*The round voyageur nickel dollar was issued in all three collectors' sets in 1987. This dollar was never issued as a circulation dollar.

SPECIMEN & PROOF SETS

From the early days of the 19th century, mints around the world have struck small quantities of coins in superior quality for presentation to visiting dignitaries, etc. In some years these "specimen" sets were made available to the general public to add to their collections. These coins are from immaculately treated dies and planchets and are struck on slow-moving presses under higher than normal pressure. The coins so produced all have unusually sharp details and sharp edges. Although the device is usually frosted, the fields can be either frosted or mirror-like. Specimen coins from the 1858 Province of Canada and the 1870 Dominion of Canada issues were made available to collectors. Since its inception in 1908, the Royal Canadian Mint, Ottawa has produced in most years a small number of specimen sets, although sets were offered for sale to the public only in the years 1908, 1911 and 1937. The appearance of some specimen pieces of Canadian coins has rivalled that of coins produced as "proof" in the United States, but the Royal Canadian Mint has never considered them to be of the superlative quality of Royal Mint (London) proofs. Hence Canada's strikings prior to 1980 have been officially designated as specimen quality. Beginning in 1981, the Royal Canadian Mint began offering proof quality coins as well as Specimen sets.

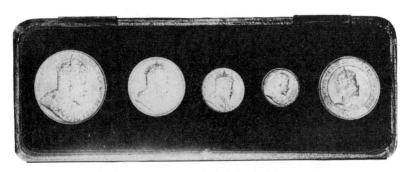

CANADA
Specimen Sets, 1858-1965

Date	Description	Case	MS-65
1858	Victoria 1¢, 5¢ (small date), 10¢, 20¢	None	25,000
1858	Victoria 1¢, 5¢ (large date), 10¢, 20¢	None	28,000
1858	Victoria double set – 2 each 1¢, 5¢ (small date), 10¢, 20¢	Leather pouch	50,000
1870	Victoria 5¢, 10¢, 25¢, 50¢	None	45,000
1870	Victoria double set – 2 each 5¢, 10¢, 25¢, 50¢	Leather	85,000
1902	Edward VII 1¢, 5¢, 10¢, 25¢	None	30,000
1908	Edward VII 1¢, 5¢, 10¢, 25¢, 50¢	Leather	3,200
1911	George V 1¢, 5¢, 10¢, 25¢, 50¢	Leather	10,000
1911-12	George V 1¢, 5¢, 10¢, 25¢, 50¢, £1, $5, $10	Leather	85,000
1921	George V 1¢, 5¢, 10¢, 25¢, 50¢	None	175,000
1929	George V 1¢, 5¢, 10¢, 25¢, 50¢	None	25,000
1930	George V 1¢, 5¢, 10¢, 25¢	None	12,000
1934	George V 1¢, 5¢, 10¢, 25¢, 50¢	None	30,000
1936	George V 1¢, 5¢, 10¢, 25¢, 50¢	None	25,000
1937	George VI 1¢, 5¢, 10¢, 25¢, 50¢, $1.00 (mirror finish)	Leather	4,500
1937	George VI 1¢, 5¢, 10¢, 25¢, 50¢, $1.00 (mirror finish)	Cardboard	4,000
1937	George VI 1¢, 5¢, 10¢, 25¢, 50¢, $1.00 (matte finish)	Cardboard	950.00
1937	George VI 1¢, 5¢, 10¢, 25¢ (mirror finish)	Leather	3,500
1938	George VI 1¢, 5¢, 10¢, 25¢, 50¢, $1.00	Leather	25,000

Date	Description	Case	MS-65
1944	George VI 1¢, 5¢, 10¢, 25¢, 50¢	None	25,000
1945	George VI 1¢, 5¢, 10¢, 25¢, 50¢, $1.00	Leather	12,000
1946	George VI 1¢, 5¢, 10¢, 25¢, 50¢, $1.00	Leather	12,000
1947	George VI 1¢, 5¢, 10¢, 25¢, 50¢, $1.00	Leather	22,500
1947ML	George VI 1¢, 5¢, 10¢, 25¢, 50¢, $1.00 (50¢ curved right)	Leather	15,000
1947ML	George VI 1¢, 5¢, 10¢, 25¢, 50¢, $1.00 (50¢ curved left)	Leather	15,000
1948	George VI 1¢, 5¢, 10¢, 25¢, 50¢, $1.00	Leather	12,500
1949	George VI 1¢, 5¢, 10¢, 25¢, 50¢, $1.00	Leather	6,000
1950	George VI 1¢, 5¢, 10¢, 25¢, 50¢, $1.00	Leather	5,000
1951	George VI 1¢, 5¢ (both types), 10¢, 25¢, 50¢, $1.00	None	5,000
1952	George VI 1¢, 5¢, 10¢, 25¢, 50¢, $1.00 (water lines)	Leather	7,500
1953	Elizabeth II 1¢, 5¢, 10¢, 25¢, 50¢, $1.00 (no shoulder fold)	Leather	3,000
1953	Elizabeth II 1¢, 5¢, 10¢, 25¢, 50¢, $1.00 (shoulder fold)	Leather	2,000
1964	Elizabeth II 1¢, 5¢, 10¢, 25¢, 50¢, $1.00	Leather	1,000
1965	Elizabeth II 1¢, 5¢, 10¢, 25¢, 50¢, $1.00	Leather	900.00

Centennial Presentation Set, 1967

In 1967, the Mint produced two special cased coin sets to celebrate the 100th anniversary of Confederation. The Gold Presentation set, containing 1¢ to $1 and a $20 gold coin, was sold to the public for $40.00. The coins were contained in a black leather box and were of specimen quality. In addition to the Gold Presentation set, a special set was offered in a red presentation case containing the 1¢ to $1 plus a sterling silver medallion designed by Thomas Shingles. The coins were all of proof-like quality.

Date		Qty. Minted	Issue Price	MS-65
1967	1¢ to $1, plus $20.00 gold (specimen quality)	337,687	40.00	250.00
1967	1¢ to $1, plus silver medal (proof-like quality)	72,463	12.00	30.00

V.I.P. Specimen Presentation Sets, 1969-1976

A very limited number of cased Specimen sets were produced by the Mint beginning in 1969 for presentation to dignitaries visiting the Royal Canadian Mint or other parts of Canada. (A small quantity of 1970 cased Specimen sets were sold to the public for $13.00 each.) The coins, 1¢ to $1 were cased in long narrow leather cases (black and other colours).

Date	Qty. Issued	Value	Date	Qty. Issued	Value
1969	2 known	2,000	1973	26	800.00
1970	100	750.00	1974	72	800.00
1971	69	800.00	1975	94	800.00
1972	25	800.00	1976	Unknown	800.00

NOTE: Sets may have been issued from 1977 to date (information not available).

Custom and Prestige Sets, 1971-1980

In 1971 the mint began offering three coin sets of different qualities to the public. In addition to the popular Proof-like sets which had been issued in a sealed pliofilm pack since 1961, the mint now offered Custom and Prestige sets.

Custom set This set has one piece of each denomination 1¢ to $1 (nickel), plus an extra cent to show the obverse, packaged in a square, vinyl covered box. The quality was proof-like from 1971 to 1976 and specimen from 1977 to 1980.

Prestige set The set consists of one piece of each denomination 1¢ to $1 (nickel) plus the commemorative silver dollar (except in 1971 and 1972 when the extra dollar was nickel), in a rectangular black leather case. The coin quality was specimen. From 1974 to 1980 the coins were mounted in a plastic page frame.

DOUBLE CENT "CUSTOM" SET

Date	Qty. Minted	Issue Price	MS-65
1971	33,517	6.50	7.00
1972	38,198	6.50	7.00
1973 25¢ large bust ...	49,376	6.50	175.00
1973 25¢ small bust incl. above		6.50	7.00
1974	44,296	8.00	7.00
1975	36,851	8.15	7.00
1976	28,162	8.15	12.00
1977	42,198	8.15	7.00
1978	41,000	8.75	9.00
1979	31,174	10.75	12.00
1980	41,447	12.50	14.00

DOUBLE DOLLAR "PRESTIGE" SET

Date	Qty. Minted	Issue Price	MS-65
1971	66,860	12.00	20.00
1972	36,349	12.00	50.00
1973 25¢ large bust ...	119,891	12.00	175.00
1973 25¢ small bust incl. above		12.00	25.00
1974	85,230	15.00	20.00
1975	97,263	15.00	27.00
1976	87,744	16.00	25.00
1977	142,577	16.00	25.00
1978	147,000	16.50	40.00
1979	155,698	18.50	35.00
1980	162,875	36.00	90.00

Specimen and Proof Sets, 1981 -

In 1981 the Royal Canadian Mint began producing sets of specimen and proof quality to replace the previous Custom and Prestige sets.

Specimen set This set consists of one encapsulated coin of each of the six denominations, from 1¢ to nickel dollar, all of specimen quality, displayed in a blue box.

Proof set This set consists of one encapsulated coin of each denomination 1¢ to nickel $1 plus the .500 silver dollar for each year. The coins are of proof quality and the set is issued in a black leather case.

SPECIMEN SET

Date	Qty. Minted	Issue Price	Value
1981	71,300	10.00	16.00
1982	62,298	11.50	16.00
1983	60,329	12.75	16.00
1984	60,511	12.75	16.00
1985	61,533	12.95	16.00
1986	67,152	13.50	16.00
1987 (voyageur dollar)*	77,212	14.00	16.00
1988 (Loon dollar)	70,205	14.75	16.00
1989	75,306	16.95	18.00
1990	76,611	17.95	19.00
1991	54,462	17.95	19.00
1992	N/A	18.95	—
1993	N/A		—

PROOF SET

Date	Qty. Minted	Issue Price	Value
1981	199,000	36.00	50.00
1982	180,908	36.00	25.00
1983	166,779	36.00	25.00
1984	161,786	40.00	25.00
1985	153,950	40.00	28.00
1986	176,224	40.00	33.00
1987 (voyageur dollar)*	175,686	43.00	35.00
1988 (Loon dollar) ...	175,259	45.00	53.00
1989	170,928	46.95	53.00
1990	158,068	48.00	53.00
1991	114,629	48.00	53.00
1992	N/A	49.75	—
1993	N/A		—

*The nickel voyageur dollar in these sets was a special collectors' dollar issued for the Proof, Specimen and Select Uncirculated sets only and was not issued as a circulating dollar for 1987.

Proof Loon Dollar, 1987

Diameter: 26.72 mm; weight: 7.0 grams; thickness: 1.95 mm;
composition: aureate bronze plated on pure nickel; edge: plain

Late in 1987 it was decided to issue the new circulating "Loon" dollar in proof quality for collectors. The Loon dollar was not included in any of the three collectors' sets issued by the Numismatic Section of the mint in 1987, and was only available as a circulation strike or in proof condition.

Date	Qty. Minted	Issue Price	Value
1987 Loon dollar, proof	178,120	13.50	20.00

OLYMPIC COINS
Silver $5 & $10, 1973-1976

$5: Diameter: 38.00 mm; weight: 24.30 grams; composition: .925 silver, .075 copper; edge: reeded
$10: Diameter: 45.00 mm; weight: 48.60 grams; composition: .925 silver, .075 copper; edge: reeded

$5 Obverse

$10 Obverse

Struck by the Royal Canadian Mint at its satellite mint in Hull, Quebec, these coins were intended to play a large part in financing the cost of the XXI Olympiad, held in Montreal in 1976.

In total twenty-eight silver coins were issued in 7 series of four coins each from 1973 to 1976. Each series of four coins (two $5 and two $10), was issued in both uncirculated and proof condition, in a variety of packaging.

$100 Gold The numismatic program for the 1976 olympics also included two $100 gold pieces. These are described on page 104.

Deluxe Proof Sets Poof silver coins were issued only in these sets, consisting of the four proof coins for the series in a case made of Canadian white birch with a tanned steer-hide cover and black insert.

Prestige Set This set was comprised of the four uncirculated coins for the series in a black leatherette case with matte finish and blue insert.

Custom Set The Custom set also contained the four uncirculated coins for the series in a black gold- trimmed case with red insert.

Individual Coins Individual uncirculated coins were released in three different forms: (1) in a "standard" black case with red interior; (2) encapsulated with no case; and (3) some individual coins were released through the banks at face value (without encapsulation) to monetize the issue.

The Patrick Brindley modification of Arnold Machin's bust of Queen Elizabeth II appears on all obverses with a simplified legend and the date of issue.

	Issue Price	Value		Issue Price	Value
$5 Uncirculated			**Custom Sets**		
Encapsulated Series I	6.50	7.50	(two $5 and two $10 coins)		
Encapsulated Series II	7.50	7.50	Series I	45.00	$42.00
Encapsulated Series III-VII	8.00	7.50	Series II-VII	55.00	$42.00
$10 Uncirculated			**Prestige Sets**		
Encapsulated Series I	12.00	15.00	(two $5 and two $10 coins)		
Encapsulated Series II	15.00	15.00	Series I	50.00	42.00
Encapsulated Series III-VII	15.75	15.00	Series II-VII	60.00	42.00
			Deluxe Proof Sets (two $5 and two $10 coins)		
Total quantities minted (1973-1976)			Series I	72.50	50.00
$5.00 - 12,733,789; $10.00 - 12,458,048			Series II-VII	82.50	50.00

Series I: Geographic, 1973

Release date: December 13, 1973; **Designer:** (by invitation) Georges Huel;
Modellers: *$5 and $10 Map issues* – None (designs photographically etched)
Kingston – Terrence Smith; *Montréal* – Ago Aarand.

$5 Landmarks of Kingston

$5 Map of North America

$10 Montreal Skyline

$10 Map of the World

Series II: Olympic Motifs, 1974

Release date: September 16, 1974.
Designer: (winner of invitational competition) Anthony Mann.
Modellers: *Head of Zeus and Athlete with Torch* – Patrick Brindley;
Olympic Rings and Temple of Zeus – Walter Ott.

$5 Athlete with Torch

$5 Olympic Rings and Wreath

$10 Head of Zeus $10 Temple of Zeus

Series III: Early Canadian Sports, 1974

Release date: April 16, 1975; **Designer:** (winner of invitational competition) Ken Danby.
Modellers: *Canoeing* – Patrick Brindley; *Lacrosse* – Walter Ott;
Others – combined work of Brindley, Ott, Smith and Aarand.

$5 Canoeing $5 Rowing

$10 Cycling $10 Lacrosse

Series IV: Olympic Track and Field Sports, 1975

Release date: August 12, 1975; **Designer:** (winner of invitational competition) Leo Yerxa
All designs include stylized Algonquin quill-work.
Modellers: *$10 issues* – Patrick Brindley; *$5 issues* – Walter Ott.

$5 Marathon Runner $5 Women's Javelin

$10 Women's Shot Put $10 Men's Hurdles

Series V: Olympic Water Sports, 1975

Release date: December 1, 1975; **Designer:** (winner of open national competition) Lynda Cooper.
Modellers: None (designs were photographically etched).

$5 Diver $5 Swimmer

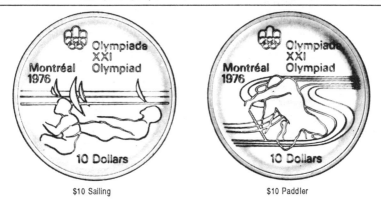

$10 Sailing $10 Paddler

Series VI: Olympic Team Sports and Body Contact Sports, 1976

Release date: March 1, 1976. **Designer:** (winner of open international competition) Shigeo Fukada.
Modellers: None (designs were photographically etched).

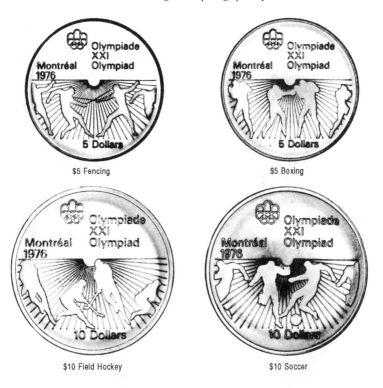

$5 Fencing $5 Boxing

$10 Field Hockey $10 Soccer

Series VII: Olympic Souvenir Issue, 1976

Release date: June 1, 1976. **Designer:** (winner of invitational competition among several Canadian design houses) Elliot Morrison, using architectural drawings by Roger Taillibert for the $10 pieces.

Modellers: *Village* – Sheldon Beveridge; *Flame* – Walter Ott (principally) and Patrick Brindley; *Stadium* – Ago Aarand; *Velodrome* – Terrence Smith.

$5 Olympic Village

$5 Olympic Flame

$10 Stadium

$10 Velodrome

IOC Issue
Silver $15, 1992
Diameter: 40.0 mm; weight: 33.63 grams; thickness: 3.1 mm;
composition: .925 silver, .075 copper; edge: lettered

To celebrate the centennial of the modern olympics, the IOC commissioned five national mints to produce a fifteen-piece set of gold and silver commemorative coins from 1992 to 1996, the centennial year. Each of the mints – Canada, Australia, France, Austria and Greece in that order – to produce a three-coin series in one of the five years, each series to consist of one gold and two silver coins. All fifteen coins in the set will bear the five olympic rings and the dates 1896-1996, with the olympic motto CITIUS, ALTIUS, FORTIUS on the coin edge.

The Royal Canadian Mint issued the first series *THE OLYMPIC VISION* in 1992, consisting of one gold $175 coin and two silver $15 coins.

Speed Skater, Pole Vaulter and Gymnast
The reverse was designed by David Craig, the obverse bears the Dora de Pédery-HUNT effigy of the queen.

The Spirit of the Generations
The reverse was designed by Stewart Sherwood, the obverse bears the Dora de Pédery-HUNT effigy of the queen.

Date	Qty. Minted	Issue Price	Value
1992 Speed Skater, etc., Proof	275,000	46.95	55.00
1992 Spirit of the Generations, Proof	275,000	46.95	55.00

Silver $20, 1985-1988

Diameter: 40 mm; weight: 34.107 grams; thickness: 3.00 mm;
composition: .925 silver, .075 copper; edge: lettered

To assist in financing the XV Winter Olympic Games in Calgary, Alberta in 1988, the mint issued a series of ten commemorative sterling silver coins in proof quality only. With the release of the first pair of coins in September, 1985, it was announced that 250,000 complete sets of ten coins would be struck, with a maximum total production of five million coins.

Each obverse bears the Arnold Machin effigy of the Queen and the year of issue. The reverse designs all bear the date of the games, 1988. The legend XV WINTER OLYMPIC GAMES • XVES JEUX OLYMPIQUES D'HIVER appears on the edge of each coin in the series.

1985 Issues

Downhill Skiing

Speed Skating

1986 Issues

Hockey

Biathlon

Cross-country Skiing

Free-style Skiing

1987 Issues

Figure Skating

Curling

Ski Jumping

Bobsled

Description	Designer	Issue Date	Qty. (31/12/87)	Issue Price	Value
$20 Downhill Skiing	Ian Stewart	Sept. 1985	350,522	37.00	40.00
$20 Speed Skating	Friedrich Peter	Sept. 1985	311,830	37.00	40.00
$20 Hockey	Ian Stewart	Feb. 1986	345,203	37.00	40.00
$20 Biathlon	John Mardon	Feb. 1986	280,188	37.00	40.00
$20 Cross-country Skiing	Ian Stewart	Sept. 1986	267,790	37.00	65.00
$20 Free-style Skiing	Walter Ott	Sept. 1986	263,820	37.00	65.00
$20 Figure Skating	Raymond Taylor	Mar. 1987	283,720	37.00	65.00
$20 Curling	Ian Stewart	Mar. 1987	253,220	37.00	65.00
$20 Ski Jumping	Raymond Taylor	Sept. 1987	246,651	37.00	65.00
$20 Bobsled	John Mardon	Sept. 1987	216,709	37.00	65.00

IOC Issue
Gold $175, 1992

Diameter: 28.0 mm; weight: 16.97 grams, thickness: 2.00 mm;
composition: .9167 gold, .084 copper; edge: lettered

To celebrate the centennial of the modern olympics, the IOC commissioned five national mints to produce a fifteen-piece set of gold and silver commemorative coins from 1992 to 1996, the centennial year. Each of the mints – Canada, Australia, France, Austria and Greece in that order – to produce a three-coin series in one of the five years, each series to consist of one gold and two silver coins. All fifteen coins in the set will bear the five olympic rings and the dates 1896-1996, with the olympic motto CITIUS, ALTIUS, FORTIUS on the coin edge.

The Royal Canadian Mint issued the first series *THE OLYMPIC VISION* in 1992, consisting of one gold $175 coin and two silver $15 coins.

The reverse was designed by Stewart Sherwood, the obverse bears the Dora de Pédery-HUNT effigy of the queen.

Date	Qty. Minted	Issue Price	Value
1992 Proof 35,000		429.75	430.00

PIONEERS OF POWERED FLIGHT IN CANADA
$20 Silver, 1990-1994

Diameter: 38.0 mm; weight: 31.103 grams;
composition: .925 silver, .075 copper; gold insert: 0.8 grams; edge; interrupted seration

Common obverse

This ten-coin series salutes aviation heroes and achievements during the first fifty years of powered flight in Canada (1900-1949). Each sterling silver coin contains 1 Troy ounce of silver, with a 24-carat gold-covered cameo, and is issued encapsulated in proof finish only.

Each coin is housed in an aluminum case in the shape of an airplane wing with a propeller design on the lid. A larger case of similar design houses all ten coins in the series.

All coins feature an interrupted reeded edge, with alternate sections reeded and smooth.

The common obverse features the new effigy of Queen Elizabeth II by Dora de Pédery-HUNT.

1990 Issues

Anson & Harvard / Robert Leckie

Lancaster 683 AVRO / John Emilius Fauquier

Harvard & Anson / Robert Leckie

The reverse design, by Nova Scotia artist Geoff Bennett, depicts a Harvard in flight while, on the ground, two pilots are boarding an Anson.
Cameo: Air Marshal Robert Leckie, who was instrumental in setting up schools for the British Commonwealth Air Training Plan. Leckie served as RCAF Chief of the Air Staff from 1944 until his retirement in 1947.

Lancaster 683 AVRO / John Emilius Fauquier

The reverse was designed by Ontario artist Robert Ralph Carmichael and depicts a Lancaster 638 AVRO bomber in flight.
Cameo: John Emilius Fauquier, one of Canada's pre-eminent aviators to be associated with the Lancaster bomber. Often decorated during his three tours of duty, Fauquier is probably best known as the commanding officer of No. 617 "Dambuster" squadron.

Date	Qty. Minted	Issue Price	Value
1990 Harvard & Anson / Robert Leckie	43,500	52.00	55.00
1990 Lancaster 683 AVRO / John Emilius Fauquier	45,000	52.00	55.00

1991 Issues

Silver Dart / John McCurdy & F.W. Baldwin   The de Havilland Beaver / Phillip Clarke Garratt

Silver Dart / John A.D. McCurdy & F.W. (Casey) Baldwin

The reverse showing the Silver Dart in flight above Bras d'Or Lake, Nova Scotia, on a test run, was designed by Quebec artist George Velinger. The Silver Dart made the first powered, controlled, heavier-than-air machine flight in Canada on February 23, 1909.

Cameo: John A.D. McCurdy (left), principal designer and pilot of the Silver Dart, and F.W. (Casey) Baldwin, the first Canadian to have flown previous prototypes.

The de Havilland Beaver / Phillip Clarke Garratt

The Beaver, one of Canada's most famous bush planes, was introduced in 1947 and is still used in more than sixty countries. The reverse design by Ontario artist Peter Mossman depicts a Beaver landing on a remote lake.

Cameo: Aviator Phillip Clarke Garratt who joined de Havilland Aircraft of Canada in 1936 and was instrumental in the development of the Beaver.

Date	Qty. Minted	Issue Price	Value
1991 Silver Dart / A.D. McCurdy & F.W. (Casey) Baldwin	30,500	52.00	—
1991 The de Havilland Beaver / Phillip Clarke Garratt	31,500	52.00	—

1992 Issues

Curtiss JN-4 Canuck / Sir Frank Wilton Bailie   The de Havilland Gypsy Moth / Murton A. Seymour

Curtiss JN-4 Canuck / Sir Frank Wilton Baillie

The reverse, designed by George Velinger of Beaconsfield, Quebec, depicts a Curtiss JN-4 (Canadian) above Camp Borden, Ontario. Informally known as the Canuck, the Curtiss was the first aircraft mass produced in Canada.

Cameo: Sir Frank Wilton Baillie, was president of Canadian Aeroplanes Limited, the most efficient aircraft manufacturer in North America during WWI.

de Havilland Gypsy Moth / Murton A. Seymour

Designed by John Mardon, the reverse depicts a Gypsy Moth flying over Camp Borden in the late 1920s. The two-seater aircraft became the standard equipment of most of the world's flying clubs during the late 1920s.

Cameo: Aviator Murton A Seymour was the first pilot trained by the Aero Club of British Columbia in 1915. He became president of the Canadian Flying Club Association in 1939.

Date	Qty. Minted	Issue Price	Value
1992 Curtiss Canuck / Sir Frank Wilton Baillie	50.000	54.35	—
1992 de Havilland Gypsy Moth / Murton A. Seymour	50,000	54.35	—

1993 issues

The Fairchild 71C / James A. Richardson   Lockheed 14 Super Electra / Zebulon Lewis Leigh

The Fairchild 71C / James A. Richardson

The reverse showing the Fairchild 71C landing on a northern lake, was designed by artist Robert R. Carmichael. This aircraft served as a freighter in Northern Canada and was used for photographic serveys, as well as technical training by the RCAF during World War II.

Cameo: James A. Richardson's active interest as well as his extensive contribution to the Canadian air transport industry led him to become director of Fairchild aerial surveys Limited of Canada.

Lockheed 14 Super Electra / Zebulon Lewis Leigh

The Lockheed 14 Super Electra was developed in 1937 to provide passenger and cargo transportation service. The design on the reverse of the coin, by artist Robert R. Carmichael. de[octs a Lockheed 14 in front of the Malton Terminal, near Toronto.

Cameo: Zebulon Lewis Leigh was awarded the Trans Canada Trophy in 1946 for his exceptional achievement in both civil and military aviation.

Date	Qty.Minted	Issue Price	Value
1993 The Fairchild 71C / James A. Richardson	50,000	54.35	—
1993 Lockheed 14 Super Electra / Zebulon Lewis Leigh	50,000	54.35	—

4
CANADIAN BULLION ISSUES

MAPLE LEAF COINAGES

The gold Maple Leaf was introduced in 1979 as a bullion coin for investors, each coin containing one Troy ounce of gold. Until 1982, the $50 maple leaf was produced in a fineness of .999 gold. In 1982 the mint raised the fineness to .9999 and began issuing maple leaf bullion coins in two smaller sizes, the $5 (1/10 ounce) and the $10 (1/4 ounce). The $20 (1/2 ounce) size was added to these in 1986.

In 1988 the Mint introduced five additional maple leaf coins, one in silver (1 Troy ounce) and four in platinum (1/10, 1/4, 1/2 and 1 Troy ounce). The fineness of the silver maple leaf is .9999, while the platinum issues have a fineness of .9995.

All maple leaf bullion coins bear the same obverse and reverse designs, differing only in date, fineness, size (1/4 oz., 1 oz., etc.) and metal specified in the legends.

The obverse, until 1989, bears the Arnold Machin effigy of the Queen, with the simple legend ELIZABETH II above and the nominal value and date beneath. The reverse device, a single maple leaf, was designed by the staff at the mint. The reverse legend includes the fineness of the coin and the word CANADA.

PHYSICAL SPECIFICATIONS

	Years Issued	Bullion Content	Diameter (mm)	Weight (grams)	Thickness (mm)	Fineness
Gold Issues						
$50	1979-1990 ...... 1 Troy ounce		30.00	31.150	2.80	.999
$20	1986-1990 ..... 1/2 Troy ounce		25.00	15.584	2.30	.9999
$10	1982-1990 ..... 1/4 Troy ounce		20.00	7.797	1.70	.9999
$5	1982-1990 .... 1/10 Troy ounce		16.00	3.131	1.22	.9999
Platinum Issues						
$50	1988-1990 ...... 1 Troy ounce		30.00	31.160	2.52	.9995
$20	1988-1990 ..... 1/2 Troy ounce		25.00	15.590	2.02	.9995
$10	1988-1990 ..... 1/4 Troy ounce		20.00	7.800	1.50	.9995
$5	1988-1990 .... 1/10 Troy ounce		16.00	3.132	1.01	.9995
Silver Issues						
$5	1988-1990 ...... 1 Troy ounce		38.00	31.390	3.21	.9999

Elizabeth II, Tiara Obverse, 1979-1989
QUANTITIES MINTED

Date	1/10 Troy ounce	1/4 Troy ounce	1/2 Troy ounce	1 Troy ounce
1979 gold	—	—	—	1,000,000
1980 gold	—	—	—	1,215,000
1981 gold	—	—	—	863,000
1982 gold	184,000	246,000	—	883,000
1983 gold	224,000	130,000	—	695,000
1984 gold	226,000	355,200	—	1,098,000
1985 gold	476,000	607,200	—	1,747,500
1986 gold	483,000	879,200	386,400	1,093,500
1987 gold	459,000	376,800	332,800	978,000
1988 gold	412,000	380,000	521,600	800,500
platinum	46,000	87,200	23,600	26,000
silver	—	—	—	1,062,000
1989 gold	53,900	82,200	129,600	856,000
platinum	1,800	800	2,400	10,000
silver	—	—	—	1,708,800

Commemorative Proof Sets, 1989

To celebrate the tenth anniversary of the maple leaf coins, commemorative sets and singles were issued in 1989 in proof quality only. All coins were encapsulated and both single coins and sets were packaged in solid maple cases with brown velvet liners.

Physical specifications and composition remain the same as other issues.

Item	Qty. Issued	Issue Price	Value
Gold 4-coin set (1/10, 1/4, 1/2 and 1 Troy ounce) 6,823		1,395.00	1,300.
Platinum 4-coin set (1/10, 1/4, 1/2 and 1 Troy ounce) 1,995		1,995.00	2,200.
Combination set, 3 coins, 1 Troy ounce each			
(1 gold, 1 platinum and 1 silver) 2,550		1,795.00	1,400.
Combination $5 set (gold 1/10 oz., platinum 1/10 oz.			
and silver 1 oz. maple leaf coins) 9,979		195.00	200.00
Single gold 1 Troy ounce maple leaf 5,510		795.00	600.00
Single silver 1 Troy ounce maple leaf 29,999		39.00	70.00

Elizabeth II, Diadem Obverse, 1990 -
QUANTITIES MINTED

Date	1/10 Troy ounce	1/4 Troy ounce	1/2 Troy ounce	1 Troy ounce
1990 gold	47,600	63,400	87,200	815,000
platinum	900	400	1,300	15,100
silver	—	—	—	1,708,800
1991 gold	32,200	41,600	48,100	290,000
platinum	1,300	1,800	2,800	31,900
silver	—	—	—	644,300
1992 gold	N/A	N/A	N/A	N/A
platinum	N/A	N/A	N/A	N/A
silver	—	—	—	N/A
1993 gold	N/A	N/A	N/A	N/A
platinum	N/A	N/A	N/A	N/A
silver	—	—	—	N/A
1994 gold	N/A	N/A	N/A	N/A
platinum	N/A	N/A	N/A	N/A
silver	—	—	—	N/A

PLATINUM PROOF SETS, 1990 -

In 1990, the mint began issuing four-coin proof sets struck in platinum. Each set is housed in a burled walnut case lined with black ultra suede. The mintage of each set is restricted to 3,500 sets worldwide.

PHYSICAL SPECIFICATIONS

	Bullion Content	Diameter (mm)	Weight (grams)	Fineness
$300	1 Troy ounce	30.00	31.1035	.9995
$150	½ Troy ounce	25.00	15.552	.9995
$75	¼ Troy ounce	20.00	7.776	.9995
$30	⅒ Troy ounce	16.00	3.111	.9995

Polar Bear, 1990

$300 $150 $75 $30

The polar bear, Canada's monarch of the north, was chosen as the subject for the first platinum proof set, featuring reverse designs by the renowned Canadian naturalist painter, Robert Bateman.

The obverse of each coin features the new portrait of Queen Elizabeth II by Canadian artist Dora de Pédery-HUNT.

Snowy Owl, 1991

$300 $150 $75 $30

The snowy owl is depicted on the second platinum proof set, featuring the designs of renowned Canadian sildlife artist Glen Loates on the reverse of the coins. The obverses again show the Dora de Pédery-HUNT effigy of the queen.

Date	Quantity Issued	Issue Price	Value
1990 Polar Bears – Proof set of 4 coins	2,629	1,990.	2,000.
1991 Snowy Owls – Proof set of 4 coins	873	1,990.	2,000.

Cougar, 1992

| $300 | $150 | $75 | $30 |

The majestic cougar is featured on the 1992 platimum proof set. The four reverse designs are by wildlife artist George McLean. The obverse again features the Dora de Pédery-HUNT effigy of the queen.

Date	Quantity Issued	Issue Price	Value
1992 Cougars – Proof set of 4 coins .... N/A		1,955.	2,000.

5
OTTAWA MINT GOLD SOVEREIGNS

Like other branches of the Royal Mint, the Ottawa Mint was authorized to strike gold sovereigns, and did so during the period 1908-19. The designs and physical specifications were identical to those of the corresponding English issues, except for the presence of the C mint mark for Canada, just above the date on the Ottawa strikings. Sovereigns struck in London had no mint mark while pieces with mint marks I, M, P, S and SA were from the mints in India, Australia and South Africa.

During the First World War, these coins were used to help pay for war materials purchased by England from the United States. England was thus saved the risk of sending London-minted gold across the Atlantic.

Such "branch mint" sovereigns are generally considered to form part of the coinage of the country in which they were struck, and so are included here.

Edward VII, Gold Sovereigns, 1908-1910
Diameter: 22.05 mm; weight: 7.988 grams; composition: .917 gold, .083 copper; edge: reeded

Position of C mint mark
for Ottawa mint

The obverse was derived from a portrait model by G.W. De Saulles (DES below neck) and the reverse is a slight modification of the original 1816 St. George and the dragon design by Benedetto Pistrucci (B.P. at lower right).

Date	Qty. Minted	VF-20	EF-40	AU-50	MS-60	MS-63
1908C*	636	2,500	3,000	3,500	4,000	6,000
1909C	16,237	300.00	350.00	500.00	850.00	2,500
1910C	28,012	250.00	300.00	400.00	725.00	2,500

*Originally struck in specimen only; however, some circulated.

George V, Gold Sovereigns, 1911-1919

VF: *Wear on head spreads near the ear and slight wear developed on the beard*
EF: *Hair over ear is only slightly worn; beard is still sharp*

The obverse was derived from a portrait model by Sir E.B. MacKennal (B.M. on truncation) and the reverse is the same as on the Edward VII issues.

1916C. Despite the reported mintage of more than 6,000, specimens of this date are rare, with only about 10 known today. Most were probably melted, as undoubtedly happened with the 1917 London issue and some Australian issues.

Date	Qty. Minted	VF-20	EF-40	AU-50	MS-60	MS-63
1911C	255,946	125.00	135.00	150.00	175.00	300.00
1913C	3,715	725.00	1,000	1,500	2,000	3,500
1914C	14,891	375.00	450.00	600.00	1,000	1,600
1916C	6,111	15,000	20,000	25,000	30,000	40,000
1917C	58,845	130.00	140.00	160.00	200.00	450.00
1918C	105,516	130.00	140.00	160.00	200.00	450.00
1919C	135,889	130.00	140.00	160.00	200.00	500.00

6
PRE-CONFEDERATION
PROVINCIAL DECIMAL ISSUES

NEW BRUNSWICK DECIMAL COINAGE

HALF CENT
Victoria, Half Cent, 1861

Diameter: 20.65 mm; weight: 2.835 grams; composition: .950 copper, .040 tin, .010 zinc; edge: plain

G: *Hair over ear worn through*
VG: *Little detail to hair over ear or braid*
F: *Strands of hair over ear begin to merge; braid is worn*
VF: *Hair over ear is worn; braid is clear but no longer sharp*
EF: *Slight wear on hair over ear; braid that holds knot in place is sharp and clear*

In 1860 New Brunswick adopted a monetary system consisting of dollars and cents, with the dollar equal to the United States gold dollar. This made the British shilling worth slightly more than 24 cents and the 6d slightly more than 12 cents. Consequently, it was not necessary for the province to issue half cents to make change for the 6d. The Royal Mint nevertheless struck over 200,000 New Brunswick half-cents. The mistake was soon discovered and most of the coins melted. The only ones to escape were a few proofs and an unknown number of business strikes (perhaps in the hundreds) that were mixed with the Nova Scotia half-cents and sent to Halifax.

The obverse design is identical to that used for the Nova Scotia half-cents and is one of those used for the British bronze farthing (Peck's obv. 3).

The reverse is similar to that for the Nova Scotia half cent.

Date	Qty. Minted	G-4	VG-8	F-12	VF-20	EF-40	AU-50	Unc-60	BU-63
1861 .... (originally 222,800)		50.00	75.00	100.00	140.00	1750.00	300.00	550.00	1,250

1 CENT
Victoria, Cents, 1861-1864

Diameter: 25.53mm; weight: 5.670 grams; composition: .950 copper, .040 tin, .010 zinc; edge: plain

Short tip 6   Long tip 6

The obverse is identical to that for the Nova Scotia coins of the same denomination and is one of those used for the British halfpenny (Peck's obv. 6). The designer and engraver was L.C. Wyon.

The reverse design is very similar to that used for the Nova Scotia issue; the wreath differs only in minor respects. The design was adapted from a model by C. Hill.

Date	Qty. Minted	G-4	VG-8	F-12	VF-20	EF-40	AU-50	Unc-60	BU-63
1861 1,000,000		2.50	4.00	3.00	6.00	12.00	30.00	85.00	250.00
1864 short tip 6 1,000,000		2.50	4.00	3.00	6.00	12.00	30.00	85.00	250.00
long tip 6 .... incl. above		2.50	4.00	3.00	6.00	12.00	30.00	85.00	250.00

5 CENTS
Victoria, 5 Cents Silver, 1862-1864

Diameter: 15.49 mm; weight: 1.162 grams; composition: .925 silver, .075 copper; edge: reeded

G: Braid around ear worn through
VG: No details in braid around the ear
F: Segments of braid begin to merge into one another
VF: Braid is clear but not sharp
EF: Braid is slightly worn but generally sharp and clear

The obverse, designed and engraved by L.C. Wyon, has a portrait of Victoria that would later be used on the Dominion of Canada five cents of 1858.

Small 6   Large 6

Date	Qty. Minted	G-4	VG-8	F-12	VF-20	EF-40	AU-50	Unc-60	BU-63
1862 100,000		25.00	40.00	75.00	150.00	300.00	700.00	1,500	3,000
1864 small 6 100,000		25.00	40.00	75.00	150.00	300.00	700.00	1,500	3,000
large 6 .... incl. above		25.00	40.00	75.00	150.00	300.00	700.00	1,500	3,000

10 CENTS
Victoria, 10 Cents Silver, 1862-1864

Diameter: 17.91 mm; weight: 2.324 grams; composition: .925 silver, .075 copper; edge: reeded

The obverse is virtually identical to and was derived from Portrait No. 6 of the Canadian 10-cent piece. (This particular Canadian obverse existed long before it appeared on the issues of 1892). The designer and engraver was L.C. Wyon.

The reverse design, the device of which is a wreath of maple surmounted by the St. Edward's crown, is identical to that used for the Province of Canada ten cents of 1858.

Normal 2   Double-punched 2

Date	Qty. Minted	G-4	VG-8	F-12	VF-20	EF-40	AU-50	Unc-60	BU-63
1862 normal date 150,000		25.00	40.00	70.00	140.00	250.00	650.00	1,300	2,500
double-punch 2 ...... incl. above		25.00	40.00	70.00	140.00	250.00	650.00	1,300	2,500
1864 150,000		25.00	40.00	70.00	140.00	250.00	650.00	1,300	2,500

20 CENTS
Victoria, 20 Cents Silver, 1862-1864

Diameter: 22.99 mm; weight: 4.648 grams; composition: .925 silver, .075 copper; edge: reeded

The obverse, designed and engraved by L.C. Wyon, has a portrait similar to that on the Province of Canada 20-cent issue.

The reverse is also similar to that used for the Province of Canada issue and, indeed, was probably initially intended for that coin. The designer and engraver may have been L.C. Wyon, but this is not known with certainty.

Date	Qty. Minted	G-4	VG-8	F-12	VF-20	EF-40	AU-50	MS-60	MS-63
1862	150,000	12.00	20.00	30.00	60.00	200.00	500.00	1,350	2,500
1864	150,000	12.00	20.00	30.00	60.00	200.00	500.00	1,350	2,500

NEWFOUNDLAND DECIMALS, 1865-1947

In an act of 1863 Newfoundland turned to decimal currency and adopted the Spanish dollar as its unit. This made the British shilling equivalent to 24 cents and the sixpence to 12 cents

LARGE CENTS
Victoria, Large Cents, 1865-1896

Diameter: 25.33 mm; weight: 5.670 grams; composition: .950 copper, .040 tin, .010 zinc; edge: plain

G: *Hair over ear worn through*
VG: *Little detail to hair over ear or braid*
F: *Strands of hair over ear begin to merge, braid is worn*
VF: *Hair over ear is worn, braid is clear but no longer sharp*
EF: *Slight wear on hair over ear, braid that holds knot in place is sharp and clear*

The obverse, designed and engraved by L.C. Wyon, is unusual in two respects. First, the portrait was one of those used for the British halfpence (Peck's obv. 6) and second, the lettering is in simple, very bold type.

The reverse was engraved by Wyon's assistant, T.J. Minton, from a design by Horace Morehen. The wreath consists of pitcher plant and oak.

1880 date varieties. Two styles for the 0 are known, narrow and wide. The position of the wide 0 also varies, these positional differences, however, are considered trivial and will not be perpetuated here.

Die axis varieties. With the exception of the 1872H, all of the Victorian Newfoundland cents were *medal-struck* (die axes arranged ↑↑). The opposite alignment (die axes arranged ↑↓) of the 1872H is probably because the alignment was not specified and Heaton's assumed it was to be the same as on the silver coins.

Date	Approx. Minted	G-4	VG-8	F-12	VF-20	EF-40	AU-50	Unc-60	BU-63
1865	240,000	1.50	2.75	4.00	8.50	20.00	80.00	200.00	500.00
1872H	200,000	1.50	2.75	4.00	8.50	20.00	60.00	140.00	300.00
1873	200,025	1.50	2.75	4.00	8.50	20.00	100.00	225.00	625.00
1876H	200,000	1.50	2.75	4.00	8.50	20.00	100.00	250.00	650.00

Narrow 0  Wide 0

Date	Approx. Minted	G-4	VG-8	F-12	VF-20	EF-40	AU-50	Unc-60	BU-63
1880 narrow 0	400,000	60.00	100.00	125.00	175.00	300.00	450.00	900.00	2,100
wide 0	incl. above	1.50	2.75	4.00	8.00	18.00	70.00	175.00	500.00
1885	40,000	15.00	25.00	35.00	50.00	90.00	150.00	400.00	1,000
1888	50,000	15.00	20.00	30.00	45.00	70.00	125.00	350.00	850.00
1890	200,000	1.25	2.50	4.00	6.50	16.00	75.00	200.00	475.00
1894	200,000	1.25	2.50	4.00	6.50	16.00	75.00	200.00	475.00
1896	200,000	1.25	2.50	4.00	6.50	16.00	75.00	200.00	475.00

Edward VII, Large Cents, 1904-1909

Diameter: 25.53 mm; weight: 5.670 grams; composition: .950 copper, .040 tin, .010 zinc; edge: plain

G: *Band of crown worn through*
VG: *Band of crown is worn through at highest point*
F: *Jewels in band of crown will be blurred*
VF: *Band of crown is still clear but no longer sharp*
EF: *Band of crown slightly worn but generally sharp and clear*

The obverse was derived from a portrait model by G.W. DeSaulles; the portrait is unusually large for the size of the coin.

The reverse design is the same as used for the Victoria series, except for the substitution of the Imperial State crown for the St. Edward's crown. The modification was made by W.H.J. Blakemore.

Date	Approx. Minted	G-4	VG-8	F-12	VF-20	EF-40	AU-50	Unc-60	BU-63
1904H	100,000	5.00	7.50	12.00	25.00	35.00	120.00	300.00	900.00
1907	200,000	1.25	2.00	3.50	6.00	15.00	85.00	175.00	450.00
1909	200,000	1.25	2.00	3.50	6.00	15.00	85.00	175.00	425.00

George V, Large Cents, 1913-1936

Diameter: (1913, 1929, 1936) 25.53 mm, (1917-20) 25.40 mm; weight: 5.670 grams; composition: (1913-20) .950 copper, .040 tin, .010 zinc, (1929-36) .955 copper, .030 tin, .015 zinc; edge: plain

G: *Band of crown worn through*
VG: *Band of crown is worn through at highest point*
F: *Jewels in band of crown will be blurred*
VF: *Band of crown is still clear but no longer sharp*
EF: *Band of crown slightly worn but generally sharp and clear*

The obverse, from a portrait model by Sir E.B. MacKennal (B.M. on truncation), is identical to that for the Canadian issues of the same denomination.

The reverse is a continuation of the design introduced in the Edward VII series.

Date	Qty. Minted	G-4	VG-8	F-12	VF-20	EF-40	AU-50	Unc-60	BU-63
1913	400,000	.75	1.25	2.50	4.00	6.50	28.00	65.00	180.00
1917C	702,350	.75	1.25	2.50	4.00	6.50	28.00	70.00	280.00
1919C	300,000	.75	1.25	2.50	4.00	6.50	45.00	125.00	325.00
1920C	302,184	.75	1.25	2.50	4.00	6.50	45.00	125.00	400.00
1929	300,000	.75	1.25	2.50	4.00	6.50	45.00	90.00	265.00
1936	300,000	.60	1.00	2.00	3.00	5.50	22.50	45.00	125.00

George VI, Small Cents, 1938-1947

Diameter: 19.05 mm; weight: 3.240 grams; composition: .955 copper, .030 tin, .015 zinc; edge: plain

VG: *Band of crown almost worn through; little detail in hair*

F: *Band of crown considerably worn; strands of hair begin to merge together*

VF: *Wear extends along band of crown; hair is clear but no longer sharp*

EF: *Band of crown shows slight wear; hair is sharp and clear*

Because of the need to have new obverses for the George VI coinage, the New-foundland government considered the question of changing to a smaller one-cent and larger five-cent pieces, similar to those already in circulation in Canada and the U.S. Despite the economic advantages of such a change, there was a strong conservative element in favor of retaining the old sizes. The final decision was to alter only the one-cent size.

The obverse for the new small cent was derived from a portrait model for British colonial coinages by Percy Metcalfe (P.M. below neck). The reverse device is the insectivorous pitcher plant, *Sarracenia purpurea,* which is native to the island. The die was engraved by W.J. Newman, a senior engraver at the Royal Mint, from designs submitted from Newfoundland.

The 1938 issue was produced in London. However, due to the danger of loss of trans-Atlantic shipments during World War II, all later coinages were struck at the Royal Canadian Mint in Ottawa.

The C mint mark was inadvertently omitted in 1940 and 1942.

1938	500,000	.50	.75	1.00	2.00	4.00	10.00	25.00	50.00
1940(C)	300,000	1.25	2.75	3.75	6.00	12.50	27.50	60.00	175.00
1941C	827,662	.25	.50	.75	1.25	3.00	10.00	20.00	50.00
1942(C)	1,996,889	.25	.50	.75	1.25	3.00	10.00	20.00	50.00
1943C	1,239,732	.25	.50	.75	1.25	3.00	10.00	20.00	50.00
1944C	1,328,776	1.00	2.00	3.00	4.00	6.00	25.00	50.00	135.00
1947C	313,772	.50	1.00	1.50	2.50	4.50	20.00	40.00	250.00

5 CENTS
Victoria, Five Cents Silver, 1865-1896

Diameter: 15.49 mm; weight: 1.178 grams; composition: .925 silver, .075 copper; edge: reeded

G: *Braid around hair worn through*

VG: *No detail in braid around ear*

F: *Segments of braid begin to merge into one another*

VF: *Braid is clear but not sharp*

EF: *Braid slightly worn but generally sharp and clear*

The initial obverse was derived from that used for New Brunswick by modifying the legend. Periods are present on both sides of NEWFOUNDLAND. A second variety lacks the periods. On the final obverse the Queen has more aged facial features with repressed upper lip and recessed forehead, and the period after NEWFOUNDLAND was restored (closer to the D).

Two noteworthy reverses are known for this series. The first has a Roman I in the date, while the second has the more conventional Arabic 1.

The first and probably all later obverse and reverse varieties were designed and engraved by L.C. Wyon.

The weights of the silver denominations were made proportional to those of the equivalent values in English silver coin; that is, 5.6552 grams per shilling (12 pence). The value of the 5 cents was 2½ d.

| Obv. 1 | Obv. 2 | Obv. 3 | Obv. 1-2 | Obv. 3 |

Roman 'I'   Arabic '1'

Date	Qty. Minted	G-4	VG-8	F-12	VF-20	EF-40	AU-50	MS-60	MS-63
Roman "I" Reverse (1865)									
1865 .... obv. 1, 2 80,000		20.00	35.00	50.00	90.00	200.00	350.00	1,200	2,500
Arabic "1" Reverse (1870-1896)									
1870 .... obv. 1, 2 40,000		30.00	50.00	70.00	120.00	275.00	500.00	1,700	3,250
1872H .... obv. 2 40,000		20.00	35.00	50.00	90.00	200.00	350.00	1,000	2,200
1873 .... obv. 2 44,260		30.00	50.00	80.00	150.00	300.00	6725.00	1,800	3,500
1873H .... obv. 2 .... incl. above		750.00	1,200	2,000	3,000	3,500	5,000	—	—
1876H .... obv. 2 20,000		50.00	125.00	175.00	300.00	500 .00	1,000	3,000	5,000
1880 .... obv. 2 40,000		25.00	40.00	65.00	115.00	225.00	350.00	1,600	3,000
1881 .... obv. 2 40,000		15.00	25.00	40.00	75.00	180.00	300.00	1,250	2,500
1882H .... obv. 3 60,000		12.50	20.00	35.00	55.00	150.00	300.00	1,000	2,000
1885 .... obv. 2 16,000		75.00	135.00	200.00	325.00	600.00	1,400	3,500	6,000
1888 .... obv. 2, 3 40,000		20.00	30.00	45.00	80.00	200.00	300.00	1,000	2,500
1890 .... obv. 3 160,000		7.00	12.00	25.00	50.00	120.00	300.00	900.00	2,000
1894 .... obv. 3 160,000		7.00	12.00	25.00	50.00	120.00	300.00	900.00	2,000
1896 .... obv. 3 400,000		4.00	17.00	12.00	30.00	65.00	225.00	800.00	2,000

Edward VII, Five Cents Silver, 1903-1908

Diameter: 15.49 mm; weight: 1.178 grams; composition: .925 silver, .075 copper; edge: reeded

G: *Band of crown worn through*
VG: *Band of crown worn through at highest point*
F: *Jewels in band of crown will be blurred*
VF: *Band of crown still clear but no longer sharp*
EF: *Band of crown slightly worn but generally sharp and clear*

The obverse, designed and engraved by G.W. DeSaulles (DES. below bust), is identical to that for the Canadian issues.

The reverse was also the work of De Saulles.

1903 100,000		3.50	5.50	12.00	30.00	75.00	225.00	800.00	2,000
1904H 100,000		3.00	5.50	9.00	25.00	60.00	175.00	500.00	1,000
1908 400,000		2.50	4.00	8.00	20.00	50.00	150.00	450.00	750.00

George V, 5 Cents Silver, 1912-1929

Diameter: (1912-19) 15.49 mm, (1929) 15.69 mm; weight: (1912) 1.178 grams, (1917-29) 1.166 grams; composition: .925 silver, .075 copper; edge: reeded

G: *Band of crown worn through*
VG: *Band of crown worn through at highest point*
F: *Jewels in band of crown will be blurred*
VF: *Band of crown still clear but no longer sharp*
EF: *Band of crown slightly worn but generally sharp and clear*

The obverse bears a portrait derived from a model by Sir E.B. MacKennal (B.M. on truncation) and is identical to that for the Canadian issues.

The reverse is as for the Edward VII series.

Date	Qty. Minted	G-4	VG-8	F-12	VF-20	EF-40	AU-50	MS-60	MS-63
1912	300,000	1.00	1.50	3.50	10.00	30.00	80.00	350.00	550.00
1917C	300,319	1.00	1.50	3.50	9.00	25.00	75.00	350.00	700.00
1919C	100,844	2.00	3.50	6.00	20.00	50.00	125.00	600.00	1,000
1929	300,000	1.00	1.50	3.00	6.00	20.00	75.00	250.00	500.00

George VI, 5 Cents Silver, 1938-1947

Diameter: (1938) 15.69 mm, (1940-47) 15.49 mm; weight: 1.166 grams; composition: (1938-44) .925 silver, .075 copper, (1945-47) .800 silver, .200 copper; edge: reeded

VG: *Band of crown almost worn through*
F: *Band of crown considerably worn; strands of hair begin to merge together*
VF: *Wear extends along band of crown; hair is clear but no longer sharp*
EF: *Band of crown shows slight wear; hair is sharp and clear*

The obverse is derived from a portrait model by Percy Metcalfe (P.M. below neck) intended for English colonial coinages.

The reverse is as for the Edward VII and George V issues.

1938	100,000	1.00	2.00	3.00	4.00	8.00	40.00	125.00	325.00
1940C	200,000	1.00	1.50	2.00	4.00	5.00	20.00	70.00	250.00
1941C	612,641	.60	1.00	1.50	3.00	4.00	12.00	30.00	50.00
1942C	298,348	1.00	1.50	2.00	4.00	7.00	20.00	55.00	100.00
1943C	351,666	.60	1.00	1.50	3.00	4.00	12.00	30.00	50.00
1944C	286,504	1.00	1.50	2.50	4.00	6.00	25.00	60.00	175.00
1945C	203,828	.60	1.00	1.50	3.00	4.00	12.00	30.00	50.00
1946C	2,041	200.00	300.00	400.00	600.00	700.00	1,100	2,500	3,500
1947C	38,400	3.00	5.00	8.00	12.00	25.00	60.00	100.00	200.00

10 CENTS
Victoria, 10 Cents Silver, 1865-1896

Diameter: 17.98 mm; weight: 2.356 grams; composition: .925 silver, .025 copper; edge: reeded

G: *Braid around ear worn through*
VG: *No details in braid around ear*
F: *Segments of braid begin to merge together*
VF: *Braid is clear but not sharp*
EF: *Braid slightly worn but generally sharp and clear*

The initial obverse was derived from that for the New Brunswick 10-cent piece by modifying the legend. A second variety lacks the period after NEWFOUND-LAND. A third variety has the period restored (but closer to the D) and depicts the

Queen with more aged facial features. Two noteworthy reverses are known for this series. The first has Roman Is in the l0 and date, while the second has the more conventional Arabic 1s. There are also slight differences in the devices and rim denticles.

1871H Newfoundland / Canada mule. Quite possibly the result of an inadvertent muling of a Canadian 1871H reverse with a Newfoundland obverse. The two known examples of this interesting and extremely rare variety are in well circulated condition, adding credence to the proposition that it is not a pattern.

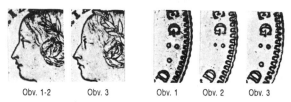

| Obv. 1-2 | Obv. 3 | Obv. 1 | Obv. 2 | Obv. 3 |

1880 2nd 8 over 7. All of the 10- and 50-cent pieces of 1880 examined have the second 8 in the date punched over a 7. By the latter part of the 1870s, the dies for these denominations were sunk from reverse punches bearing the partial date 187-; the final digit was hand punched into each die. In 1880, then, the Mint was faced with either making new punches or using the old ones and correcting the 7 in each die, in addition to adding the final digit. The latter course of action was chosen in 1880, probably because of a lack of time and the small number of dies which had to be made for Newfoundland in that year. The reverse punches for the other denominations lacked both the third and the fourth digits, so this problem did not arise for them.

Roman 'I'	Arabic '1' (note 2nd 8 over 7)

Date	Qty. Minted	G-4	VG-8	F-12	VF-20	EF-40	AU-50	MS-60	MS-63
Roman "I" Reverse (1865-1870)									
1865 .... obv. 1 80,000		10.00	20.00	40.00	100.00	275.00	700.00	2,000	4,000
1870 .... obv. 1, 2 30,000		150.00	250.00	350.00	600.00	1,100	2,250	5,000	10,000
Arabic "1" Reverse (1872-1896)									
1871H mule 40,000							Extremely Rare		
1872H .... obv. 2 40,000		14.00	22.00	40.00	90.00	225.00	600.00	1,500	3,250
1873 .... obv. 1, 2 23,614		16.00	25.00	45.00	115.00	325.00	900.00	3,200	7,500
1876H .... obv. 2 10,000		25.00	40.00	70.00	160.00	450.00	1,100	3,000	6,000
1880 2nd 8 over 7 obv. 2 10,000		25.00	40.00	70.00	160.00	450.00	1,100	3,000	6,000
1882H .... obv. 3 20,000		14.00	22.00	40.00	90.00	225.00	550.00	1,500	3,250
1885 .... obv. 3 8,000		65.00	100.00	200.00	425.00	900.00	1,700	3,500	6,500
1888 .... obv. 3 30,000		14.00	22.00	40.00	100.00	275.00	650.00	2,300	6,000
1890 .... obv. 3 100,000		6.00	9.00	20.00	45.00	135.00	400.00	1,200	3,000
1894 .... obv. 2, 3 100,000		6.00	9.00	20.00	45.00	135.00	400.00	1,200	3,000
1896 .... obv. 3 230,000		4.00	6.00	15.00	40.00	110.00	325.00	1,000	3,000

Edward VII, 10 Cents Silver, 1903-1904
Diameter: 17.96 mm; weight: 2.356 grams; composition: .925 silver, .025 copper; edge: reeded

The obverse, designed and engraved by G.W. De Saulles (DES. below bust), is identical to that for the Canadian issues.

The reverse was also done by De Saulles.

G: *Band of crown worn through*
VG: *Band of crown worn through at highest point*
F: *Jewels in band of crown will be blurred*
VF: *Band of crown still clear but no longer sharp*
EF: *Band of crown slightly worn but generally sharp and clear*

Date	Qty. Minted	G-4	VG-8	F-12	VF-20	EF-40	AU-50	MS-60	MS-63
1903	100,000	3.00	5.00	13.00	45.00	110.00	250.00	1,150	2,750
1904H	100,000	2.00	4.00	10.00	35.00	90.00	200.00	600.00	1,000

George V, 10 Cents Silver, 1912-1919

Diameter: (1912) 17.96 mm, (1917, 1919) 18.03 mm; weight: (1912) 2.356 grams, (1917, 1919) 2.333 grams; composition: .925 silver, .075 copper; edge: reeded

G: *Band of crown worn through*
VG: *Band of crown worn through at highest point*
F: *Jewels in band of crown will be blurred*
VF: *Band of crown still clear but no longer sharp*
EF: *Band of crown slightly worn but generally sharp and clear*

The obverse bears a portrait derived from a model by Sir E.B. MacKennal (B.M. on truncation) and is identical to that for the Canadian issues.

The reverse is identical to that of the Edward VII series.

1912	150,000	1.50	3.00	5.00	16.00	50.00	200.00	550.00	900.00
1917C	250,805	1.25	2.50	4.00	10.00	35.00	150.00	700.00	1,700
1919C	54,342	2.00	3.50	6.00	16.00	50.00	200.00	325.00	600.00

George VI, 10 Cents Silver, 1938-1947

Diameter: 18.03 mm; weight: 2.333 grams; composition: (1938-44) .925 silver, .075 copper, (1945-47) .800 silver, .200 copper; edge: reeded

VG: *Band of crown almost worn through; little detail in the hair*
F: *Band of crown considerably worn; strands of hair begin to merge together*
VF: *Wear extends along band of crown; hair is clear but no longer sharp*
EF: *Band of crown shows slight wear; hair is sharp and clear*

The obverse is derived from a portrait model by Percy Metcalfe (P.M. below neck) intended for English colonial coinages.

The reverse is as for the Edward VII and George V issues.

Date	Qty. Minted	VG-8	F-12	VF-20	EF-40	AU-50	MS-60	MS-63
1938	100,000	1.50	3.00	6.50	12.00	40.00	200.00	400.00
1940(C)	100,000	1.50	3.00	6.00	10.00	35.00	150.00	375.00
1941C	483,630	1.50	2.50	4.50	8.00	20.00	60.00	150.00
1942C	292,736	1.50	2.50	4.50	8.00	20.00	70.00	150.00
1943C	104,706	1.50	2.50	4.50	8.00	20.00	70.00	175.00
1944C	151,471	1.50	2.50	5.00	9.00	25.00	100.00	275.00
1945C	175,833	1.50	2.50	4.00	8.00	20.00	60.00	150.00
1946C	38,400	6.00	10.00	20.00	30.00	70.00	200.00	400.00
1947C	61,988	3.00	5.00	8.00	20.00	50.00	150.00	400.00

20 CENTS
Victoria, 20 Cents Silver, 1865-1900
Diameter: 23.19 mm; weight: 4.713 grams; composition: .925 silver, .075 copper; edge: reeded

G: *Braid around ear worn through*
VG: *No details in braid around ear*
F: *Segments of braid begin to merge together*
VF: *Braid is clear but not sharp*
EF: *Braid is slightly worn but generally clear and sharp*

The first obverse was derived from the New Brunswick 20-cent obverse by modifying the legend. A second design, derived from the first, shows the Queen with more aged facial features: slight double chin, repressed upper lip and recessed forehead.

The reverses for the 1865 and 1880 issues have a Roman 'I' in the date; later issues have the more conventional Arabic '1' in the date.

The weights of the silver denominations were made proportional to those of the equivalent values in English silver coins; that is, 5.6552 grams per shilling (12 pence). The value of the 20 cents was 10d.

	Obv. 1	Obv. 2			Roman I		Arabic 1			
Date		**Qty. Minted**	**G-4**	**VG-8**	**F-12**	**VF-20**	**EF-40**	**AU-50**	**MS-60**	**MS-63**
Roman "I" Reverse (1865-1880)										
1865	obv. 1	100,000	9.00	15.00	25.00	70.00	200.00	540.00	1,800	3,600
1870	obv. 1	50,000	14.00	22.00	40.00	100.00	250.00	675.00	2,300	4,950
1872H	obv. 1	90,000	8.00	13.00	23.00	55.00	160.00	500.00	1,600	3,150
1873	obv. 1	45,799	10.00	17.00	30.00	80.00	200.00	600.00	2,400	5,400
1876H	obv. 1	50,000	12.00	20.00	35.00	90.00	250.00	650.00	2,300	4,950
1880	obv. 1	30,000	15.00	25.00	45.00	110.00	300.00	700.00	2,300	4,950
Arabic "1" Reverse (1881-1900)										
1881	obv. 1	60,000	5.00	8.00	18.00	45.00	140.00	400.00	1,500	3,150
1882H	obv. 2	100,000	5.00	8.00	18.00	45.00	140.00	400.00	1,500	3,150
1885	obv. 1	40,000	8.00	13.00	23.00	55.00	175.00	563.00	2,250	4,950
1888	obv. 2	75,000	5.00	8.00	18.00	50.00	160.00	450.00	1,500	3,600
1890	obv. 2	100,000	4.00	6.00	13.00	33.00	100.00	350.00	1,000	2,700
1894	obv. 1, 2	100,000	4.00	6.00	13.00	33.00	100.00	300.00	1,000	2,700
1896 small 96	obv. 2	125,000	4.00	6.00	12.00	33.00	90.00	300.00	1,000	2,700
1896 large 96	obv. 1	incl. above	5.00	8.00	18.00	45.00	125.00	360.00	1,200	2,700
1899 small 99	obv. 2	125,000	5.00	8.00	18.00	45.00	150.00	400.00	1,200	2,700
1899 large 99	obv. 2	incl. above	4.00	6.00	12.00	33.00	90.00	300.00	1,000	2,700
1900	obv. 2	125,000	4.00	6.00	10.00	25.00	80.00	300.00	1,000	2,700

Edward VII, 20 Cents Silver, 1904

Diameter: 23.19 mm; weight: 4.713 grams; composition: .925 silver, .075 copper; edge: reeded

G: *Band of crown worn through*
VG: *Band of crown worn through at highest point*
F: *Jewels in band of crown will be blurred*
VF: *Band of crown still clear but no longer sharp*
EF: *Band of crown slightly worn but generally sharp and clear*

The obverse was derived from a portrait model by G.W. De Saulles (DES. below bust).

The reverse was designed and engraved by W.H.J. Blakemore.

Date	Qty. Minted	G-4	VG-8	F-12	VF-20	EF-40	AU-50	MS-60	MS-63
1904H	75,000	9.00	14.00	30.00	85.00	200.00	550.00	1,800	3,500

George V, 20 Cents Silver, 1912

Diameter: 23.19 mm; weight: 4.713 grams; composition: .925 silver, .075 copper; edge: reeded

G: *Band of crown worn through*
VG: *Band of crown worn through at highest point*
F: *Jewels in band of crown will be blurred*
VF: *Band of crown still clear but no longer sharp*
EF: *Band of crown slightly worn but generally sharp and clear*

The obverse was derived from a portrait model by Sir E.B. MacKennal (B.M. on truncation).

The reverse was a continuation of that used for the Edward VII series.

1912	350,000	2.50	3.50	6.00	18.00	65.00	250.00	650.00	1,500

25 CENTS
George V, 25 Cents Silver, 1917-1919

Diameter: 23.62 mm; weight: 5.32 grams; composition: .925 silver, .075 copper; edge: reeded

G: *Band of crown worn through*
VG: *Band of crown worn through at highest point*
F: *Jewels in band of crown will be blurred*
VF: *Band of crown still clear but no longer sharp*
EF: *Band of crown slightly worn but generally sharp and clear*

Because of continuing public confusion between Canadian 25-cent and New-foundland 20-cent pieces, the latter denomination was discontinued and a 25-cent piece was struck instead.

The obverse, from a portrait model by Sir E.B. Mackennal (B.M. on truncation), is identical to that for the Canadian issues of the same denomination.

W.H.J. Blakemore designed and engraved the reverse.

Date	Qty. Minted	G-4	VG-8	F-12	VF-20	EF-40	AU-50	MS-60	MS-63
1917C	464,779	1.50	2.00	4.00	8.00	16.00	55.00	175.00	375.00
1919C	163,939	2.00	3.00	5.00	11.00	25.00	90.00	250.00	700.00

50 CENTS
Victoria, 50 Cents Silver, 1870-1900

Diameter: 29.85 mm; weight: 11.782 grams; composition: .925 silver, .075 copper; edge: reeded

G: Braid around ear worn through
VG: No details in braid around ear
F: Braid segments begin to merge together
VF: Braid is clear but not sharp
EF: Braid is slightly worn but generally clear and sharp

This denomination bears a laureate bust, distinctly different from the crowned effigy on the Canadian 50-cent issues. There are two portrait varieties; the first is a youthful effigy with prominent upper lip, while the second, derived from the first, is a more aged representation with repressed upper lip, a drooping mouth and a longer depression over the eye.

The initial reverse is characterized by the presence of thick loops near the rim denticles. A second design has thin loops.

L.C. Wyon was the designer and engraver of the first and probably the later designs as well.

The weights of the silver denominations were made proportional to those of the equivalent values in English silver coins; that is, 5.6552 grams per shilling (12 pence). The value of the 50 cents was 2s. 1d.

1880 2nd 8 over 7. See 10-cent copy for details.

Thick Loops	Thin Loops	Obv. 1	Obv. 2

Date	Qty. Minted	G-4	VG-8	F-12	VF-20	EF-40	AU-50	MS-60	MS-63
Thick Loops Reverse (1870-1880)									
1870 .... obv. 1 50,000		9.00	16.00	25.00	75.00	225.00	675.00	2,700	7,200
1872H .... obv. 1 48,000		9.00	16.00	25.00	75.00	225.00	675.00	2,025	6,300
1873 .... obv. 1 37,675		15.00	25.00	40.00	85.00	338.00	788.00	3,600	10,800
1874 .... obv. 1 80,000		9.00	16.00	25.00	75.00	248.00	743.00	3,600	10,800
1876H .... obv. 1 28,000		15.00	25.00	40.00	115.00	405.00	1,035	4,050	9,000
1880 2nd 8 over 7 .. obv. 1 24,000		18.00	28.00	45.00	125.00	428.00	1,125	4,050	9,000
Thin Loops Reverse (1881-1900)									
1881 .... obv. 1 50,000		9.00	16.00	30.00	90.00	293.00	788.00	3,150	8,100
1882H .... obv. 2 100,000		8.00	14.00	23.00	65.00	225.00	675.00	2,250	5,850
1885 .... obv. 1 40,000		11.00	16.00	25.00	70.00	248.00	743.00	3,150	8,100
1888 .... obv. 1 20,000		14.00	20.00	40.00	125.00	450.00	900.00	3,600	9,000
1894 .... obv. 1 40,000		8.00	12.00	20.00	65.00	225.00	630.00	2,700	6,750
1896 .... obv. 1, 2 60,000		6.00	10.00	15.00	50.00	180.00	540.00	2,250	5,850
1898 .... obv. 1, 2 76,607		6.00	10.00	15.00	50.00	180.00	518.00	2,250	5,850

Narrow, bold 9's 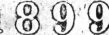 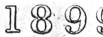 Wide, delicate 9's

Date	Qty. Minted	G-4	VG-8	F-12	VF-20	EF-40	AU-50	MS-60	MS-63
1899 narrow 9s . obv. 2 150,000		6.00	9.00	15.00	45.00	162.00	495.00	2,250	5,850
wide 9s .... included above		6.00	9.00	15.00	45.00	162.00	495.00	2,250	5,850
1900 .... obv. 2 150,000		5.00	8.00	15.00	40.00	135.00	428.00	2,250	5,850

Edward VII, 50 Cents Silver, 1904-1909

Diameter: 29.85 mm; weight: 11.782 grams; composition: .925 silver, .075 copper; edge: reeded

G: *Band of crown worn through*
VG: *Band of crown worn through at highest point*
F: *Jewels in band of crown will be blurred*
VF: *Band of crown still clear but no longer sharp*
EF: *Band of crown slightly worn but generally sharp and clear*

The obverse, designed and engraved by G.W. De Saulles (DES. below bust), is identical to that used for the Canadian issues.

The reverse was designed by W.H.J. Blakemore.

Date	Qty. Minted	G-4	VG-8	F-12	VF-20	EF-40	AU-50	MS-60	MS-63
1904H 140,000		5.00	7.00	10.00	25.00	75.00	150.00	425.00	1,500
1907 100,000		5.00	8.00	12.00	33.00	85.00	220.00	450.00	1,800
1908 160,000		5.00	7.00	10.00	25.00	70.00	125.00	325.00	1,000
1909 200,000		5.00	7.00	10.00	25.00	70.00	125.00	325.00	1,000

George V, 50 Cents Silver, 1911-1919

Diameter: (1911) 29.85 mm, (1917-19) 29.72 mm; weight: (1911) 11.782 grams, (1917-19) 11.664 grams; composition: .925 silver, .075 copper; edge: reeded

G: *Band of crown worn through*
VG: *Band of crown worn through at highest point*
F: *Jewels in band of crown will be blurred*
VF: *Band of crown still clear but no longer sharp*
EF: *Band of crown slightly worn but generally sharp and clear*

The obverse was derived from a model by Sir E.B. MacKennal (B.M. on truncation) and is identical to that used for the 1912-36 Canadian issues. It should be noted that the legend contains DEI GRA : (by the Grace of God), a feature which was absent on the 1911 Canadian issue of the same denomination.

The reverse is as for the Edward VII series.

Date	Qty. Minted	G-4	VG-8	F-12	VF-20	EF-40	AU-50	MS-60	MS-63
1911 200,000		4.00	5.50	10.00	23.00	55.00	140.00	440.00	1,000
1917C 375,560		4.00	5.50	8.00	18.00	45.00	100.00	260.00	600.00
1918C 294,824		4.00	5.50	8.00	18.00	45.00	100.00	260.00	600.00
1919C 306,267		4.00	5.50	8.00	18.00	45.00	112.00	260.00	600.00

GOLD 2 DOLLARS
Victoria, 2 Dollars Gold, 1865-1888
Diameter: 17.983 mm; weight: 3.328 grams; composition: .917 gold, .083 copper; edge: reeded

F: *Segments of braid begin to merge together*
VF: *Braid is clear but not sharp*
EF: *Braid slightly worn but generally sharp and clear*

This interesting series of "double dollars" as they were sometimes called, gives Newfoundland the distinction of being the only English colony with its own issue of gold.

This denomination is the same diameter as the 10-cent piece, and obverses in both cases were derived from the same matrices and punches (and perhaps dies). See 10-cent description for details on the three obverse varieties.

The reverse was designed and engraved by L.C. Wyon.

Date	Obverse	Qty. Minted	VF-20	EF-40	AU-50	MS-60	MS-63
1865	obv. 1	10,000	225.00	325.00	550.00	1,400	3,500
1870	obv. 1, 2	10,000	275.00	350.00	600.00	1,600	4,000
1872	obv. 2	6,050	350.00	500.00	1,100	3,000	8,000
1880	obv. 2	2,500	1,600	2,000	3,500	7,500	15,000
1881	obv. 2	10,000	180.00	250.00	350.00	850.00	3,000
1882H	obv. 3	25,000	170.00	210.00	275.00	600.00	2,500
1885	obv. 2	10,000	210.00	260.00	350.00	750.00	3,000
1888	obv. 2, 3	25,000	170.00	210.00	275.00	600.00	2,500

NOVA SCOTIA DECIMALS, 1861-1864

In 1859 Nova Scotia adopted a monetary system of dollars and cents, but set its dollar at the rate of $5 per £ sterling. This enabled the province to utilize British silver (the shilling was equal to 25 cents and the 6d to 12½ cents); however, it necessitated the issue of a half-cent piece to make change for the 6d. Only cents and half cents were issued prior to Confederation in 1867.

HALF-CENT
Victoria, Half-Cent, 1861-1864

Diameter: 20.65 mm; weight: 2.835 grams; composition: .950 copper, .040 tin, .010 zinc; edge: plain

G: *Hair over ear worn through*
VG: *Little detail in hair over ear or braid*
F: *Strands of hair over ear begin to merge; braid is worn*
VF: *Hair over ear is worn; braid is clear but no longer sharp*
EF: *Slight wear on hair over ear; braid that holds knot in place is sharp and clear*

The obverse, with a laureated bust of Victoria, is identical to the New Brunswick coins of the same denomination and is one of those used for the British bronze farthing (Peck's obv. 3). The designer and engraver was L.C. Wyon.

The original pattern for the issue had a reverse device of the Imperial crown and a wreath of roses and rose leaves. However, as a result of a propaganda campaign led by J.S. Thompson (father of Sir John Thompson), the wreath of the adopted issue consisted of both roses and mayflowers. The mayflower, *Epigea repens*, being the provincial flower of Nova Scotia.

Date	Qty. Minted	G-4	VG-8	F-12	VF-20	EF-40	AU-50	Unc-60	BU-63
1861	400,000	2.00	4.00	7.00	10.00	18.00	35.00	75.00	200.00
1864	400,000	2.00	4.00	7.00	10.00	18.00	35.00	75.00	200.00

1 CENT
Victoria, Large Cent, 1861-1864

Diameter: 25.53 mm; weight: 5.670 grams; composition: .950 copper, .040 tin, .010 zinc; edge: plain

The obverse is identical to that used for the New Brunswick coins of the same denomination and is one of those used for the British bronze halfpence (Peck's obv. 6). Two reverses, stemming from different matrices, are known. The first was used only for some of the 1861 issue. The crown is very detailed and a rosebud at the lower right is large. The second reverse saw use in 1861-64 and has a somewhat plainer crown with a thinner headband and a smaller rosebud at the lower right; and a repositioned inner circle and NOVA SCOTIA. All designs were by L.C. Wyon, the reverses being adapted from a model by C. Hill.

1862 issue. Although the reported mintages for the 1861 and 1862 cents were 800,000 and 1,000,000 respectively, the latter date is very scarce. Some, probably most, of the 1862 strikings are believed to have been made with dies dated 1861. Consequently, the figures have been combined for these two years.

Large bud

Small bud

Note position of I, relative to ribbon tip.

Date	Qty. Minted	G-4	VG-8	F-12	VF-20	EF-40	AU-50	Unc-60	BU-60
Large Rosebud Reverse (1861)									
1861 large rosebud 1,800,000		1.50	2.50	4.00	7.00	14.00	35.00	110.00	250.00
Small Rosebud Reverse (1861-1864)									
1861 small rosebud .... included above		1.50	2.50	4.00	7.00	14.00	35.00	110.00	250.00
1862 .... included above		18.00	27.50	40.00	70.00	150.00	225.00	400.00	1,100
1864 800,000		1.50	2.50	4.50	8.00	15.00	35.00	220.00	250.00

P.E.I. DECIMAL ISSUE, 1871

1 CENT
Victoria, Large Cent, 1871

Diameter: 25.40 mm; weight: 5.670 grams; composition: .950 copper, .040 tin, .010 zinc; edge: plain

G: Hair over ear worn through
VG: No details in hair over ear
F: Strands of hair over ear begin to merge
VF: Hair and jewels no longer sharp, but clear
EF: Hair over ear sharp and clear; jewels in diadem must show sharply and clearly

In 1871 the island adopted a decimal system with a dollar equal to the U.S. gold dollar, as in Canada. Only the 1-cent denomination was issued prior to entry into Confederation in 1873.

The obverse was designed and engraved by L.C. Wyon, based on a portrait model by William Theed, and is identical to that for the Jamaica halfpenny of the same year.

The reverse was adapted by L.C. Wyon from the Government seal of the island. The device is composed of a large oak tree (representing England) sheltering three oak saplings. (representing the three countries of the island); beneath these is the Latin phrase PARVA SUB INGENTI (The small beneath the great).

The issue is distinctive in that it was struck at the Heaton Mint in Birmingham, but lacks the familiar H mint mark and has English titles rather than Latin on the obverse.

Date	Qty. Minted	G-4	VG-8	F-12	VF-20	EF-40	AU-50	Unc-60	BU-60
1871 2,000,000		—	1.75	3.00	8.00	15.00	45.00	125.00	300.00

7
THE FRENCH REGIME

None of the coins of the French regime is strictly Canadian. They were all general issues for the French colonies of the New World. The coinage of 1670 was authorized by an edict of Louis XIV dated February 9, 1670, for use in New France, Acadia, the French settlements in Newfoundland and the French West Indies. The copper of 1717 to 1722 was authorized by edicts of 1716 and 1721 for use in New France, Louisiana, and the French West Indies.

ISSUE OF 1670

The coinage of 1670 consisted of silver 5 and 15 sols. A copper 2 deniers was also authorized but never struck. A total of 200,000 of the 5 sols and 40,000 of the 15 sols was struck at Paris. Old copper coin was to have been melted down at Nantes, but this was not done; the reasons for this may never be known, since the archives of the Nantes mint before 1700 were destroyed. The only known specimen is a pattern struck at Paris. The coins were not popular in New France. The silver coins were raised in value by a third in 1672 to keep them circulating, but in vain. They rapidly disappeared, and by 1680 none was to be seen. Later they were restored to their original value.

Note: Silver pieces similar to the 5 and 15 sols, with other dates and inscribed SIT NOMEN DOMINI BENEDICTUM were struck for use in France. Their use in the colonies was not intended at first. Most of the pieces are much more common than the colonial issue of 1670.

Copper

Date and value	VG	F	VF	EF
Double or 2 Deniers 1670				(Unique)

Silver

	VG	F	VF	EF
5 sols 1670	600.00	900.00	1,200	1,750
15 sols 1670	7,000	9,000	15,000	27,500

COINAGE OF 1717-1720

The copper 6 and 12 deniers of 1717, authorized by an edict of Louis XV dated December 1716, were to be struck at Perpignan. The order could not be carried out because the supply of copper was too brassy. A second attempt in 1720 also failed, probably for the same reason. All these coins are extremely rare, the 6 deniers of 1720 probably being unique.

Copper

Date and value	VG	F	VF	EF
6 deniers 1717	2,000	3,000	5,000	
6 deniers 1720				Unique
12 deniers 1717	2,000	3,000	5,000	

COINAGE OF 1721-1722

The copper coins of 1721-1722, authorized by an edict of Louis XV dated June 1721, were struck on copper blanks imported from Sweden. Rouen and La Rochelle struck pieces of 9 deniers in 1721 and 1722. New France received 534,000 pieces, mostly from the mint of La Rochelle, but only 8,180 were successfully put into circulation as the colonists disliked copper. In 1726 the rest of the issue was sent back to France.

Copper

1722, 2 over 1

Date and value	VG	F	VF	EF
9 deniers 1721B	275.00	385.00	550.00	715.00
9 deniers 1721H	80.00	110.00	150.00	275.00
9 deniers 1722H, 2 over 1	110.00	165.00	220.00	385.00
9 deniers 1722, normal date	80.00	110.00	15000	275.00

FRENCH BILLON COINS USED IN CANADA

Almost every type of French coin minted between 1600 and 1759 sooner or later found its way into Canada. To enumerate all these would be unwise, therefore we have confined the listings to the billon coinages, large shipments of which were known to have been sent to Canada. There are several types which were brought to New France. They are:

(a) The countermarked douzains of 1640. In 1640 all old douzains in France
     were stamped with a fleur de lys in an oval and re-issued at 15 deniers.
(b) The douzain of 1658. This was issued at 12 deniers, but raised to 15 deniers
     four months later.
(c) The 15 deniers of 1692-1707.
(d) The mousquetaire of 30 deniers 1709-1713, with its half, already listed.
(e) The 23 deniers of 1738-1760 and its half, already listed.

The John Law Coinage. At the instigation of John Law, many changes were
made in the French coinage. Copper pieces of 3, 6 and 12 deniers were introduced in 1719 and 1720 and coined till 1724. A coinage of silver ecus, halves,
thirds, sixths, and twelfths was introduced in 1720 and coined till 1724. The petit
Louis d'argent of 3 livres was coined in 1720, and a pure silver livre was also
coined. Gold Louis and halves were coined from 1720 to 1723.

Date and value	VG	F	VF	EF
15 deniers 1710-1713AA	138.00	220.00	330.00	550.00
30 deniers 1709-1713AA	110.00	165.00	220.00	358.00
30 deniers 1709-1713D	110.00	165.00	220.00	358.00

Half sol marque 1738-54	100.00	140.00	200.00	275.00
Sol marque 1738-1760*	30.00	50.00	90.00	132.00

The piece of 30 deniers was called a *mousquetaire*, and was coined at Metz and
Lyons. The 15 deniers was coined only at Metz. The sol marque and half were
coined at almost every French mint, those of Paris being most common.

*Specimens of the sol marque dated after 1760 were not used in Canada, which by then was firmly in British hands.

Mint marks on French Regime coins:
Paris – A; Metz – AA; Rouen – B; Lyons – D; LaRoche – H; Perpignan – Q.

PLAYING CARD MONEY

In the early days of New France the first ship arriving from France in the spring
of each year carried a supply of coins to be used for paying the troops and purchasing furs and other raw products. Everything that New France could not
produce for itself had to be imported from France, with payment in cash. Taxes
were also paid in cash. In spite of a rich trade in furs, New France imported more
than it exported with the result that most of the coinage received from France
was shipped back (sometimes on the next ship) in payment to France. The resultant shortage of coins (particularly in winter when no ships would arrive from
France) caused considerable inconvenience.

In 1685 the Intendant, Jacques de Meulles, decided to introduce an emergency issue of paper money for paying the troops. There were no printing presses in New France and the only available paper was writing paper which was not durable enough to be used as currency. Playing cards were plentiful in New France and made to be handled repeatedly, so de Meulles issued the first such notes on the backs of playing cards.

The first series of playing card money was issued in three denominations; four livres (equivalent to four English pounds) written on an entire card; two livres written on half a card; and 15 sols (the sol or sou being considered equivalent to the English shilling) written on a quarter card.

The measure adopted by de Meulles brought only temporary relief and the need for card money was met in the same manner by successive Governors and Intendants. Each new issue replaced the previous issue and stiff penalties were imposed on anyone keeping old cards after new ones were issued. It is for this reason that not a single specimen of the first eight issues of card money is known to exist today. After the first five issues, plain card was used rather than the backs of playing cards and a few of these can be found today in museum collections.

From 1685 to 1760 there were no fewer than 22 issues of card money used in New France. In the latter part of this period the supply of card money was supplemented by the issue of ordonnances (notes drawn on the treasury of Quebec) which were printed and written on ordinary paper. Although the issuance of card money was originally intended as a temporary expedient, the economy of New France was run almost entirely on locally produced paper money of this nature for a period of seventy-five years (two and a half generations).

All playing card money is very rare and is now protected from export from Canada by the Heritage and Culture Act.

8
PRE-CONFEDERATION
COLONIAL ISSUES

MAGDALEN ISLANDS

The penny token was issued by Isaac Coffin, who planned to rule the islands like a feudal baron. At this time the islands belonged to the colony of Lower Canada. Coffin soon learned that he did not have the powers of a colonial governor, but his pennies must have circulated for a long time, since they are rather rare in very fine or better condition. The islands had been granted to Coffin, but were taken from him and put under the direct administration of Lower Canada, now the province of Quebec. There is evidence that this token was used in Halifax, Nova Scotia after being rejected by the Magdalen Islanders, and that it circulated in Halifax to a considerable extent at one time.

Breton			G	VG	F	VF	EF
1	520	Penny token 1815	20.00	40.00	75.00	200.00	450.00

NEWFOUNDLAND

Newfoundland was discovered by John Cabot in 1497 and claimed for England. The city of St. John's dates from about 1500. English authority was firmly established by Sir Humphrey Gilbert in 1583. Further settlements took place after 1600, but the French planted some colonies along the south coast, at and near Placentia. These were ceded to the British in 1710.

Rutherford Tokens

There was no coinage specifically for Newfoundland until 1841, when the first copper tokens appeared. These were issued by R. & I.S. Rutherford of St. John's. The Rutherford family arms on the reverse contains the Latin phrase PER MARE PER TERRAS, meaning "by land, by sea."

2-3 obv.   2 rev.   4 rev.

Breton			G	VG	F	VF	EF
2	952	RUTHERFORD etc., reverse no date	2.00	5.00	10.00	25.00	100.00
3		Same, 1841	2.00	5.00	10.00	30.00	150.00

The second Rutherford tokens were issued by Rutherford Bros. of Harbour Grace. These latter pieces were struck by Ralph Heaton & Sons, whose initials RH appear above the date. Eventually the Rutherford tokens became too plentiful and fell into discredit.

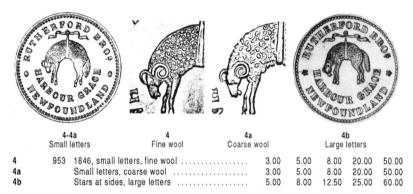

4-4a	4	4a	4b
Small letters	Fine wool	Coarse wool	Large letters

4	953	1846, small letters, fine wool	3.00	5.00	8.00	20.00	50.00
4a		Small letters, coarse wool	3.00	5.00	8.00	20.00	50.00
4b		Stars at sides, large letters	5.00	8.00	12.50	25.00	60.00

M'Auslane Token

Number 5, of farthing size, appeared about 1845. It was not a farthing but an advertising piece issued by Peter M'Auslane, a general merchant whose business at St.John's was destroyed by fire shortly afterward. He then quit the island and settled in Ontario.

5

5	956	PETER M'AUSLANE etc., brass	Extremely Rare

Anonymous Issues

At this time lightweight halfpennies were being brought over by the barrel from Prince Edward Island, and in 1851 and again in 1860 the government had to forbid their further importation and use. The rare ship token of 1858 was struck by Heaton and issued anonymously at St. John's. It has been faked, but according to Breton, the fakes were easily exposed.

The FISHERY RIGHTS token of 1860 commemorates the signing of a treaty by the major fishing nations to regulate the fisheries. Shore limits were fixed, the rights of local fishermen were recognized, and steps were taken to control the behaviour of foreign seamen whose vessels had to use local harbours for shelter or repairs.

Breton		VG	F	VF	EF
6	954 Ship, 1858	225.00	300.00	450.00	900.00
7	955 FISHERY RIGHTS etc., 1860	30.00	40.00	50.00	80.00

PRINCE EDWARD ISLAND

Prince Edward Island was colonized by France and originally named Isle St-Jean. Acquired by Great Britain in 1758, it was governed from Nova Scotia until 1770, when it was given the status of separate colony. In 1794 it was given its present name in honour of Edward, Duke of Kent, the father of Queen Victoria.

The "Holey Dollar" and "Plug" of 1813

In 1813 the newly-arrived governor found a serious commercial crisis resulting from a lack of coined money on the island. His solution was to issue mutilated Spanish-American "dollars" (8 reales pieces), as was being done in some of the colonies in the West Indies and elsewhere. He directed that up to 1,000 dollars would be perforated, forming "plugs" (the discs punched out of the centre) and "holey dollars" (the rings that remained). The plugs were to pass for 1 shilling and the rings for 5 shillings; this over-rating (the whole dollars went for only 5 shillings), plus the mutilation was believed to be sufficient to keep these pieces in circulation.

Unfortunately, some individuals saw a chance to make a quick profit, and soon the colony was plagued with additional holey dollars (and plugs?) privately issued in imitation of those officially issued by the government treasury. This forced the recall of the official issue in 1814. Interestingly, the merchants then agreed to continue accepting the imitations in trade, thus raising them to the status of tokens.

Although we know of no documentary evidence regarding how the official issues were marked, purely circumstantial evidence points to a counterstamp, consisting of 10 triangles arranged in a circle, resembling a rayed sun. Furthermore, it is quite possible that the countermark was applied such that it overlapped the King's forehead on the dollars and his throat on the plugs.

There is presently no way of positively authenticating the supposed government counterstamp punch (or punches). The official and imitation issues are listed together for that reason.

Unfortunately, the situation is further complicated by the fact that later forgeries have been produced to deceive collectors. Some are complete fabrications which can be easily detected; however, others are made from genuine Spanish-American dollars and can be very difficult to differentiate from the pieces that circulated in P.E.I. Needless to say, great caution should be exercised in purchasing a purported P.E.I. "holey" dollar or "plug."

	VG	F	VF	EF	UNC
Holey dollar, original or contemporary imitation	1,500	2,500	3,000	3,500	—
Plug, original or contemporary imitation	2,500	3,500	4,500	—	—

Ships, Colonies & Commerce Tokens

The inscription on these pieces is an allusion to a remark made by Napoleon at the battle of Ulm. Ships, colonies, and commerce, he said, were the three British advantages that would defeat him in the end. The first tokens came out about 1829. These were struck in New York by Wright & Bale, and bear a striped flag superficially resembling the United States flag. These pieces were popular, and later issues were imported from England. Most were designed by Thomas Halliday. The two brass pieces dated 1815 were struck after 1830, being antedated to evade laws against anonymous tokens. The reverse of No. 9 is that of a private token of the Isle of Man.

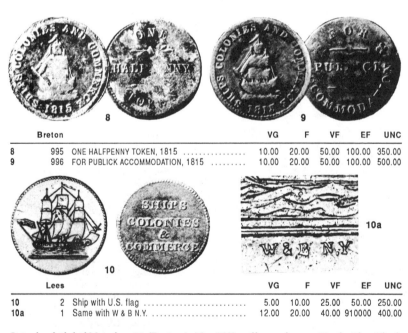

Breton			VG	F	VF	EF	UNC
8	995	ONE HALFPENNY TOKEN, 1815	10.00	20.00	50.00	100.00	350.00
9	996	FOR PUBLICK ACCOMMODATION, 1815	10.00	20.00	50.00	100.00	500.00

Lees			VG	F	VF	EF	UNC
10	2	Ship with U.S. flag	5.00	10.00	25.00	50.00	250.00
10a	1	Same with W & B N.Y.	12.00	20.00	40.00	910000	400.00

It is doubtful if Number **11** (Breton's No. 999) will ever be positively identified. Its obverse, as drawn by Breton, shows a small ship very much like that of such Nova Scotia tokens as the Starr & Shannon pieces. Its reverse die has yet to be identified. The high poopdeck variety (**12**) has been said to be Breton 999, but this is not so. Judge lees, who published these pieces in *The Numismatist* in 1926, made this point very clear.

12

Lees			VG	F	VF	EF	UNC
11		Small ship					Existence doubted
12	5a	High poopdeck, blank flag					Extremely Rare

Note: Tokens No. 10-12 are also known to have been used in Lower Canada.

The next three varieties bear the same reverse, characterized by very large, bold lettering. The first, Lees 5b, is very rare. It has been called fraudulent, and its status is still in question.

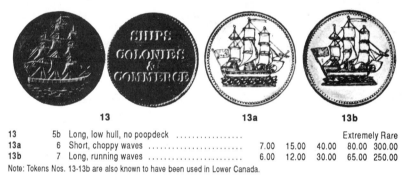

13   **13a**   **13b**

Lees			VG	F	VF	EF	UNC
13	5b	Long, low hull, no poopdeck					Extremely Rare
13a	6	Short, choppy waves	7.00	15.00	40.00	80.00	300.00
13b	7	Long, running waves	6.00	12.00	30.00	65.00	250.00

Note: Tokens Nos. 13-13b are also known to have been used in Lower Canada.

The following tokens, numbered 997 by Breton, have over forty minor die varieties, some of which are very rare. They were struck in Birmingham and designed by Thomas Halliday. Most of the varieties are in the reverse inscription. For example, four styles of "&" are found on varieties of **14**, **14b** and **14c**. The varieties of **14a** all have the "&" ending in a short horizontal bar.

14a

Lees			VG	F	VF	EF	UNC
14	23-33	Raised H on exergue line	3.00	6.00	15.00	30.00	150.00
14a	9-13	No H on exergue line	6.00	10.00	20.00	50.00	200.00
14b	14-22	Two guys at top of spritsail	30.00	55.00	75.00	150.00	400.00
14c	34-46	H on exergue line and in water	6.00	10.00	20.00	40.00	180.00

 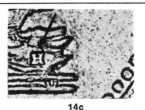

14b   **14c**

The next three pieces are all characterized by ships having a drooping flag at the stern. Numbers **15** and **15a**, which correspond to Lees 3, are from complete dies in which all of the design (including rim beads) is present. There are thick (presumably struck first) and thin varieties. Lees 4, a lightweight piece of "blacksmith-like" character, was produced from the obverse die of **15, 15a** and a reverse die lacking rim beads. Care should be taken not to confuse worn lightweight specimens of Lees 3 (**15a**) for Lees 4 (**15b**).

15-15b obv.   **15-15a rev.**   **15b rev.**

	Lees		Average Condition
15	3	Drooping flag, beads on both sides, thick	100.00
15a	3	Same, lightweight	125.00
15b	4	Same, no beads on reverse	Very Rare

Note: Numbers 15, 15a and 15b are also known to have been used in Lower Canada.

Local Tokens, 1840-1858

Local tokens appeared first in 1840, the rarest being the sheaf of wheat halfpenny. It was struck by James Milner of Charlottetown with dies and machinery imported from the United States. The "Success to the Fisheries" tokens (**17- 17c**) were issued by E. Lydiard and F. Longworth of Charlottetown. Those with a clevis to the plow were issued in 1840, and those with a hook in 1857. The large tail to the fish fillet is well struck up, while the small tail is weak. These and all later tokens were struck by Ralph Heaton & Sons.

16

	Breton		VG	F	VF	EF	UNC
16	916	Sheaf of wheat 1840	350.00	525.00	750.00	950.00	—

Clevis   Hook

Weak Tail   Bold Tail

	Breton		VG	F	VF	EF	UNC
17	917	Clevis, weak tail	2.00	5.50	11.50	25.00	250.00
17a		Clevis, bold tail	5.00	10.00	20.00	32.00	300.00
17b		Hook, weak tail	3.00	5.00	10.00	30.00	175.00
17c		Hook, bold tail	3.00	5.00	10.00	30.00	175.00

The *Cent* of 1855 was issued by James Duncan, a hardware merchant who moved to Charlottetown from Montreal. This is the first Canadian decimal piece. It is doubtful if it was accepted as a hundredth of a dollar, for it weighed the same as the other tokens which were halfpennies and which went at 150 to the Spanish dollar. Specimens on thicker flans may have been an attempt to pass them as cents by increasing the weight.

The token showing the paddle steamer was issued in 1858, probably by James Duncan, though this has not been established. Early writers attributed it to Newfoundland.

18   19

18	920	*one cent* 1855	3.00	6.00	10.00	20.00	90.00
19	921	Paddle steamer	4.00	7.00	15.00	30.00	200.00

The tokens inscribed SELF GOVERNMENT AND FREE TRADE were issued by Henry Haszard and George and Simeon Davies. Numerous minor varieties are known. The most noticeable differences are in the island name and the style of 5 in the date. The first issues have the name rendered as PRINCE EDWARD'S ISLAND, and have 5s with short, thick tops. Later issues show first a change to 5s with longer, thinner tops, followed by a change to PRINCE EDWARD ISLAND.

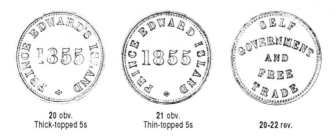

20 obv.   21 obv.
Thick-topped 5s   Thin-topped 5s   20-22 rev.

	Breton		VG	F	VF	EF	UNC
20	918	PRINCE EDWARD'S 1855, thick-topped 5s	2.50	5.00	9.00	20.00	185.00
20a		Same, thin-topped 5s	3.50	7.00	12.00	25.00	200.00
21	919	PRINCE EDWARD 1855	2.50	5.00	9.00	20.00	200.00
22		Same, 1857	2.50	5.00	9.00	20.00	200.00

NOVA SCOTIA

Nova Scotia was colonized for the first time in 1604 by Sieur de Monts, who claimed the land for France under the name of Acadia. Captured several times by the British, it was always returned to France, but in 1713 it passed permanently into British hands and was renamed Nova Scotia.

Very little coined money was available in the early days under the British. Some Spanish dollars and occasional shipments of British halfpennies and farthings were almost the only coins to be had. The Spanish dollar was accepted in Halifax at five shillings, which rating became legal by 1758. Halifax Currency, as this rating was called, was destined to become the standard of all the Canadian colonies.

Trade & Navigation Tokens, 1812-1814

After 1800 the shortage of copper began to become serious, and about 1812 local merchants started to import tokens from England and Ireland. The first were the "Trade & Navigation" tokens, struck over the tokens of Samuel Guppy of Bristol. The farthing is known to have been imported by a Halifax merchant named Haliburton.

For many years there have been reports of a penny bearing the date 1812, but in recent years none has been found. Early auction sales record specimens dated 1812, but none has been traced.

23

24-25

26-27

1814, 1 over 0
(blundered die)
27a

23	964	Farthing 1813	32.50	45.00	75.00	120.00	325.00
24	963	Halfpenny 1812	4.00	8.00	15.00	40.00	160.00
25		Halfpenny 1813	5.00	10.00	20.00	40.00	150.00
	(962)	Penny 1812			Existence doubtful		

	Breton		VG	F	VF	EF	UNC
26	962	Penny 1813	10.00	20.00	30.00	60.00	150.00
27		Penny 1814, normal date	15.00	25.00	35.00	70.00	300.00
27a		Penny 1814, 2nd 1 over 0	25.00	45.00	70.00	150.00	500.00

28

| 28 | 965 | Ship under topsails, 1813 .... | 4.00 | 8.00 | 15.00 | 40.00 | 225.00 |

Broke Token of 1814

The Broke tokens were struck in honour of Captain P.B. Vere Broke, who commanded H.M.S. *Shannon* and captured U.S.S. *Chesapeake in 1813*. This was the first British naval victory in the War of 1812.

29

| 29 | 879 | Broke, 1814 .... | 8.00 | 15.00 | 35.00 | 75.00 | 250.00 |

Local Merchants' Tokens, 1814-1820

In 1814 merchants began to issue tokens of their own design, a few being issued anonymously. There was a great variety of these pieces issued from 1814 to 1816, and in 1817 the government ordered their removal from circulation within three years because they had become too plentiful. Most were struck in England.

31   32

| 31 | 880 | FOR TRADE, 1814 .... | 20.00 | 35.00 | 60.00 | 100.00 | 450.00 |
| 32 | 881 | CARRITT & ALPORT, 1814 .... | 10.00 | 20.00 | 40.00 | 80.00 | 350.00 |

Tokens **33** to **38** were engraved and struck by Thomas Halliday of Birmingham. The smaller pieces (**34-37**) show a close relationship through the use of common obverse dies.

Breton			VG	F	VF	EF	UNC
33	882	HOSTERMAN & ETTER, 1814	8.00	12.00	25.00	60.00	225.00

34-37
Typical obv.

Hosterman rev.   Barry rev.   British Copper rev.   Halifax rev.

			VG	F	VF	EF	UNC
34	883	HOSTERMANN & ETTER, 1815	5.00	10.00	20.00	40.00	150.00
35	891	JOHN A. BARRY, 1815	6.00	10.00	20.00	45.00	160.00
36	886	GENUINE BRITISH COPPER, 1815	5.00	8.00	15.00	50.00	165.00
37	889	HALIFAX, 1815	5.00	10.00	20.00	55.00	165.00

38	888	SUCCESS TO NAVIGATION & TRADE, ...1815	5.00	10.00	25.00	60.00	175.00
39	887	GENUINE BRITISH COPPER, 1815	20.00	35.00	60.00	125.00	300.00

The crude pieces **41** and **42** were made, probably locally, for a merchant *J. Brown,* and the bust and harp piece (**40**) may also have been made for him. All are of a "blacksmith-like" character.

Bust obv.   Harp in wreath rev.

Warehouse obv.   JB rev.

Breton No.			Average Condition
40	—	Bust, 1815, harp in wreath	Extremely Rare
41	—	Warehouse, harp in wreath	Extremely Rare
42	—	Warehouse, script ᴊʙ	350.00

The halfpenny of J. Brown (43) was once attributed to Scotland because of its
design. It has an obverse with a thistle and the Latin legend NEMO ME IMPUNE
LACESSIT. The translation is "No one may hurt me with impunity."

Breton No.			VG	F	VF	EF	UNC
43	896	PAYABLE J. BROWN	4.50	7.50	15.00	45.00	300.00
44	895	SUCCESS	30.00	50.00	75.00	175.00	500.00

45 obv.   46 obv.   45-46 rev.

45	885	COMMERCIAL CHANGE 1815	5.00	10.00	25.00	75.00	275.00
46	884	STARR & SHANNON 1815	4.00	10.00	20.00	50.00	200.00

Breton		VG	F	VF	EF	UNC
47	890 MILES W. WHITE etc., 1815	5.00	10.00	25.00	75.00	275.00

			VG	F	VF	EF	UNC
48	892	HARDWARE 1816	8.00	15.00	25.00	100.00	300.00
49	893	W.A. & S BLACK, 1816	8.00	15.00	35.00	75.00	300.00

The TRADE & NAVIGATION tokens of 1820 are attributed to Nova Scotia because of the inscription. Since they are dated 1820, they would have been issued in violation of the law, for by 1820 all private tokens were to be out of circulation as required by a law passed in 1817. A variety with two shamrocks growing under the harp has been reported, but none has been seen in Canada.

			VG	F	VF	EF	UNC
50	894	TRADE & NAVIGATION, 1820 copper	6.50	12.00	45.00	80.00	325.00

SEMI-REGAL TOKENS, 1823-1843

The withdrawal of private tokens after 1817 created a fresh shortage of small change which by the early 1820s became quite serious. Because British regal coppers could not be obtained, the provincial government made arrangements with a private coiner in England to provide coppers that were slightly lesser in weight than the corresponding official coins. This was done without the knowledge of the British government, who would surely not have allowed such a local issue at that time. These coppers are therefore best described as semi-regal tokens, as they lacked the authority of the home government.

George IV Thistle Tokens, 1823-1832

The first government of semi-regal tokens were issued in 1823. These and the later issues through 1843 are known as the Thistle Tokens because of their reverse design. All the issues were struck in Birmingham. There was an issue of 400,000 halfpennies in 1823 and in 1824 there was an issue of 217,776 pennies and 118,636 halfpennies.

In 1832 there was an issue of 200,000 pennies and 800,000 halfpennies bearing the bust of George IV, although coined two years after his death. Presumably the order for coins "similar in design" to those of 1824 was taken too literally.

51 obv.　　　　　　　51a obv.　　　　　　Typical rev.

Breton			VG	F	VF	EF	UNC
51	867	Halfpenny 1823	4.00	7.50	12.00	40.00	180.00
51a		Same, no hyphen in NOVA SCOTIA	8.00	15.00	25.00	50.00	225.00
52	869	Halfpenny 1824	6.50	10.00	20.00	55.00	350.00
53	871	Halfpenny 1832	3.00	6.00	12.00	30.00	160.00

54-55

54	868	Penny 1824	7.00	10.00	25.00	60.00	200.00
55	870	Penny 1832	5.00	8.00	15.00	50.00	175.00

Imitations of George IV Thistle Tokens

56

Among the products of the clandestine "mints" of Lower Canada in the 1830's were struck imitations of the 1832 thistle tokens. They were shipped to Nova Scotia and for a time circulated along with the government issue. One much prized variety of the imitation halfpenny has the date 1382, resulting from a blundered die. This was apparently soon discovered, for a second variety with the date altered to 1832 exists. Pieces from this altered die at first glance appear to be dated 1882. Fakes have been made of the 1382 variety in order to deceive collectors; these, however, have a round topped 3 in the date as opposed to a flat topped 3 on the true 1382s.

Imitation Halfpennies

		Error date		Corrected date			
	Breton		VG	F	VF	EF	UNC
56	871	Imitation, normal date 1832	5.00	10.00	15.00	70.00	—
56a	872	Imitation, error date 1382	300.00	450.00	900.00	—	—
56b	873	Imitation, corrected date 1832	8.00	15.00	35.00	75.00	—

Imitation Pennies

57

57	870	Imitation penny 1832		7.00	12.00	25.00	60.00	—

Victoria Thistle Tokens, 1840-1843

On the 1840 and 1843 issues of thistle tokens the portrait was that of the current British monarch, Victoria. The coiners attempted to copy William Wyon's beautiful bust used on the British regal coinage, but were not very successful. The weight and size of the Victorian thistles, particularly the 1840 halfpennies, is somewhat variable. The quantities issued were 300,000 halfpennies and 150,000 pennies of each date. Very rare cast imitations of the 1840 halfpenny are know.

58

1840 0 varieties

Large 0   Medium 0   Small 0

58	874	Halfpenny 1840, large 0	6.00	12.00	25.00	50.00	300.00
58a		Same, medium 0	4.00	8.00	15.00	30.00	200.00
58b		Same, small 0	5.00	10.00	20.00	40.00	300.00
59		Halfpenny 1843	5.00	10.00	20.00	50.00	200.00

60

Breton			VG	F	VF	EF	UNC
60	873	Penny 1840	4.00	8.00	15.00	50.00	225.00
61		Penny 1843, 3 over 0	30.00	60.00	150.00	350.00	—
61a		Penny 1843, normal date	5.00	10.00	20.00	55.00	250.00

Imitations of Victoria Thistle Tokens

62

62	874	Imitation halfpenny 1840	Very Rare

PRE-DECIMAL COINAGE
Mayflower Coinage, 1856

63   64

By the 1850s the attitude in Great Britain was more favourable toward the issue of local coppers in British North America and the Nova Scotia government applied for a coinage of halfpennies and pennies. Their application was accepted and the first true coins were struck for this province. They are popularly known as the Mayflower coppers because of their reverse designs and are among the most beautiful of all the Canadian colonial coppers. The master tools were engraved by Leonard C. Wyon, using his own design for the obverse and that of Halifax botanist John S. Thompson for the reverse. The halfpennies with L.C.W. under the bust exist only in proof and are most likely patterns; hence, they are not listed here (see comments in the Introduction). The coinage was executed by

Heaton's Mint in Birmingham because the Royal Mint in London was too busy with the Imperial coinage at the time. Most of the pieces were struck in bronze, although the halfpenny is also known in brass.

	Breton		VG	F	VF	EF	UNC
63	876	Halfpenny 1856, bronze	4.00	6.00	10.00	45.00	250.00
63a		Same, brass	35.00	70.00	150.00	300.00	—
64	875	Penny 1856, L.C.W. under bust	4.50	7.00	15.00	30.00	250.00
64a		Same, no L.C.W.	5.00	9.00	20.00	40.00	300.00

NEW BRUNSWICK

New Brunswick was claimed by France as part of Acadia. It was not settled until 1631, when a fort was built at the mouth of the St. John River. When Acadia was ceded to Great Britain in 1713, the French continued to dispute the British claim to New Brunswick, but gave up all claims in 1763.

Under British rule it was governed from Nova Scotia until 1784, when it was detached from Nova Scotia at the request of the inhabitants. New Brunswick was not as seriously short of coin as were the other colonies. A brisk trade with Nova Scotia kept the colony supplied to a limited extent with copper. The need for copper was not serious before 1830, when a halfpenny was anonymously issued at Saint John.

Miscellaneous Tokens, ca. 1830-1845

The first piece was not issued because the name of the city was spelled incorrectly. Saint John is the largest city of New Brunswick, St. John's is the capital city of Newfoundland. Evidently this rarity was made by the manufacturers of the almost equally rare Montreal Ropery halfpenny.

The second piece appeared about 1830. Its reverse die was used also for an anonymous token issued at the same time in Lower Canada (**101**).

65						
65	—	ST. JOHN'S ... TOKEN	Extremely Rare (Only Two Known)			
66	913	FOR PUBLIC ACCOMMODATION	5.00	10.00	20.00	55.00	300.00

SEMI-REGAL TOKENS, 1843

In 1841 the provincial government took steps to solve their growing shortage of copper currency by importing £3000 worth of British Imperial pennies and halfpennies. Being sterling, these coins were worth a fraction more in local currency than their face value. The government soon found that they could circulate them only at 1d and ½d local currency, because there was no way to make change for small numbers of pieces.

Only about £150 worth of the Imperial coppers had been put into circulation when the New Brunswick government decided to return the unissued remainder to England and obtain in their place tokens payable in local currency. The government entered into a contract with Mr. William Hammond of Halifax to choose the designs and make the other necessary arrangements for obtaining the new coppers. When the British government was informed of the colony's plan, it was furious. Thus rebuked, the colonial government informed the Colonial Office in London that the contract with Hammond had been cancelled and plans for the new coinage shelved.

The subsequent events are most interesting. The evidence at hand suggests that the New Brunswick government quietly went ahead with their plans and obtained coppers from Boulton & Watt of Soho. The British government knew nothing about them until 1853, when application was made for a fresh coinage of coppers by the unknowing successor of the Lt. Governor under whom the 1843s had been obtained.

67

Breton			VG	F	VF	EF	UNC
67	910	Halfpenny 1843	4.00	6.00	12.50	35.00	250.00

68

68	909	Penny 1843	4.00	7.00	15.00	45.00	300.00

PRE-DECIMAL COINAGE, 1854

By 1853, when a fresh coinage of pennies and halfpennies was required by the New Brunswick government, the climate in the Colonial Office was more favourable for the issue of local coinages by the British North American colonies. The master tools from the 1843 tokens were forwarded from New Brunswick to the Royal Mint, where they were used as a source of modified designs. These alterations, probably by L.C. Wyon, consisted of the substitution on the obverse of William Wyon's portrait for the British shilling on the halfpenny and that for the British halfpenny on the penny. In addition, the word CURRENCY was used in place of TOKEN on the reverse. The use of CURRENCY indicated the official nature of the issue and also implied Halifax Currency, the standard at the time. Due to a heavy schedule at the Royal Mint, the new dies were sent to the Heaton Mint, where 480,000 pieces of each denomination were struck.

Breton No.			VG	F	VF	EF	UNC
69	912	Halfpenny 1854	3.50	5.50	15.00	35.00	200.00

70	911	Penny 1854	4.00	7.00	18.00	50.00	300.00

LOWER CANADA

New France was conquered by the British in 1760 and ceded to Great Britain in 1763. It was known as the colony of Quebec until 1791. Originally the colony included the St. Lawrence basin and the Great Lakes region, and large areas of territory extending south to the Ohio River. In 1783 the Great Lakes and the upper St. Lawrence were made the boundary with the United States. In 1791 the Great Lakes area was separated from Quebec, which now became the colony of Lower Canada. Lower Canada was predominantly French, and was the largest and most populous of the Canadian colonies.

WELLINGTON TOKENS

No special coinage was struck for Lower Canada until 1837. About 1813 anonymous tokens began to appear. The earliest were the Wellington tokens, brought over by British troops sent to Canada to fight the Americans in 1814. These tokens depicted a bust of the Duke of Wellington, and were very popular. They were often struck over other tokens. Some of them are antedated in order to evade laws passed in 1825 against private tokens.

In 1808 Napoleon sent an army into Spain and Portugal, deposed the king of Spain, and placed his brother Joseph on the Spanish throne. In the same year the British invaded Portugal and won major victories at Vimeira, Talavera, Busaco and Almeida, finally driving the French out in 1811. The action in Spain continued until 1813. Major British victories were scored at Ciudad Rodrigo, Badajoz, Salamanca, Madrid, San Sebastian, Vitoria and Pamplona. Wellington commanded the British forces during most of the period of conflict.

The wellington pieces dated 1805 and 1811 are of questionable connection to British North America. The reverse of the 1805 token would seem to be the work of Peter Wyon for an Irish piece (also see No. **237**).

In honour of the Peninsular campaigns J.K. Picard of Hull had the battle tokens (**73-75**) struck by Sir Edward Thomason of Birmingham. Specimens in silver were struck for presentation at Court, Picard having been invited by the Prince Regent to come to London and shows his coppers. They are halfpenny size, but there is no expression of denomination, perhaps because they were initially intended to be more in the nature of medalets. In any case they were ultimately used as halfpenny tokens and there was even a brass imitation of one of the varieties which circulated in Canada. Note that only on **74b** is the Spanish word *ciudad* (city) spelled correctly.

Numbers **76-79, 81-89** were all designed by Thomas Halliday, the Cossack penny being considered an example of his best work. Of these pieces, most varieties of **76-79, 85-86** were struck over Guppy tokens of Bristol. Specimens of **86** were overstruck with other designs for use in England, proving that not all the anonymous Wellington tokens of these listed types were sent to Canada.

71

72

73

73b

	Breton		VG	F	VF	EF	UNC
71	976	WELLINGTON, HIBERNIA, 1805	10.00	20.00	45.00	80.00	300.00
72	977	TRADE & COMMERCE, 1811	30.00	50.00	75.00	225.00	500.00
73	987	CUIDAD &c.&c.&c, copper	6.00	10.00	20.00	45.00	160.00
73a		Same, silver	100.00	200.00	300.00	400.00	500.00
73b		Imitation No. 73, brass	20.00	40.00	60.00	95.00	—

74 obv.   74 rev.   74b rev.

			VG	F	VF	EF	UNC
74	986	CUIAD MADRID,copper	5.00	10.00	20.00	40.00	125.00
74a		Same, silver	100.00	200.00	300.00	400.00	500.00
74b		CIUDAD (correct spelling), copper	5.00	10.00	20.00	40.00	125.00

Breton		VG	F	VF	EF	UNC
75	988 SALAMANCA PAMPLUNO	8.00	20.00	40.00	125.00	400.00

Halfpennies

All of the undated halfpennies with HALFPENNY TOKEN on the reverse were produced by Thomas Halliday of Birmingham and most (if not all) were struck over halfpennies of Samuel Guppy.

76	972	Undated, trident	3.00	7.50	15.00	50.00	200.00
76a		Undated, spear	6.50	15.00	30.00	75.00	300.00
77	971	Undated, large letters	3.00	7.50	15.00	35.00	250.00

The next three pieces, showing Britannia surrounded by a continuous wreath on the reverse, are lightweight and are believed to have been struck by Thomas Halliday on Canadian order. They are linked to the Britannia-eagle tokens of Lower Canada through their reverses.

| Field Marshall obv. | Halfpenny obv. | Clockwise wreath | Counterclockwise wreath |

	Breton		VG	F	VF	EF	UNC
78	973	FIELD MARSHALL, clockwise wreath				Extremely Rare	
78a		Same, counterclockwise wreath				Extremely Rare	
79	980	HALFPENNY, counterclockwise wreath	50.00	90.00	200.00	400.00	—

The Marquis Wellington halfpenny was struck by Isaac Parkes of Dublin. It is antedated, since Wellington did not become a marquis until 1814. The tokens of 1814, struck on Canadian order, also were antedated to evade the law against private tokens.

80

80	978	MARQUIS WELLINGTON, 1813	6.00	10.00	20.00	125.00	500.00

The other halfpennies dated 1813, including the lightweight one dated 1814, were produced by Thomas Halliday. The 1813s were struck over Guppy halfpennies and the 1814 was probably struck on Canadian order.

81-81a   **82**

81	969	1813, plain edge	3.75	6.50	16.00	35.00	125.00
81a		1813, engraved edge	6.00	12.50	25.00	50.00	200.00
82	979	Wellington 1814	3.75	5.50	15.00	50.00	200.00

The halfpenny tokens dated 1816 are lightweight pieces struck by Halliday on Canadian order about 1830.

83   **84**

83	981	WATERLOO 1816	3.75	8.50	15.00	40.00	200.00
84	531	MONTREAL 1816	3.75	8.00	25.00	100.00	300.00

Pennies

In most cases the pennies produced by Thomas Halliday of Birmingham were struck over penny tokens of Samuel Guppy. It is questionable whether any of the Wellington pennies, particularly the "Cossack" penny (see below), circulated to a large degree in British North America.

			Obverse		85			86	
	Breton			VG	F	VF	EF	UNC
85	970	Undated, no wreath on reverse		55.00	75.00	125.00	250.00	600.00
86		Undated, wreath on reverse		20.00	30.00	45.00	90.00	300.00

The following three pennies form a group called the Peninsular Pennies because they were struck for use by Wellington's troops in Portugal and Spain. They were specially designed so that they could not be mistaken for British, Spanish or Portuguese copper coins. The "Cossack" piece is a tribute to the Russian Cossacks, who gave Napoleon's Grande Armée such an uncomfortable time in Russia in 1812 and 1813. All these pieces were struck by Sir Edward Thomason, undoubtedly from dies made by Halliday.

87

87	985	COSSACK PENNY TOKEN	15.00	25.00	37.50	60.00	300.00

88

Breton			VG	F	VF	EF	UNC
88	974	1813 under bust	30.00	40.00	55.00	150.00	450.00

89

| 89 | 984 | 1813 on reverse .... | 15.00 | 25.00 | 40.00 | 100.00 | 250.00 |

Anonymous Tokens

Until the mid-1830s when some of the banks began issuing tokens of their own, the copper currency was provided by merchants and other individuals. It consisted largely of anonymous halfpenny tokens. Some were brought into the colony from the other British North American provinces or from the British Isles in the pockets of immigrants or visitors. Others were surreptitiously imported in quantity and still others were produced locally. The imported tokens were often English or Irish types which had circulated in the British Isles; however, some were new designs struck on Canadian order.

In 1825 the governments of Upper and Lower Canada passed laws forbidding the further importation of private tokens. Due to a loophole in the wording, it was not illegal to import coppers that lacked a date or bore a date prior to 1825. The laws were never corrected and the way was paved for the importation of undated or antedated pieces.

The first anonymous halfpenny attributable to Lower Canada is No. **90**, the VICTORIA NOBIS EST token. It was produced by Birmingham coiner Thomas Halliday and the stylistic relationship to the Wellington is unmistakable. Indeed its reverse die is that of the Wellington halfpenny No. **76a**. The bust is thought to be that of Lord Nelson and the Latin legend means, "Victory is ours!". Most of this issue was struck over Guppy tokens.

90

| 90 | 982 | VICTORIA NOBIS EST .... | 3.75 | 7.50 | 15.00 | 35.00 | 175.00 |

Britannia-Eagle Tokens
Original Issue, 1813

The original Britannia-eagle tokens of 1813 were struck over Guppy tokens of Bristol, probably for a Boston merchant who settled in Montreal in 1813. Other lightweight pieces dated 1813-1815 are believed to have been struck much later than the dates they bear. Aside from the difference in weight, the original 1813 issue can be distinguished from the later strikings having the same date by the larger reverse lettering on the later strikings. Most of the 1815s were discovered in 1867 still in mint state in a barrel in a warehouse.

91

Breton			VG	F	VF	EF	UNC
91	994	Eagle 1813	5.00	10.00	20.00	40.00	150.00

Lightweight Antedated Issues, 1813-1815

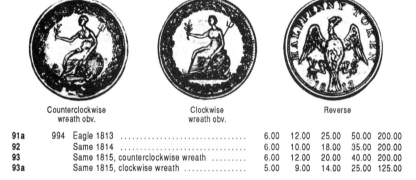

Counterclockwise wreath obv.	Clockwise wreath obv.	Reverse

91a	994	Eagle 1813	6.00	12.00	25.00	50.00	200.00
92		Same 1814	6.00	10.00	18.00	35.00	200.00
93		Same 1815, counterclockwise wreath	6.00	12.00	20.00	40.00	200.00
93a		Same 1815, clockwise wreath	5.00	9.00	14.00	25.00	125.00

The following group of lightweight halfpennies presumably all come from the same coiner, as they stem from a small number of dies used in various combinations. Some of these combinations were quite inappropriate because the dies were originally designed for coining various size pieces. For example, the small bust obverse appears to have been made for use with the COMMERCIAL CHANGE reverse; when it was used with the larger SHIPS COLONIES & COMMERCE reverse, a very broad rim resulted on the obverse. Conversely, the large bust obverse, when used with the smaller COMMERCIAL CHANGE reverse, produced a piece that had little or no rim design on the obverse.

These pieces were imported about 1830. Their linkage with Lower Canada is unmistakable, since they were later found in hoards in the province of Quebec. It is interesting to note that among the tokens in one large hoard was a variety of the Ships Colonies & Commerce token, **13a**, which has always been considered a variety of Breton 997, but portrays a very different ship. The hull is much shorter than on the varieties of Breton 997, and the water is very rough.

Obverses

Ship

Large bust

Medium bust

Small bust

Military bust
(open sleeve)

Military bust
(closed sleeve)

Reverses

WELLINGTON
WATERLOO

SHIPS, etc.

COMMERCIAL
CHANGE

TRADE

	Breton		VG	F	VF	EF	UNC
94	1003	Ship, rev. WELLINGTON WATERLOO 1815	6.00	12.00	22.50	40.00	150.00
95	1006	Large bust, rev. WELLINGTON WATERLOO 1815 ..	6.00	12.00	25.00	45.00	150.00
96	1002	Large bust, rev. SHIPS, etc.	6.00	10.00	25.00	45.00	150.00
96a		Medium bust, rev. SHIPS, etc.	14.00	22.50	35.00	65.00	175.00
96b		Small bust (broad rim), rev. SHIPS, etc.	20.00	35.00	50.00	80.00	—
97	1007	Large bust, rev. COMMERCIAL CHANGE (no rim) .... Very Rare					
97a		Small bust, rev. COMMERCIAL CHANGE	5.00	8.00	15.00	50.00	200.00
98	992	Large bust, rev TRADE 1825 .... Extremely Rare					
98a		Military bust (open sleeve), rev. TRADE 1825 ...	3.75	7.50	15.00	35.00	125.00
98b		Same, closed sleeve	15.00	35.00	100.00	250.00	—

Other Anonymous Issues

			VG	F	VF	EF	UNC
99	1011	Bust 1820, rev. "Commerce"	5.50	10.00	25.00	50.00	200.00
100	1001	Ship, rev. "Commerce" .... Extremely Rare					

The halfpennies inscribed FOR PUBLIC ACCOMMODATION were issued about 1830. They were struck with the same reverse die used for **66**, the token of Saint John, New Brunswick.

Breton			VG	F	VF	EF	UNC
101	533	FOR PUBLIC ACCOMMODATION	5.00	10.00	20.00	50.00	200.00

The seemingly anonymous "Canada" tokens of 1830 and 1841, are known to have been issued by James Duncan, a hardware merchant of Montreal. He later settled in Charlottetown, Prince Edward Island, where he circulated these pieces until issuing his "cents" in 1855 (Nos. **18-22**).

			VG	F	VF	EF	UNC
102	532	CANADA 1830	5.00	10.00	20.00	75.00	275.00
103		CANADA 1841	5.00	10.00	20.00	60.00	250.00

Private Tokens
Bearing the Issuer's Name

The private tokens bearing their issuer's names are extremely variable in weight and quality. The only really honest token in this regard is the Molson halfpenny of 1837. The Montreal Ropery halfpenny was issued about 1824, shortly before the firm changed hands. The Mullins token was issued in anticipation that the son would enter into partnership, but this did not happen.

			VG	F	VF	EF	UNC
104	564	R.W. OWEN ROPERY					Extremely Rare
105	563	FRANCIS MULLINS & SON MONTREAL	8.00	15.00	25.00	60.00	200.00

104   105

T.S. Brown, the issuer of **106**, was a hardware merchant who took up arms in the Rebellion of 1837, and had to flee to the United States when the rebellion was put down. He remained there until amnesty was granted in 1844.

John Shaw's halfpenny was issued at Quebec in 1837, Shaw withdrew his tokens when the Quebec Bank issued its Habitant tokens the following year.

106   107

Breton			VG	F	VF	EF	UNC
106	561	T.S. BROWN ... MONTREAL	5.00	10.00	25.00	70.00	300.00
107	565	J. SHAW ... QUEBEC	6.00	10.00	25.00	50.00	225.00

The Molson halfpenny was struck in Montreal by Jean Marie Arnault, who also engraved the dies, probably from designs submitted by the Company. The obverse is a copy in reverse of that of a halfpenny token issued in Perth, Scotland, in 1797.

108

			VG	F	VF	EF	UNC
108	562	MOLSON, copper	120.00	175.00	275.00	400.00	800.00
108a		Same, silver (not struck for circulation)	—	—	—	3,000	4,500

The Roy token was issued in 1837. Specimens on thin flans were made by a journeyman employed by the manufacturer. This individual would run off a few extra specimens from the dies whenever he needed money for liquor. The appearance of these lightweight sous forced Roy to withdraw his tokens to avoid discredit.

Breton			VG	F	VF	EF	UNC
109	671	J. ROY, thick flan	25.00	50.00	75.00	175.00	350.00
109a		Same, thin flan	25.00	50.00	75.00	175.00	350.00

109

The Bust and Harp Tokens, 1820-1825

These halfpennies first appeared in Lower Canada about 1825. Their design was undoubtedly inspired by the Irish regal halfpennies. The originals were struck in Dublin and are dated 1825. They have denticles at the rims. A second pair of dies, with the reverse also dated 1825 but without rim denticles, was prepared. It is assumed that upon instructions from those who ordered the tokens, the date on this second die was altered to 1820 and pieces struck. One may further assume the purpose in overdating was to antedate the tokens so they would not be excluded from importation by the law passed in Lower Canada in 1825. A non-overdated 1820 reverse dies was also used.

Originals

1820 – 0 over 5　　　　　　　　　　　　　　　Normal date

	Breton		VG	F	VF	EF	UNC
110	1012	Bust and harp 1825				Extremely Rare	
111		Same, 1820, 0 over 5				Extremely Rare	
111a		Same, 1820 normal date	15.00	25.00	75.00	175.00	—

Imitations

Vast quantities of imitations (mostly in brass) of the bust and harp halfpennies were locally produced, probably about 1837. The next two tokens were very likely the product of the same "mint." No. **112** is of moderately good quality and is by far the most common today. No. **113** is noticeably cruder, almost of "blacksmith" style (see No. **259**).

112　　　　　　　　　　　　　　　　113

112	Bust and harp imit., good quality dies	3.00	6.00	12.00	25.00	200.00
113	Same, "blacksmith-like"	—	—	—	—	200.00

— 184 —

The next piece is perhaps Lower Canadian, but its attribution to British North America is hardly firm. Considered by some to be part of the "blacksmith" series, its uncertain status dictates that it should be listed here temporarily until conclusive evidence can be found. Note that the bust faces right.

114

Breton	VG	F	VF	EF	UNC
114 Bust and harp, legend	400.00	—	—	—	—

The Tiffin Tokens

About 1832 a Montreal grocer named Joseph Tiffin imported copper halfpennies from England, the design of which was a copy of pieces which had circulated twenty years earlier in Great Britain (and perhaps to a much lesser degree in British North America as well). The original pieces had been struck by Birmingham coiner Thomas Halliday. These are of good weight, have an engrailed edge and bear Halliday's "H" on the truncation of the bust of George III. Collectors have come to call "Tiffins" any tokens of the bust and commerce 1812 design, whether or not they are the variety issued by him.

The pieces actually circulated by Tiffin appeared later (see below).

Halliday Copper Originals

115

			VG	F	VF	EF	UNC
115	960	Halfpenny 1812, with H	2.50	6.50	15.00	40.00	200.00

116 Obv.   116-117 Rev.

117-118 Obv.   118-119 Rev.

Breton			VG	F	VF	EF	UNC
116	959	Penny, 1812 on reverse	6.00	12.50	25.00	60.00	325.00
117	957	Penny, 1812 on both sides	10.00	15.00	30.00	65.00	350.00
118	958	Penny, 1812 on obverse	5.00	10.00	20.00	40.00	150.00
119	958	Penny, 1813 on obverse	12.00	20.00	40.00	80.00	325.00

Halfpennies Probably Circulated by Tiffin

Writings of R.W. MacLachlan suggest that the tokens ordered by Joseph Tiffin in 1832 were halfpennies of the kind shown below. These are of medium weight, well executed and struck in copper. They are most easily separated from the original strikings by their plain edge and lack of the letter "H" on the truncation.

120

120	960	Halfpenny 1812, no H	3.00	6.00	12.00	30.00	100.00

Lightweight Imitations in Copper Alloys

Like the bust and harp halfpennies, Tiffin's pieces were soon buried by a vast quantity of lightweight, poorly executed imitations. Various copper alloys were used, so the colour of the imitations varies from brassy yellow to the brown of nearly pure copper. These pieces were quite probably produced by the same "mint" that was responsible for the bust and harp imitations. There were two basic obverse designs (wreath running counterclockwise or clockwise) and two reverses (legend and date or date only).

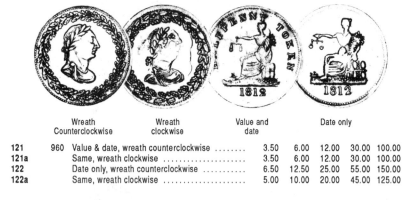

	Wreath Counterclockwise	Wreath clockwise	Value and date	Date only		
121	960	Value & date, wreath counterclockwise	3.50	6.00	12.00	30.00	100.00
121a		Same, wreath clockwise	3.50	6.00	12.00	30.00	100.00
122		Date only, wreath counterclockwise	6.50	12.50	25.00	55.00	150.00
122a		Same, wreath clockwise	5.00	10.00	20.00	45.00	125.00

The Vexator Canadiensis Tokens

These pieces appeared perhaps in the mid-1830's and are close relatives of the "blacksmiths" (see Nos. **261** and **262**) in that their devices, though very crudely executed, resemble those on the British regal halfpennies. The "classical" Vexators, Breton 558 and 559, have legends which are satirical and at the same time cleverly designed to evade the laws against forgery, sedition and the issue of private tokens.

To ensure that they would be accepted in change, the tokens bore a bust on the obverse and a seated female figure on the reverse, thus superficially resembling English regal copper. To avoid being prosecuted for forgery, the issuers made use of inscriptions quite different from those seen on regal copper.

They are satirical pieces in that the types are caricatures and the legends definitely provocative. The obverse legend as usually read means, "The Tormentor of Canada." The reverse legend means, "Wouldn't you like to catch them." and could allude to those who put the coins into circulation. However, the toils of the law were foreseen here and cleverly avoided. The third letter in the obverse legend is very vague in form, and could as easily be an N as an X. The word could then be read as VENATOR and the legend translated as "A Canadian Trapper." The bust is very shaggy and appears to be wearing a fur cap such as trappers wore in those days. The reverse legend could as easily have referred to fur-bearing ani mals as to the issuers of the tokens. Thus, if caught, the issuers could plead that the pieces were really medalets honouring the fur trade, of which Montreal was in those days an important centre.

The date 1811 is clearly an antedate. After going to all the trouble to evade prosecution for forgery and sedition, the issuers were not going to run afoul of the law of 1825 against private tokens. This method of evasion was very easy. The light and variable weight of these tokens also indicates that they are antedated, for nothing as light as these would have been acceptable in 1811.

Who was the "Tormentor of Canada"? Since the tokens are antedated, it certainly was not Sir James Craig, autocratic though he was. It probably was King William IV, whose attitude toward colonies, especially those acquired from other countries in warfare, was very harsh. Almost any of the governors of Lower Canada from 1830 to 1838, or some particularly obnoxious local officials of the period, also could have qualified for this dubious title.

The fur-trade aspect of these tokens is the fruit of brilliant reasoning by Dr. J.P.C. Kent of the British Museum and R.H.M. Dolley of Belfast. The evasion of the laws against forgery was suggested to the author by R.C. Bell of Newcastle-on Tyne, who pointed out that it was in the technique of the makers of the old English "Bungtown" tokens. It has been known since the time of R.W. McLachlan that these pieces were antedated, but the fact had been almost forgotten in recent years

There are two very rare Vexators in addition to the "classical" ones. The first is from the reverse die of Breton 558, but has a new obverse, apparently with only the date 1810 and the crude bust. The second is from entirely new dies. There seems to be only a bust on the obverse. The so-called "variety" of Breton 559 with a ML in the obverse legend is not a variety at all. The ML simply doesn't show on many of the pieces; they were all struck from the same obverse die.

123 Obverse   **124** Obverse   **123-124** Reverse

Breton					Average Condition

123	558	VEXATOR CANADIN SIS 1811 .... 450.00
124		Obverse dated 1810, but no legend .... Extremely Rare

125

125	559	VEXATOR ML. CANADIENSIS 1811 .... 450.00

126

126		No (?) obverse legend or date .... Unique

THE FIRST BANK TOKENS, 1835-1837

Bank of Montreal

In 1835 the banks refused to take any more anonymous brass pieces and other metallic trash except by weight. To supply a copper coinage, the Bank of Montreal began issuing halfpenny tokens of good weight. The value was inscribed in French on the reverse, but was incorrectly expressed by the plural form SOUS rather than SOU. This did not hinder their circulation at all. In 1836 the bank received government authority to supply copper, and added its name to the reverse inscriptions, but did not correct the value, for the error was taken by everyone as a guarantee of authenticity. The Bank of Montreal sous were struck in Birmingham. Each year there was an issue of about 72,000.

Breton			VG	F	VF	EF	UNC
127	713	BANK TOKEN MONTREAL	4.00	8.00	15.00	40.00	200.00
128	714	BANK OF MONTREAL TOKEN	4.00	8.00	15.00	60.00	300.00

BANQUE DU PEUPLE

The first sou of the Banque du Peuple was the so- called "Rebellion Sou," issued in 1837. It received its name because of the addition of a small star and a liberty cap on the reverse, said to have been done at the instigation of an accountant who favoured the cause of the rebels of 1837. It was soon discovered, and the token was replaced with another type in 1838. The Rebellion Sou was engraved by Jean Marie Arnault of Montreal, who struck about 12,000 pieces. There is considerable variation in size and weight.

The second sou of the Bank du Peuple (130) was issued in 1838 to replace the Rebellion sou. About 84,000 were struck in Belleville, New Jersey.

Breton			VG	F	VF	EF	UNC
129	716	"Rebellion" sou	6.00	12.50	30.00	65.00	250.00
130	715	BANQUE DU PEUPLE, "oak" wreath	2.50	5.00	12.00	30.00	100.00

BOUQUET SOUS

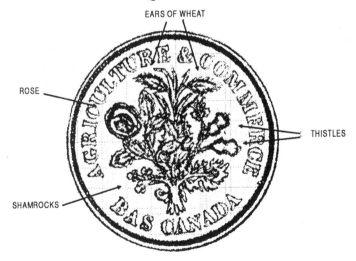

The Bouquet Sous are imitations of the Bank of Montreal tokens. The latter were so popular that lightweight imitations soon appeared, bearing a similar obverse bouquet of roses, thistles, shamrocks, and wheat. Inscriptions were entirely in French, however (with the words AGRICULTURE and COMMERCE the same in both languages), and the value was correctly rendered in the singular.

Because of the wide usage of the Bouquet Sous, they became the first series to achieve great popularity with collectors. They have been more thoroughly studied than other colonial issues, and it has been traditional to collect them by die variety.

Bouquet Sous are most easily identified by first counting the number of leaves in the reverse wreath. This number will serve to locate a general area in one of the groups below, after which details may be compared with the notes below the illustrations. Such points as the number and location of shamrocks and relative position of letters, berries, and leaves will serve as guides to identification. To illustrate, an enlarged bouquet token (in this case No. **157**) is shown with arrows pointing to the shamrocks, roses, thistles and ears of wheat on obverse. The number of leaves on the wreath can be counted.

I. Belleville Issues

The Belleville mint was a private company in Belleville, New Jersey, whose production was mainly American tokens.

Sixteen leaves in reverse wreath:

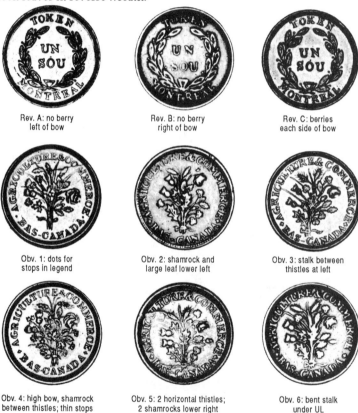

Rev. A: no berry
left of bow

Rev. B: no berry
right of bow

Rev. C: berries
each side of bow

Obv. 1: dots for
stops in legend

Obv. 2: shamrock and
large leaf lower left

Obv. 3: stalk between
thistles at left

Obv. 4: high bow, shamrock
between thistles; thin stops

Obv. 5: 2 horizontal thistles;
2 shamrocks lower right

Obv. 6: bent stalk
under UL

	Breton		VG	F	VF	EF	UNC
131	680	Rev. A, obv. 1	10.00	20.00	80.00	160.00	400.00
132		Same, obv. 2					Unique
133	678	Same, obv. 3	5.00	10.00	20.00	80.00	325.00
134	679	Same, obv. 4	4.50	8.50	15.00	30.00	125.00
135		Same, obv. 5	—	—	—	—	—
136	681	Rev. B, obv. 5	165.00	250.00	450.00	—	—

	Breton		VG	F	VF	EF	UNC
137	682	Same, obv. 6	8.50	15.00	40.00	70.00	200.00
138	675	Rev. C, obv. 2					Very Rare
139	677	Same, obv. 3					Rare
140	676	Same, obv. 6	18.00	30.00	50.00	100.00	300.00

Seventeen leaves in reverse wreath:

Rev D: 17 leaves

Obv. 7: rose flanked by 2 pairs of stalks

			VG	F	VF	EF	UNC
141	683	Rev. D, obv. 1	7.50	15.00	30.00	60.00	300.00
142		Same, obv 5					Extremely Rare
143		Same, obv. 7					Unique

Eighteen leaves in reverse wreath, no bow:

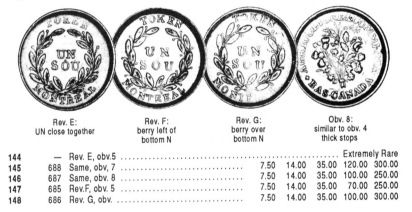

Rev. E: UN close together

Rev. F: berry left of bottom N

Rev. G: berry over bottom N

Obv. 8: similar to obv. 4 thick stops

			VG	F	VF	EF	UNC
144	—	Rev. E, obv. 5					Extremely Rare
145	688	Same, obv, 7	7.50	14.00	35.00	120.00	300.00
146	687	Same, obv. 8	7.50	14.00	35.00	100.00	250.00
147	685	Rev.F, obv. 5	7.50	14.00	35.00	70.00	250.00
148	686	Rev. G, obv.	7.50	14.00	35.00	100.00	300.00

Eighteen leaves in reverse wreath, with bow:

Rev. H: leaf points straight up to U of sou

Rev. J: L below middle of leaf

Rev. K: letters REAL repunched

Rev. L: leaf tip above centre of M

Rev. M: SOU very low

Obv. 9: colon stops; S-C closely spaced

Obv. 10: colon stops; S-C widely spaced

Obv. 11: shamrock, small leaf above ribbon ends

Obv. 12: rose at left; no punctuation

Obv. 13: "broken" leaf at top left

Obv. 14: 1 large, 2 small leaves above ribbon ends

Obv. 15: ribbon ends left; bouquet base over A

Obv. 16: ribbon ends left; bouquet base over N

	Breton		VG	F	VE	EF	UNC
149	696	Rev. H, obv. 1	20.00	40.00	80.00	165.00	425.00
150	691	Rev. J, obv. 9	3.00	5.00	10.00	30.00	175.00
151	695	Rev. K, obv. 1	10.00	25.00	50.00	100.00	250.00
152	692	Same, obv. 4	3.00	5.00	10.00	35.00	200.00
153	693	Same, obv. 7	10.00	20.00	40.00	75.00	300.00
154	694	Same, obv. 10	3.00	5.00	10.00	40.00	200.00
155	697	Rev. L, obv. 11	10.00	15.00	20.00	40.00	200.00
156	698	Same, obv. 12	15.00	25.00	45.00	90.00	300.00
157	699	Rev. M, obv. 12	7.50	15.00	30.00	60.00	250.00
158	703	Same, obv. 13	375.00	550.00	900.00	—	—
159	702	Same, obv.14	4.50	8.50	15.00	30.00	175.00
160	700	Same, obv. 15	5.50	9.50	20.00	40.00	200.00
161	701	Same, obv. 16	12.00	25.00	60.00	100.00	275.00

Twenty leaves in reverse wreath:

	Obv. 17: 2 shamrocks lower right	Rev. N: small bow	Obv. 18: no shamrocks lower right	Rev. P: large bow		

	Breton		VG	F	VF	EF	UNC
162	704	Rev. N, obv. 14	3.50	5.50	10.00	35.00	175.00
163	705	Rev. P, obv. 18	5.00	10.00	22.50	40.00	225.00

II. Birmingham Issues

The sous numbered **164** through **169** were struck in Birmingham, England by the same firm that produced the early sous of the Bank of Montreal. These issues can be readily distinguished by the large number of leaves (32-42) in the wreath on the reverse. The bouquet sou assigned number 712 by Breton was exposed as fraud by McLachlan, who described how it was made. All specimens of this variety seen by the authors are fabrications. It is therefore not assigned a number in this catalogue.

Thirty-two leaves in reverse wreath:

Rev. R: 32 leaves

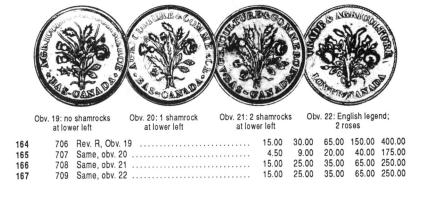

	Obv. 19: no shamrocks at lower left	Obv. 20: 1 shamrock at lower left	Obv. 21: 2 shamrocks at lower left	Obv. 22: English legend; 2 roses		

			VG	F	VF	EF	UNC
164	706	Rev. R, Obv. 19	15.00	30.00	65.00	150.00	400.00
165	707	Same, obv. 20	4.50	9.00	20.00	40.00	175.00
166	708	Same, obv. 21	15.00	25.00	35.00	65.00	250.00
167	709	Same, obv. 22	15.00	25.00	35.00	65.00	250.00

Forty-two leaves in reverse wreath:

Rev. S: 42 leaves	Obv.23: 1 large, 2 small shamrocks at lower left	Obv. 23a: 1 shamrock right, 2 left

	Breton		VG	F	VF	EF	UNC
168	710	Rev. S, obv. 21	15.00	30.00	65.00	95.00	300.00
169	712	Same, obv. 23 .... Very Rare					
—	712	Same, obv. 23a .... Authenticity questionable					

III. Montreal Issues

Several varieties of the bouquet sous were produced in Montreal by Jean Marie Arnault. Nos. **171** and **172** were routinely struck over other tokens withdrawn from circulation, quite possibly in 1837. No. **170** was long thought to be No. **171** struck over an Upper Canada sloop token (No. **199**); however, closer examination shows that neither of the dies used for the overstriking was that of No. **171** or any other catalogued sou. The lettering is quite small and the bouquet clearly different from that on Nos. **173- 174**. It is very possible that the "small letters" sou was a prototype for sou No. **171** and that the dies were created in both cases for the purpose of overstriking other tokens.

The last two varieties, which share the same obverse, were postulated by Courteau to have been "patterns" for a coinage of sous for one of the Montreal banks, perhaps the City Bank. As this is far from proven, we list these pieces here.

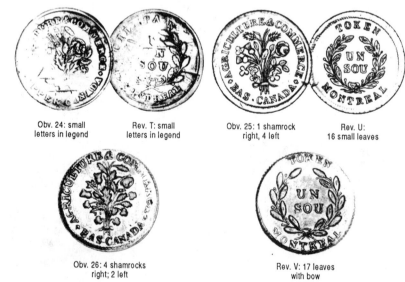

Obv. 24: small letters in legend	Rev. T: small letters in legend	Obv. 25: 1 shamrock right, 4 left	Rev. U: 16 small leaves

Obv. 26: 4 shamrocks right; 2 left	Rev. V: 17 leaves with bow

Obv. 27:	Rev. W:	Rev. X:
English legend	$\frac{1}{2}$ penny token 1837	$\frac{1}{2}$ penny bank token

	Breton		VG	F	VF	EF	UNC
170		Rev. T, Obv. 24					Unique
171	674	Rev. T, obv. 25	8.50	15.00	35.00	75.00	300.00
172	684	Rev. V, obv. 26	4.50	10.00	20.00	45.00	250.00
173	672	Rev. V, obv. 27					Unique
174	673	Rev. X, obv. 27				Extremely Rare	

IV. Miscellaneous Issues

The first two varieties probably never circulated; both were unknown until at least the 1860s and do not come in well worn condition. The dies and a few "original" specimens of No. **175** were found in Montreal. A small number of restrikes were struck in various metals after the dies had been fitted with a collar. Most specimens of No. **176** are know as "proofs" and were found in Boston. For that reason this variety has been called the "Boston" sou.

Number **177** is a heavy piece which could well have circulated more in the United States than it did in Canada. Its reverse is thought to have been originally intended for a token for Belleville butcher T.D. Seaman. The U in DUSEAMAN was deliberately made to facilitate passing these pieces off an anonymous cents in the United States.

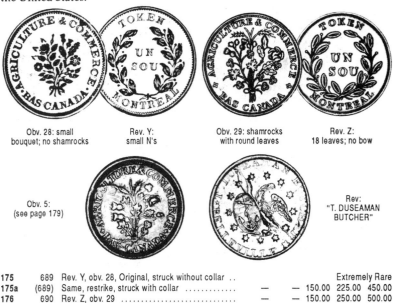

Obv. 28: small bouquet; no shamrocks	Rev. Y: small N's	Obv. 29: shamrocks with round leaves	Rev. Z: 18 leaves; no bow

Obv. 5: (see page 179)		Rev: "T. DUSEAMAN BUTCHER"

175	689	Rev. Y, obv. 28, Original, struck without collar ..				Extremely Rare	
175a	(689)	Same, restrike, struck with collar	—	—	150.00	225.00	450.00
176	690	Rev. Z, obv. 29	—	—	150.00	250.00	500.00
177	670	Rev. DUSEAMAN, obv. 5	10.00	20.00	35.00	65.00	300.00

LATER BANK TOKENS

Habitant Tokens

The Habitant tokens, so called because they show on the obverse a Canadian habitant in traditional winter costume, were struck by Boulton & Watt and released early in 1838. The Bank of Montreal, the Quebec Bank, the City Bank, and the Banque du Peuple participated in the issue, with the bank name appearing on the reverse ribbon. The Bank of Montreal issued 240,000 pennies and 480,000 halfpennies; the others issued 120,000 pennies and 240,000 halfpennies each.

179

	Breton		VG	F	VF	EF	UNC
178	522	Halfpenny, CITY BANK	2.50	5.00	10.00	25.00	75.00
179		Same, QUEBEC BANK	2.50	5.00	10.50	25.00	75.00
180		Same, BANQUE DU PEUPLE	5.00	10.00	20.00	40.00	125.00
181		SAME, BANK OF MONTREAL	5.00	10.00	20.00	40.00	125.00

183

			VG	F	VF	EF	UNC
182	521	Penny, CITY BANK	3.00	6.00	12.00	25.00	100.00
183		Same, QUEBEC BANK	4.00	7.00	15.00	30.00	110.00
184		Same, BANQUE DU PEUPLE	15.00	22.00	40.00	65.00	175.00
185		Same, BANK OF MONTREAL	6.00	12.00	25.00	40.00	150.00

Side View Tokens

The "Side View" tokens, so called because they show a corner view of the Bank of Montreal building, were struck by Cotterill, Hill & Co. of Walsall, England. In 1838 the coiners shipped 120,000 pennies and 240,000 halfpennies to Montreal. The bank returned the coins because the workmanship was far inferior to that of the Habitant tokens, and the copper was brassy. The most probable point of objection on the obverse is the trees, which appear "frizzy." The reverse is considerably more crude than that for the Habitant pieces. In 1839 another 120,000 pennies and 240,000 halfpennies arrived, but these were also returned with the complaint that they were even worse than the shipment of 1838.

The reverse of the 1839s is an improvement over the 1838 issue. The fault is in the obverse, which has the bank building rendered in atrocious perspective. Note the portico, for example. These tokens are more expensive than rare today.

	Breton		VG	F	VF	EF	UNC
186	524	Halfpenny 1838	285.00	375.00	475.00	650.00	1,300
187		Halfpenny 1839	285.00	375.00	475.00	600.00	1,100
188	523	Penny 1838	550.00	725.00	900.00	1,100	5,000
189		Penny 1839	550.00	725.00	900.00	1,100	5,000
190		Penny 1839, BANQUE DU PEUPLE				Very Rare	

UPPER CANADA

In 1791 the Great Lakes region was detached from Quebec and organized as the colony of Upper Canada. It is now the Province of Ontario. Very little coined money was in use before 1800. A few of the Wellington tokens trickled in from Lower Canada after 1814, and local tokens appeared about 1812.

The Brock Tokens

The Brock tokens were struck about 1816 to honour one of the heroes of the War of 1812, Major General Sir Isaac Brock, who was commander of the British troops in Upper Canada. In July of 1812 he captured Detroit and on 13 October of that year successfully repulsed an American invasion attempt at Queenstown (near Niagara Falls), although Brock himself was killed in the battle. The tokens are light in weight. They soon became too plentiful and fell into discredit. Note the spelling blunder on **191** (*Brook* instead of *Brock*). No. **193** is a mule struck from very worn dies.

Ship obverse	Monument obverse	Text reverse	1816 reverse

191	723	Ship, text	8.00	15.00	40.00	100.00	250.00
192	724	Monument, 1816	3.75	8.50	18.00	35.00	180.00
193	725	Ship, 1816	35.00	50.00	65.00	200.00	—

The Sloop Tokens

These tokens feature on their obverses a sloop, which was in those days the chief means of transportation on the Great Lakes. This obverse was the work of John Sheriff of Liverpool. The tokens are heavier, as Upper Canada by this time was using Halifax Currency. Most of them are antedated to evade the law against private tokens enacted in 1825. As this law became a dead letter, later issues bore the actual date of issue. The "hunter" piece (**198**) is a mule struck from very worn dies. Its reverse die was used previously to strike one of the Nova Scotia tokens (**45**).

Obverse	Anvil reverse	Upper Canada reverse

Jamaica reverse	Plow reverse	Hunter reverse

Antedated Issues

	Breton		VG	F	VF	E	UNC
194	727	Anvil, 1820	4.50	8.00	20.00	40.00	125.00
195	728	UPPER CANADA on cask, 1821	25.00	50.00	150.00	250.00	600.00
196	729	JAMAICA on cask, 1821	250.00	400.00	750.00	—	—
197	730	Plow, 1823	5.50	11.00	22.50	45.00	150.00
198	726	Hunter, 1815	22.50	35.00	75.00	—	—

Contemporaneously Dated Issues

| | | | 199 | | 200 | | |

| 199 | 730 | Plow 1833 | 3.75 | 7.50 | 15.00 | 50.00 | 300.00 |
| 200 | 731 | Tools 1833, brass | 6.00 | 12.00 | 25.00 | 75.00 | 300.00 |

The Lesslie Tokens

These tokens were issued by a drug and book firm with shops in Toronto, Dundas, and Kingston. The first halfpennies were issued from 1824 to 1827 and have a plain edge. Note the use of York, which was the old name for Toronto; the change took place in 1834. A second issue of halfpennies (1828-1830) has an engrailed edge and a comma after YORK. The twopence was engraved by Thomas Wells Ingram and was struck at least as early as 1827. A specimen was found in the cornerstone during the demolition of the old Courthouse of Hamilton, Ontario, which was built in that year. Because of its size, the twopence was never popular and many became washers. Both Leslie denominations are unique in being the only Upper Canada issues with French in their inscriptions. They have the phrase, LA PRUDENCE ET LA CANDEUR, meaning "wisdom and honesty."

201

	Breton		VG	F	VF	EF	UNC
201	718	LESSLIE & SONS, halfpenny, plain edge	7.50	15.00	30.00	75.00	250.00
201a		Same, engrailed edge	10.00	20.00	35.00	75.00	250.00

202

202	717	Twopence 1822	100.00	175.00	300.00	450.00	750.00

Miscellaneous Tokens

About 1830 tokens inscribed NO LABOUR NO BREAD were imported into Toronto by Perrins Bros., a dry goods firm. Because of the act outlawing private tokens, however, the pieces were seized by the Customs Dept. and ordered to be melted down. A large number of the coppers "fell to the floor" as it has been so quaintly said, and so escaped the melting pot and entered circulation. They were occasionally found in change as late as 1837.

203	1010	NO LABOUR, NO BREAD	5.00	10.00	20.00	40.00	300.00

In 1832 a halfpenny token (204) was issued of honest size and weight. It was struck in Birmingham by the firm which struck the thistle tokens of Nova Scotia. Like the Nova Scotia issues of 1832, this piece shows the bust of George IV, even though it was then two years after his death. It is not yet known whether this token is semi-regal or private.

Breton			VG	F	VF	EF	UNC.
204	732	Halfpenny, George IV 1832	12.00	20.00	30.00	100.00	300.00

THE NORTHWEST

FUR TRADE TOKENS

What was loosely termed "the Northwest" in colonial times included all of British North America north and west of colonial Canada to the Pacific coast and the Arctic Archipelago. This vast region was the preserve of the Hudson's Bay Company. No settlement took place anywhere in this region before Lord Selkirk opened up the valley of the Red River, later to become the province of Manitoba. Beyond this area the only permanent establishments were the trading posts of the Hudson's Bay Company and its rival, the Northwest Company. After years of bitter strife the two companies merged in 1821.

On the west coast, Vancouver Island was detached from the Company and set up as a Crown Colony. The British Columbia mainland was separated in 1858 as a second Crown Colony. The two colonies united in 1866 and the united colony entered the Dominion of Canada in 1871. The remainder of the territory of the Hudson's Bay Company was acquired by the Dominion of Canada in 1869.

Northwest Company Token, 1820

The Northwest Company token was struck in Birmingham in 1820. It is not known by whom, but its style suggests that it may have been struck by the makers of Nova Scotia coinage of 1823-1843. Many known specimens of this piece were found in the lower valley of the Columbia River in Oregon, which is now in the United States. For this reason it is sometimes considered an American piece. It is also thought of as Canadian because it was issued by a Canadian firm.

All but one of the known specimens is holed. It is believed that they were issued holed to facilitate wearing them as medalets or attaching them to garments.

205

Breton			VG	F	VF	EF	UNC.
205	925	NORTHWEST COMPANY, copper	750.00	1,000	1,450	—	—
205a		Same, brass	700.00	950.00	1,300	—	—

Hudson's Bay Company Tokens

The brass tokens of the Hudson's Bay Company were issued around 1854. At the top of the reverse is the Company's HB monogram, below which are the initials EM for the East Main district, south and east of Hudson Bay. The tokens have been found in northern Quebec and Ontario, and as far west as Manitoba. They are erroneously valued in "new beaver." The unit of the fur trade was the "made beaver," which is an adult beaver skin in prime condition. It was never cut up, so the Company thought that tokens would be the ideal way in which to express fractions of the made beaver. The indians, however, preferred to trust the Company accounts rather than take the tokens, which were easily lost. For this reason the pieces never circulated in large quantities. When it was decided to redeem them, the tokens were punched on the reverse at the top to show that they had been redeemed and cancelled. The number of unpunched pieces available now suggests that they were not all presented to be redeemed, or that not all company offices punched them as they were redeemed.

206   207

208   209

206	929	1/8 made beaver	32.00	40.00	50.00	70.00	125.00
207	928	1/4 made beaver	32.00	40.00	50.00	70.00	125.00
208	926	1/2 made beaver	32.00	40.00	50.00	70.00	125.00
209	926	1 made beaver	32.00	40.00	50.00	70.00	125.00

PROVINCE OF CANADA

Bank of Montreal
"Front View" Tokens, 1842-1845

In 1841 Upper and Lower Canada were reunited to form the colony of Province of Canada. The Bank of Montreal was given the right to coin copper, and issued 240,000 pennies and 480,000 halfpennies in 1842. A further issue of 1,440,000 halfpennies was released in 1844. The tokens were struck by Boulton & Watt. A halfpenny die was prepared in 1845, and two tokens struck, but the bank did not issue any tokens dated 1845.

In addition to the normal 1842 front view penny, a mule exists with the Habitant reverse of 1837 (with CITY BANK on the ribbon). It has long been known that dies and other tools connected with the Habitant and front view tokens later fell into the hands of an unscrupulous die sinker named W.J. Taylor and that he used them to produce proofs for sale to collectors. It is also believed that Taylor produced a number of mules which had never been issued for circulation. Many people have generally believed the front view 1837 mule pennies to be just such a concoction. Nevertheless, some pieces recently examined are clearly circulation strikes and are presumably originals produced by Boulton & Watt. Such pieces seem to be inadvertent mules. Because of the relative commonness of the Taylor restrikes compared with the originals, both are listed here.

210   213

Breton			VG	F	VF	EF	UNC
210	527	Halfpenny 1842	5.50	12.00	18.00	35.00	150.00
211		Halfpenny 1844	2.00	5.00	10.00	20.00	100.00
212		Halfpenny 1845				Extremely Rare	
213	526	Penny 1842	3.25	6.00	12.00	35.00	200.00
213a	526a	Mule penny: CITY BANK 1837; rev. original	100.00	150.00	225.00	350.00	650.00
213b	—	Same, Taylor restrike	—	—	—	—	450.00

Quebec Bank Tokens, 1852

In 1852 the Quebec Bank was allowed to issue pennies and halfpennies because of a serious shortage of copper in Quebec. The Bank of Upper Canada coinage was supposed to be enough for the whole province, but the first two issues of this bank were not delivered until 1853, and the Quebec Bank was desperate. With government sanction the bank issued 240,000 pennies and 480,000 halfpennies in 1852. A request for permission to issue more was turned down on the grounds that a change to decimal currency was under contemplation, which occurred in 1858. The Quebec Bank pieces were struck by Ralph Heaton & Sons, and are among the most attractive Canadian colonial issues. The obverse features the familiar "habitant" device and the reverse shows the coat of arms of Quebec City.

Breton			VG	F	VF	EF	UNC
214	529	Quebec Bank halfpenny 1852	2.50	5.50	10.00	25.00	120.00
215	528	Quebec Bank penny 1852	3.50	6.50	15.00	30.00	300.00

Bank of Upper Canada Tokens, 1850-1857

The Bank of Upper Canada received the right to issue copper in 1850, after the capital was transferred to Toronto from Montreal. An order was placed at the Royal Mint that same year for halfpennies and pennies. The Province of Canada's agent for coinage was the British firm of Rowe, Kentish and Co. The obverse device is the popular St. George and the Dragon motif and the reverse shows the then obsolete arms of Upper Canada. The master tools were engraved by John Pinches of London, but it is Rowe, Kentish's RK & Co. that appears on the ground line on the obverse.

The pieces dated 1850 were struck at the Royal Mint in 1851 and did not reach Canada until 1852. Some of the pennies have a dot between the cornucopia tips on the reverse. Although this dot seems to have been deliberately added, its significance is not known.

In 1852 a second order was placed. The Royal Mint began the coinage, but was unable to complete it because of more pressing demands. The remaining blanks were transferred to Heaton's Mint in Birmingham where the remainder of the order was struck. The Royal Mint striking probably have the die axes ↑↑ (medal struck), while the Heaton's pieces have the dies ↑↓ (coinage struck).

The 1854 and 1857 issues were also produced by Heaton's. No further orders were placed because of the change to the decimal system of currency in 1858.

In 1863 the Bank complained to the government that because of the introduction of the decimal coins it had not been possible for them to put much of the final order of their tokens into circulation. The government agreed to purchase the tokens and they were stored in Montreal for a number of years. It seems that, through some irregularity (after the Bank had closed in 1867), a portion of the tokens got into circulation. In any case the tokens were moved to Toronto in the early 1870s, sold as copper bullion and melted under government supervision in 1873.

216	720	Halfpenny 1850		2.00	4.00	8.00	15.00	120.00

Breton		VG	F	VF	EF	UNC
217	Halfpenny 1852, dies ↑↑	2.00	4.00	8.00	15.00	75.00
217a	Same, dies ↑↓	2.00	4.00	8.00	15.00	75.00
218	Halfpenny 1854, plain 4	2.00	4.00	8.00	15.00	60.00
218a	Same, crosslet 4	20.00	30.00	45.00	85.00	200.00
219	Halfpenny 1857	2.00	3.00	7.00	15.00	80.00

220

220a
Dot between cornucopiae tips

			VG	F	VF	EF	UNC
220	719	Penny 1850	4.00	6.00	12.00	20.00	90.00
220a		Same, dot between cornucopiae tips	5.00	10.00	25.00	45.00	150.00

Plain 4

Crosslet 4

			VG	F	VF	EF	UNC
221	719	Penny 1852, Dies ↑↑	3.25	5.00	10.00	20.00	80.00
221a		Same, dies ↑↓	2.25	4.00	7.50	15.00	75.00
222		Penny 1854, plain 4	2.25	4.00	7.00	15.00	75.00
222a		Same, crosslet 4	6.00	12.00	25.00	40.00	150.00
223		Penny 1857	2.00	4.00	8.00	15.00	60.00

ANONYMOUS AND MISCELLANEOUS TOKENS

This section contains various kinds of tokens which are not included in the sections dealing specifically with tokens of the individual colonies, provinces or geographical regions.

With the exception of the "blacksmith" tokens, most of these pieces are of English or Irish origin, some of which had been used in the British Isles before being sent to Canada. Those of light weight were probably struck on Canadian order. A few, such as the North American token, circulated to a limited extent in the United States near the Canadian border.

The North American Token

224

The North American token was struck in Dublin long after 1781. It was dated 1781 to evade Canadian laws against the importation of anonymous tokens after 1825. To add to the illusion of age, the token was struck without a collar.

Breton			VG	F	VF	EF	UNC
224	1013	NORTH AMERICAN TOKEN, copper	15.00	30.00	60.00	80.00	275.00

The Success to Trade Token

Number **225** is an anonymous English piece with altered legends. The phrase "Success to Trade" was punched over "George III Rules," and "Commerce" was punched over "Britannia."

225

			VG	F	VF	EF	UNC
225	983	SUCCESS TO TRADE	25.00	50.00	100.00	150.00	350.00

Other Issues

Pieces **226** through **231** were engraved by Thomas Halliday and struck in Birmingham. The "Irish" piece, number **226**, evidently was used in Ireland before being sent to Canada, as specimens have been found there.

226   227

226	1009	Irishman in wreath	3.00	7.00	15.00	55.00	300.00
227	996	FOR GENERAL ACCOMMODATION	5.00	10.00	20.00	40.00	175.00

The RH tokens have sometimes been attributed to Richard Hurd of Montreal. In light of available evidence, however, it is more reasonable to consider them English. Even if Hurd also ordered pieces of this design, it is likely that only the halfpenny on the thin flan was involved.

Breton			VG	F	VF	EF	UNC
228	991	RH farthing	30.00	40.00	70.00	150.00	500.00
229	990	RH halfpenny, thick flan	6.50	11.00	25.00	50.00	200.00
229a		RH halfpenny, thin flan	7.50	14.00	30.00	60.00	275.00
230	989	RH penny	15.00	25.00	50.00	125.00	325.00

| 228 | 229 | 230 |

The ship tokens, **231** through **233**, are lightweight tokens, probably struck on Canadian order. The reverse of **232** is that of a halfpenny token of Shaw, Jobson & Co. of Roscoe Mills, Sheffield, England, whose initials S.J & Co. can be seen on the bale. The ship on this piece flies a pennant from the mainmast.

A second variety dated 1812 appears to be a direct copy by another coiner and can be distinguished by the presence of a pennant flying from the foremast (the Halliday variety has none). The 1815 issue was by Halliday, using the same obverse die as in 1812 and a new reverse die.

231

	Breton		VG	F	VF	EF	UNC
231	1005	HALFPENNY TOKEN, no date; rev. ship	10.00	30.00	75.00	200.00	—

		232	No pennant		Pennant on foremast		
232	1004	HALFPENNY TOKEN 1812, rev. ship no pennant .	11.00	30.00	75.00	200.00	—
232a		Same, with pennant	5.50	11.00	22.50	45.00	200.00
233		HALFPENNY TOKEN 1815, rev. ship	3.00	6.00	15.00	35.00	150.00

The anchor and H halfpennies are rather crudely made. It has been said that they were issued in Halifax, Nova Scotia, but this has not yet been proved. An 1814 date has been reported but cannot be confirmed.

234		Anchor and H, 1816	Baker Sale 1987:	$350.00

234

Doubtful Pieces

The five tokens listed here have been traditionally included in Canadian collections but are more properly placed in the English or Irish category. While they may have circulated in British North America in very small quantities, none was specifically imported. The BRITISH COLONIES tokens were originally sent to Jamaica for circulation as pennies. No. 236 was issued for use in British Guiana.

235   236

Breton			VG	F	VF	EF	UNC
235	993	TO FACILITATE TRADE 1825	7.50	14.00	30.00	45.00	150.00
236	967	TRADE & NAVIGATION 1838	3.00	6.00	12.00	50.00	275.00

The Hibernia penny (237) is an anonymous Irish token designed by Peter Wyon.

237

237	975	HIBERNIA 1805, penny	10.00	20.00	45.00	150.00	450.00

The two pennies with the "Tiffin" obverse and the inscription COMMERCE on the reverse are English tokens, produced by Thomas Halliday.

238		COMMERCE	35.00	65.00	85.00	125.00	350.00
239		COMMERCE 1814	20.00	40.00	60.00	95.00	300.00

239

The "Blacksmith" Tokens

This fascinating group of tokens derives its name from a quaint legend that attributes their origin to a Montreal blacksmith, who made them to pay for liquor. Whatever their origin, it is clear that the blacksmith tokens were not produced by a single source and arose over a period of some years. They could have appeared as early as about 1820, when the tokens then in circulation had been largely decried and the only acceptable coppers were the battered, worn-out old British and Irish regal halfpennies of George III. In any case they were still being introduced as late as 1837. The blacksmiths were initially copper, but the late issues tended to be brass.

In a traditional sense the blacksmiths have been defined as specially produced imitations of worn British and Irish regal halfpence. The first blacksmiths were just that, but the series grew more complex with the passage of time. Later issues imitated popular tokens in circulation at the time and yet other pieces were of "original" designs resulting from the muling of various dies or the use of dies that were not copying anything.

The blacksmith technique was to leave the designs unfinished and to engrave in very low relief. The devices were often reversed compared to those being copied and usually there was no legend or date. To further heighten the appearance of age and wear, the copper pieces were darkened by heating before being passed into circulation.

The series was almost completely ignored by the earlier writers, Breton including only two in his work. They were described in detail by Howland Wood, whose 1910 monograph is still the standard reference.

The nature of blacksmiths makes them difficult to grade and, in any case, most pieces fall within a rather narrow range of condition. Therefore, the prices for pieces in this series are given for "Average Condition" only. Some of the extremely rare varieties are not priced.

Imitations of British Regal Halfpennies

Obverses:

Bust left   Bust right

Britannia
seated

Britannia
"standing"

Britannia
"on water"

Wood			Average Condition
240	1-4	Bust left, rev. seated Britannia	35.00
241	11,13-18	Same, standing Britannia	35.00
242	7,8	Same, Britannia on water	200.00
243	23	Bust right, rev. seated Britannia	25.00

The next two pieces are of a rather complex nature. There is a group of tokens generally considered U.S., called "bungtowns." These are imitations of British and Irish halfpence, where the legend has deliberately been garbled to circumvent the laws against counterfeiting. The first piece (244) could well be a U.S. "bungtown" shipped to Lower Canada. (So many of them have been found in Canada that there can be no doubt of their right to be called Canadian.) The legends are GLORIOUS III • VIS (instead of GEORGIUS III REX) on the obverse and BITIT • (instead of BRITANNIA) on the reverse. It was thought by Wood to be an *imitation* of a bungtown; however, the relatively high quality of the lettering leads us to believe it to be a U.S. product.

The legend on the second piece (245) is much cruder and more difficult to read. The letters which show suggest that this token is a copy of the "bungtown" issue.

244   **245**

244	33	Bust right, GLORIOUS III • VIS	20.00
245	34	Bust left, GLORIOUS III • III VIS (?)	550.00

Imitations of Irish Regal Halfpennies

Typical obv.

Plain harp rev.

"Surrounded" harp rev.

In addition to a plain harp on the reverse there are some curious pieces with a harp surrounded on the sides and bottom by a nondescript design. This design has generally been believed to have resulted from deterioration of the die, but this is only partially correct. Much of it was *engraved*.

Wood			Average Condition
246	6	Bust left, plain harp	40.00
247	5,12	Same, "surrounded" harp	35.00
248	35	Obverse of 245, rev. smaller harp (not shown)	Extremely rare
			(Fewer than five known)

Imitations of Regal Halfpennies
With Only a Bust

This is group consisting of uniface strikings from the obverse dies for some of the preceding pieces, but mostly from dies apparently intended to be used alone. Most were unknown to Wood and all are extremely rare and hence not priced.

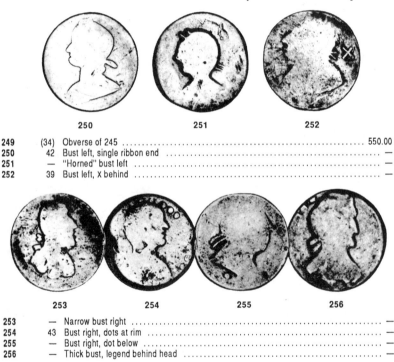

	250	251	252			253	254	255	256

249	(34)	Obverse of 245	550.00
250	42	Bust left, single ribbon end	—
251	—	"Horned" bust left	—
252	39	Bust left, x behind	—

253	—	Narrow bust right	—
254	43	Bust right, dots at rim	—
255	—	Bust right, dot below	—
256	—	Thick bust, legend behind head	—

Imitations of Ships, Colonies and Commerce Tokens

The next two pieces, not found in Wood, are rare and have both been included in Lees under 5. Recently, however, their obverses have been shown to be from different dies. The first (257) has faint rim beads on the obverse, a distinct ball at the top of each mast and a thin line extending back from between the two waves just below the ship's stern. The classical Lees 5 (258) lacks rim beads, has indistinct mast tops and no line between the waves at the rear. In addition all known examples are from a badly cracked die.

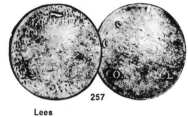 

257   258

	Lees		Average Condition
257	5	Drooping flag, incomplete ship	Extremely Rare
258	5	Same, no beads either side	Extremely Rare

Other Imitating Designs

259   260

	Wood		G	VG	F
259	21,22	"Bust-Harp-like" 1820			Extremely Rare
260	19	"Tiffin-like" 1820		250.00	400.00
260a	20	Same, brass		300.00	500.00

261   262

261		"Vexator-like" 1811 (?), uniface	Extremely Rare
262		Same, no date (?), uniface	Extremely Rare

263

263	31	"Sloop-like" wreath	Unique

Miscellaneous "Original" Designs

Some of the tokens in the blacksmith series fall into a category which can be called original designs. The dies, individually or in combination, did not copy an existing design. The first two pieces are from one die for an imitation of a regal halfpenny, and the other for an imitation of the SHIPS COLONIES & COMMERCE tokens. The reverse die of **264** is the same as the obverse die for **258**.

264   265

Wood			G	VG	F
264	9	Bust, ref. ship			Extremely Rare
265	10	SHIPS COLONIES etc., rev. "surrounded" harp		400.00	

The reverses of **266** and **267** are said to be from very worn reverse dies for standard type tokens. In the first case it is the Upper Canadian sloop **197** to **199** and in the second it is a U.S. "hard times" token (Low 19). The obverse of **267** also strongly resembles that of **98a**. Whether the dies which struck these blacksmith issues are really those that struck the tokens they resemble is not yet established.

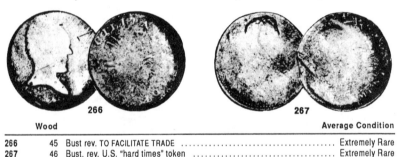

266   267

Wood			Average Condition
266	45	Bust rev. TO FACILITATE TRADE	Extremely Rare
267	46	Bust, rev. U.S. "hard times" token	Extremely Rare

The "Mexican" bouquet sou has what appears to be a copy of a State of Chihuahua copper coin (1833-1856) depicting a standing Indian for its reverse design. The obverse die is probably a copy of a bouquet sou die, rather than a deteriorated original die.

268

268	"Mexican" bouquet sou	500.00

The next group of "original" designs stems from five kinds of dies used in various combinations. The RISEING SUN TAVERN piece has been tentatively linked to a Tavern in Toronto; however, this is not certain. It is interesting that two of the dies are apparently discarded reverse dies from metallic store cards of N.S. Starbuck & Son and J. & C. Peck, both of Troy, New York.

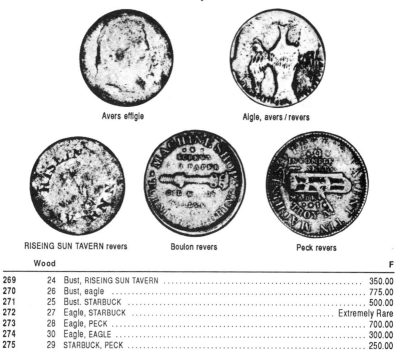

Avers effigie   Aigle, avers / revers

RISEING SUN TAVERN revers   Boulon revers   Peck revers

	Wood		F
269	24	Bust, RISEING SUN TAVERN	350.00
270	26	Bust, eagle	775.00
271	25	Bust. STARBUCK	500.00
272	27	Eagle, STARBUCK	Extremely Rare
273	28	Eagle, PECK	700.00
274	30	Eagle, EAGLE	300.00
275	29	STARBUCK, PECK	250.00

The next three tokens are of completely new designs, but are nevertheless generally considered to be part of the blacksmith series.

276

277

Wood			Average Condition
276	—	Windmill, rev. NO CREDIT .... (Fewer than ten known)	950.00
277	32	Anchor, rev. shield	900.00

278

278	—	Balance, rev. tools and star	Extremely rare

A GUIDE FOR ATTRIBUTING TOKENS

The listings of tokens in the main body are arranged according to the colony for which they were struck or where they were most used. Many of the pieces bear some indication of the colony of issue, in the form of either a city in the colony or the colony name itself. However, others do not, and as an aid to finding such pieces in the catalogue listings, the table below was constructed. To find a given token the following rules should be noted:

1. Pieces with the name of a city or the colony are NOT included in this list if they are listed under the expected colony.
2. If one or both sides of the token has a legend, consult the lists of legends.
3. Where a token has two legends on the same side - one around the outside and the second (usually the value) in a circle in the centre - the legends are listed separately.
4. When there is no legend or the legend is indistinct, the lists of designs should be consulted.

PIECES WITHOUT LEGENDS

DESIGN	Haxby-Willey Token Nos.	DESIGN	Haxby-Willey Token Nos.
Anchor / shield	277	Bust in wreath / seated female 1812	122-122a
Balance scale / tools and star	278	Bust / eagle	270
Bouquet / dancing Indian	268	Bust / harp	113-114, 246-248
Bust left (uniface)	249-52, 262	Bust / harp 1820	111-112, 259
Bust right (uniface)	253-256	Bust / harp 1825	110
Bust 1811? (uniface)	261	Bust / ship	264
Bust / seated female	240, 242-243	Eagle / eagle	274
Bust / standing female	241	Ship / 1858	6
Bust 1820 / seated female	99	Ship / seated female	100
Bust / seated female 1820	260-260a	Sloop in wreath / anvil, shovels in wreath ...	263

PIECES WITH LEGENDS

LEGEND	Haxby-Willey Token Nos.
AGRICULTURE & COMMERCE	
• BAS CANADA	117
BRITISH COLONIES	235
BRITIT	244
CANADA 1830	102
1841	103
CANADA HALF PENNY TOKEN	101
COMMERCE (undated)	80, 224
1814	239
COMMERCE RULES THE MAIN	225
COMMERCIAL CHANGE	97-97A
COSSACK PENNY TOKEN	87
EXECUTIVE EXPERIMENT	267
FARTHING TOKEN 1812	228
FIELD MARSHALL WELLINGTON	
(undated)	71, 76-78A, 81-81A, 85-86
1813	88
FISHERIES AND AGRICULTURE	18-19
FOR GENERAL ACCOMMODATION	227
FOR PUBLIC ACCOMMODATION	101, 237
FOR PUBLICK ACCOMMODATION	9
FOR THE CONVENIENCE OF TRADE	31
GENUINE BRITISH COPPER (undated)	36
1815	39
GLO III • VIS(?)	244
GLORIOUS III • VIS	245, 248-249
H	234
HALFPENNY OR HALF PENNY	40-42, 102-103
HALFPENNY OR HALF PENNY TOKEN:	
(UNDATED)	19, 24-25, 28, 39, 76-77, 90, 227, 231
1812	24, 115, 120-121a, 232
1813	25, 28, 82-81a, 91-93a
1814	31, 229-229a
1815	36, 38, 40, 233
1816	84, 234
HB EM ⅛ (¼, ½ or 1) NB	206-209
HIBERNIA 1805	71,237
HISPANIUM ET LUSITANIUM RESTITUIT WELLINGTON	73-75
JB (script)	42
MACHINE SHOP, etc.	271-272, 275
MAGDALEN ISLAND TOKEN	1
MARQUIS WELLINGTON 1813	80
NEMO ME IMPUNE LACESSIT	43
NO CREDIT	276
NO LABOUR NO BREAD	203
NORTH AMERICAN TOKEN 1781	224
NORTH WEST COMPANY	205-205a
ONE CENT 1855	18
ONE HALFPENNY TOKEN (undated)	8
1820	50
ONE PENNY	237
ONE PENNY TOKEN	
(undated)	26-27a, 85-86, 88, 118-119
1812	116-117
1813	26, 89
1814	27-27a, 230
PAYABLE AT THE STORE OF J. BROWN	43
PECK'S PATENT, etc.	273-275
PURE COPPER PREFERABLE TO PAPER	23-28, 226-227, 236
RENUNILLOS VISCAPE 1811	123-126
RH (script)	228-230
RISEING SUN TAVERN	269
SHIPS COLONIES & COMMERCE	10-15b, 96-96b, 257-258, 265
SHIPS COLONIES & COMMERCE 1815	8-9
' SPEED THE PLOUGH	17-17c
SPEED THE PLOUGH HALFPENNY TOKEN	203
SUCCESS TO THE FISHERIES	17-17c
SUCCESS TO TRADE 1812	225
SUCCESS TO NAVIGATION & TRADE	38
T. DUSEAMAN BUTCHER. BELLEVILLE	177
THE ILLUSTRIOUS WELLINGTON	83
TO FACILITATE TRADE (undated)	266
1825	98-98b, 235
TOKEN 1820	205-205a
TRADE & COMMERCE 1811	72
TRADE & NAVIGATION (undated)	50
1812	24
1813	23, 25-26, 28
1814	27-27a
1838	236
VE?ATOR CANADIN SIS	123-124
VE?ATOR CANADIENSIS	125
VICTORIA NOBIS EST	90
VIMIERA • TALAVERA • BADAJOZ • SALAMANCA • VITTORIA	89
VIMIERA • TALAVERA • BUSACO • BADAJOZ • SALAMANCA	87
WATERLOO HALFPENNY 1816	83
WELLINGTON HALFPENNY TOKEN	79, 82
WELLINGTON WATERLOO 1815	94-95

9
TRADE, ADVERTISING AND TRANSPORTATION TOKENS

Trade and advertising tokens appeared in the developing portions of the Dominion after 1880. They were issued by rural storekeepers and city firms in the West and in the north of Ontario as a means of enticing customers to return to their place of business. Given out in change, they could only be redeemed in the locality or at the shop of the issuer. In many cases they augmented the local supply of cash. Saskatchewan saw an enormous quantity and variety of these pieces in use, in denominations ranging from one cent to ten dollars. Large numbers were issued in Manitoba, Alberta, and British Columbia.

There was also a great variety of tokens issued which were redeemable in goods or services. Cordwood tokens, pool checks, hotel and restaurant tokens, barber shop tokens, cigar store tokens, dairy tokens, and bread tokens abound in all provinces. A special class of tokens good for some service are transportation tokens. These were issued to pay the fare by bus, street car or ferry in various localities, or to pay tolls for the use of bridges and tunnels. The famous Bout de l'Isle tokens are an example of tokens issued to pay tolls, in this case over a series of bridges near Montreal. One of the earliest fare tokens is the Montreal & Lachine Railroad token.

Trade Tokens

Pool check   Cigar store token   Hotel token

Another item now becoming very popular is the trade or souvenir coin. This is a sort of cross between a trade token and a commercial medal, for it is issued by a local organization or municipality for temporary use as money within the limits of a municipality, and commemorates or honours some important local event or historical personage. Usually these pieces are issued with a value of one dollar, and collectors have called them trade dollars, but their appearance in other denominations necessitates their being called by some other name, for by no conceivable stretch of the imagination ought a fifty-cent trade coin be called a trade dollar.

One of the earliest of these pieces was the dollar struck in 1960 for the golden jubilee of the founding of Prince Rupert, British Columbia, They have been most widely used in Western Canada, but have recently spread into the East.

Dairy token   Bread token

Barber shop token   Ferry token

Montreal and Lachine
Railroad Token

It was found that ordinary railway tickets were not convenient for use among the Indians and workmen on the Lachine Canal, who formed the bulk of third class travel on the Montreal & Lachine Railroad Company.

These tokens were therefore imported from Birmingham, England. The tokens were strung on a wire as they were collected by the conductor.

Article reprinted from *An Introduction to Coin Collecting* with the kind permission of the Canadian Numismatic Association.

10
DOMINION OF CANADA
NOTES 1867-1935

TRANSITIONAL ISSUES

The newly formed government of the Dominion of Canada decided to utilize the large stockpiles of Province of Canada notes which had only been in circulation for a short time. These notes were not withdrawn from circulation and became the first issue of Dominion notes. In addition to the Province of Canada type notes payable at Toronto or Montreal the newly formed Dominion government had to prepare notes payable in the Maritimes. Notes prepared for New Brunswick were overprinted with a horizontal blue ST. JOHN in addition to the regular vertical green markings PAYABLE AT TORONTO (on $1 to $50 notes). Nova Scotia notes were specially prepared ($5 note only) with a green PAYABLE AT HALIFAX ONLY appearing vertically at each end of the face.

As the types payable only at Toronto or Montreal were previously issued by the Province of Canada, they will not be listed here. All notes have the engraved signature of T.D. Harington at the right and the manuscript signature or various individuals at the left. After 1871 all Provincial issue notes were withdrawn and replaced by Dominion of Canada notes.

Toronto / St. John issue

	VG	Fine	VF
Province of Canada Type Payable at:			
$5 payable at Halifax	1,800	3,100	6,000
$1 overprinted ST. JOHN	1.500	2,250	4,500
$2 overprinted ST. JOHN	1,750	3,500	7,000
$5 overprinted ST. JOHN	1,800	3,500	6,500
$10, $20 or $50 overprinted ST. JOHN	No notes known to exist		

25 CENT NOTES (SHINPLASTERS)

The first issue of 25¢ notes was an emergency issue to halt large amount of U.S. silver coinage circulating at par in Canada. At that time the U.S. dollar was valued at only 80¢ Canadian and was discounted 20% at banks in Canada, with the result that individuals had to bear the loss. The Canadian government hoped to replace the need for U.S. silver with an issue of Canadian coins. In order to fill the time delay required to produce the large quantity of Canadian coins needed, it was decided to meet the shortage by issuing 25¢ notes. These were never intended to be more than a temporary issue but they proved so popular with the public that the government was forced to produce further issues in 1900 and 1923.

The expression "shinplaster" has been attributed to the use of such low denomination notes by soldiers of the Revolutionary war period as a lining to protect their ankles and shins from chafing by their boots.

1870 Issue

Vignette: Britannia; signatures: right T.D. Harington (engraved), left W. Dickinson (engraved). There were three series: the A series (issued 1870), the B series (issued 1871-ca. 1885) and the no letter or "plain" series (issued ca. 1885-1900). The series letter, is located at the lower left just below the 0 of 1870.

Series letter location

Variety / Signatures	G	VG	F	VF	EF	Unc
25¢ A series	35.00	80.00	125.00	250.00	500.00	1,000
B series	10.00	25.00	35.00	75.00	150.00	400.00
"Plain" series	8.00	20.00	30.00	55.00	120.00	250.00

1900 Issue

Vignette: Britannia; signature (engraved): various (see below).

Variety	G	VG	F	VF	EF	Unc
25¢ J.M. Courtney	4.00	8.00	11.50	16.00	35.00	75.00
T.C. Boville	3.00	6.00	8.00	13.50	30.00	50.00
J.C. Saunders	5.00	10.00	15.00	25.00	45.00	100.00

1923 Issue

Vignette: Britannia; signatures (engraved); various (see below). The first printing has AUTHORIZED BY R.S.C. CAP. 31. above the signature at the left and a red check letter A, B, C, D, E, H, J, K, L or M to the left of the number. Later printings lack this statement, and a black check letter (to the left of the left 25) replaces the red one. All notes bear the seal of the Department of Finance at the right.

Major Variety / Signature at Left	G	VG	F	VF	EF	Unc
		With AUTHORIZED, etc.			Without AUTHORIZED, etc.	
25¢ With AUTHORIZED, etc.						
G.W. Hyndman	12.00	20.00	30.00	50.00	100.00	250.00

Major Variety / Signature at Left	G	VG	F	VF	EF	Unc
Without AUTHORIZED, etc.						
G.W. Hyndman	10.00	20.00	40.00	65.00	125.00	300.00
S.P. McCavour	4.00	5.00	8.00	14.00	30.00	60.00
C.E. Campbell	4.50	6.00	10.00	18.00	35.00	70.00

ONE DOLLAR
1870 Issue

Vignette: Jacques Cartier (left) and "Canada" (right); signatures: T.D. Harington (engraved at right), W. Dickinson (engraved at left) and one of various others written vertically (positioned at one end, usually the left). The city payable is indicated on the back of each note. In addition the extremely rare notes issued in Manitoba have a black MANITOBA stamped vertically on the face at the right end of PAYABLE AT MONTREAL or TORONTO varieties.

The Toronto issue was heavily counterfeited. The counterfeits can be most easily recognized by the presence of D4 (check letter D, plate number 4) twice on their face and a crude black dot for Cartier's eye.

	Major Variety	G	VG	F	VF	EF	Unc
$1	**1870 Back reads Payable at:**						
	Montreal	100.00	200.00	300.00	500.00	1,100	2,500
	Toronto	100.00	200.00	300.00	500.00	1,100	2,500
	MANITOBA stamped on either of above				No notes known to exist		
	Halifax	750.00	1,500	2,500	4,000	8,000	—
	St. John	750.00	1,500	2,500	4,000	8,500	—
	Victoria	3,000	6,000	10,000	—	—	—

1878 Issue (Dufferin)

Vignette: The Countess of Dufferin, wife of the Governor General, and on the back the Great Seal of Canada; signatures: T.D. Harington (engraved at right) and one of various others (written at left). The city payable is indicated on both the face (lower left) and the back. The initial issue had a frame (border) consisting of a scallop-like design with a large "scallop" in each corner. It was replaced in 1881 with a modified design due to some notes of the original issue being altered to $4s. The frame of the new design contains 1 ONE DOLLAR repeated with a 1 in each corner, plus other differences.

Scalloped Frame   Lettered Frame

	Major Variety / Signature	G	VG	F	VF	EF	Unc
$1	**1878 Scalloped Frame on Face — Back reads Payayable at:**						
	Montreal	110.00	200.00	400.00	700.00	1,300	3,300
	Toronto	110.00	200.00	400.00	700.00	1,300	3,300
	Halifax	500.00	1,150	1,550	3,000	5,000	—
	St. John	500.00	1,150	1,550	3,000	5,000	—
$1	**1878 Lettered Frame on Face — Back reads Payayable at:**						
	Montreal	30.00	60.00	100.00	200.00	400.00	800.00
	Toronto	30.00	60.00	100.00	200.00	400.00	8700.00
	Halifax	500.00	1,000	2,000	3,000	6,000	—
	St. John	500.00	1,000	2,500	3,000	6,000	—

1897 and 1898 (Aberdeen)

Vignettes: The Countess of Aberdeen, the Earl of Aberdeen (Governor General 1893-1898), a logging scene and on the back the centre block of the Parliament buildings in Ottawa; signatures: J.M. Courtney (later T.C. Boville) engraved at the right and one of various persons written at the left.

The face tint (background colour) on the 1897 issue is green and the design on the back contains a large 1 at each end. Probably to better distinguish it from the $2 of 1897, the colour of the face tint on the $1 was changed to brown and the notes redated 1898. It had also been found that the large 1s on the back of the original design tended to disfigure the portraits on the face (by showing through the paper), so the 1898 issue has a modified back where three small counters replace each of the large 1s. The initial 1898 back has the small ONE at each end curving inward; this was later changed to have the ONEs curving outward.

These issues mark the termination of domiciling for this denomination.

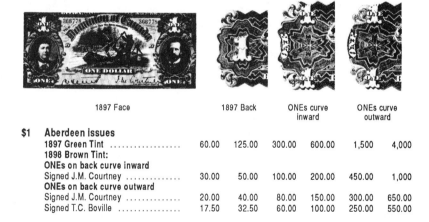

| 1897 Face | 1897 Back | ONEs curve inward | ONEs curve outward |

		G	VG	F	VF	EF	Unc
$1	**Aberdeen issues**						
	1897 Green Tint	60.00	125.00	300.00	600.00	1,500	4,000
	1898 Brown Tint:						
	ONEs on back curve inward						
	Signed J.M. Courtney	30.00	50.00	100.00	200.00	450.00	1,000
	ONEs on back curve outward						
	Signed J.M. Courtney	20.00	40.00	80.00	150.00	300.00	650.00
	Signed T.C. Boville	17.50	32.50	60.00	100.00	250.00	550.00

1911 Issue (Grey)

Vignettes: The Earl of Grey (Governor General 1904-1911) and the Countess of Grey; back design: the same as the second design for the 1898 issue; signatures: T.C. Boville (engraved at right) and one of various persons (written at left).

The first notes of this issue had a green signature pane across the bottom. On later printings a black line was added along the top edge of the panel.

			All green panel		Black line at top of panel	
	Major Variety / Signatures	**G**	**VG**	**F**	**VF**	**EF**	**Unc**

	Major Variety / Signatures	G	VG	F	VF	EF	Unc
$1	1911 all green signature panel	15.00	25.00	50.00	100.00	200.00	425.00
	black line at top of signature panel	12.00	20.00	35.00	80.00	150.00	300.00

1917 Issue (Princess Pat)

Vignettes: Princess Patricia of Connaught and on the back the centre block of the original Parliament buildings. The first printings have a plain green ONE on each side of the portrait on the face side, have the written signatures of various persons at the left and the engraved signature or T.C. Boville (later J.C. Saunders) at the right. In 1922 the government switched over to countersigning the notes by printing; as a security device the seal of the Department of Finance was added with the second signature. The initial printings involving machine countersigning were with the notes of the original design (ONE at right), so a transitional variety with the seal over the ONE was created. The final issue lacks the ONE at the right, allowing the Finance Department seal to be more easily seen.

			ONE alone at right	Seal over ONE at right	Seal alone at right	

		G	VG	F	VF	EF	Unc
$1	**1917 Plain ONE at right:**						
	Signed Boville at right	10.00	20.00	35.00	70.00	135.00	350.00
	Signed Saunders at right	10.00	25.00	40.00	80.00	150.00	400.00
	Black Seal over ONE at right						
	Signed Hyndman-Saunders	12.00	30.00	50.00	90.00	160.00	425.00
	Seal alone (No ONE) at right:						
	Signed Hyndman-Saunders	12.00	30.00	50.00	90.00	160.00	425.00

1923 Issue (George V)

Vignette: King George V and on the back the Library of Parliament; signatures: various (see below), all engraved. On this issue the seal of the Department of Finance comes in various colours, the purpose of which was to aid in sorting the notes when they came back in for destruction.

	Seal Colour / Signature	G	VG	F	VF	EF	Unc
$1	**Black Seal at right:**						
	Hyndman-Saunders	15.00	30.00	45.00	80.00	175.00	450.00
	McCavour-Saunders	15.00	30.00	45.00	80.00	165.00	350.00
	Campbell-Sellar	10.00	18.00	35.00	65.00	120.00	300.00
	Campbell-Clark	8.00	15.00	25.00	45.00	85.00	200.00
	Red Seal at right:						
	McCavour-Saunders	12.00	25.00	40.00	70.00	125.00	300.00
	Blue Seal at right:						
	McCavour-Saunders	12.00	25.00	40.00	70.00	125.00	300.00
	Green Seal at right:						
	McCavour-Saunders	15.00	30.00	45.00	80.00	160.00	350.00
	Purple-Brown Seal at right:						
	McCavour-Saunders	15.00	30.00	45.00	80.00	160.00	350.00
	Lilac Seal at right:						
	McCavour-Saunders	65.00	135.00	225.00	350.00	750.00	2,000
	Campbell-Sellar	90.00	200.00	300.00	500.00	1,000	2,500

*All of the scarce lilac seal notes have a C prefix in the note number and have a small C-1 to the right of the seal.
Purple-brown seal notes do not come with this letter.

TWO DOLLARS
1870 Issue

Vignettes: Generals Wolfe and Montcalm, the ill- fated commanders of the British and French forces in the Battle of the Plains of Abraham at Quebec City in 1759, and "civilization" (centre); signatures: T.D. Harington (engraved at right), W. Dickinson (engraved at left) and that of various persons (written, vertically positioned at one end, usually the left). The city payable is indicated on the back of each note. In addition, the extremely rare notes issued in Manitoba have a black MANITOBA stamped vertically on the face at the right end of PAYABLE AT MONTREAL or TORONTO varieties.

	Major Variety	G	VG	F
$2	**1870 Back reads Payable at:**			
	Montreal	700.00	1,500	2,500
	Toronto	700.00	1,500	2,500
	MANITOBA overprint	3,500	7,000	—
	Halifax	1,900	3,700	6,000
	St. John	2,000	4,000	6,500
	Victoria	No notes known to exist		

1878 Issue (Dufferin)

Vignettes: The Earl of Dufferin, Governor General 1872-1878 and on the back the Great Seal of Canada; signatures: T.D. Harington (engraved at right) and that of various persons (written at left). The city payable is indicated on both the face (lower left) and the back. Both the Montreal and Toronto issues were heavily counterfeited; which is likely the reason for the early retirement of the whole issue compared to the corresponding $1 issue. The counterfeits have a rather inferior portrait and all known examples have at least a single 1 in the serial number. The counterfeits have curved topped 1s, while the genuine notes have flat topped 1s. Unfortunately, most of the surviving notes of the Toronto and Montreal varieties are the counterfeits.

Flat topped 1   Curved top 1
(Genuine)   (Counterfeit)

		G	VG	F
$2	**1878 Back reads Payable at:**			
	Montreal	350.00	750.00	1,125
	Toronto	375.00	775.00	1,200
	Halifax	600.00	1,200	1,800
	St. John	750.00	1,500	2,500

1887 Issue (Lansdowne)

Vignettes: the Marchioness of Lansdowne, the Marquis of Lansdowne (Governor General 1883-1888) and on the back "Quebec!," showing Jacques Cartier and his men aboard ship. The back is bi-coloured for security reasons and is the only Dominion note to have such a back.

		G	VG	F	VF	EF	Unc
2$	1887 (Lansdowne)	100.00	200.00	300.00	500.00	1,000	2,000

1897 Issue (Wales)

Vignettes: Edward, Prince of Wales (later King Edward VII), men cod fishing from a boat and on the back field workers harvesting grain; signatures: J.M. Courtney (later T.C. Boville) engraved at the right and that of various persons written at the left. The first printings have a red-brown back; this was soon revised to dark brown.

	Major Varieties / Signature	G	VG	F	VF	EF	Unc
$2	**1897 Prince of Wales**						
	Red-brown coloured back						
	Signed J.M. Courtney	400.00	900.00	13500	2,500	5,000	—
	Dark brown coloured back						
	Signed J.M. Courtney	30.00	65.00	95.00	170.00	350.00	750.00
	Signed T.C. Boville	25.00	50.00	75.00	150.00	250.00	550.00

1914 Issue (Connaught)

Vignettes: The Duke of Connaught (Governor General 1911-1916), the Duchess of Connaught and on the back the Canadian coat-of-arms, along with those of the provinces; signatures: the initial design has the statement WILL PAY TO THE BEARER ON DEMAND in a curved line over the large 2 counter in the centre of the face. On later printings this statement is in a straight line. Initially the notes also have an olive TWO on each side of the portrait on the face side, have the written signature of various persons at the left and the engraved signature of T.C. Do-ville (later J.C. Saunders) at the right. In 1922 the government switched over to countersigning the notes by printing; as a security device the seal of the Department of Finance was added with the second signature. The first printings involving machine countersigning were with notes of the second design (straight WILL PAY, etc. and TWO at the right), so a transitional variety was created. The final issue lacks the TWO at the right, allowing the Finance Department seal to be more easily seen.

Curved WILL PAY, etc.   Straight WILL PAY, etc.

	Major Varieties / Signature	G	VG	F	VF	EF	Unc
$2	**1914 Duke and Duchess of Connaught**						
	Plain TWO at right						
	Curved WILL PAY etc.:						
	signed Boville	25.00	50.00	70.00	125.00	250.00	650.00
	Straight WILL PAY, etc.:						
	Signed Boville	25.00	55.00	100.00	175.00	350.00	950.00
	Signed Saunders	25.00	50.00	75.00	130.00	250.00	750.00
	Black seal over TWO at right						
	Straight WILL PAY, etc.:						
	Signed Saunders	75.00	125.00	200.00	375.00	700.00	1,500
	Seal alone (no TWO) at right						
	Straight WILL PAY, etc:						
	Signed Saunders	30.00	55.00	125.00	175.00	375.00	900.00

1923 Issue (Prince of Wales)

Vignettes: Edward, Prince of Wales (later King Edward VIII) and on the back the coat-of-arms of Canada; signatures: various, all machine signed, (see below). On this issue the seal of the Department of Finance comes in various colours, the purpose of which was to aid in sorting the notes when they came back in for destruction.

	Major Variety / Signatures	G	VG	F	VF	EF	Unc
$2	**Black Seal at right:**						
	Hyndman-Saunders	30.00	65.00	100.00	175.00	350.00	900.00
	McCavour-Saunders	25.00	50.00	85.00	150.00	300.00	750.00
	Campbell-Sellar	20.00	40.00	60.00	110.00	200.00	500.00
	Campbell-Clark	20.00	40.00	70.00	120.00	240.00	600.00
	Red Seal at right;						
	McCavour-Saunders	22.00	45.00	75.00	120.00	250.00	700.00
	Blue Seal at right:						
	McCavour-Saunders	22.00	45.00	75.00	120.00	250.00	700.00
	Campbell-Sellar	22.00	45.00	75.00	120.00	250.00	700.00
	Green Seal at right:						
	McCavour-Saunders	35.00	60.00	100.00	175.00	350.00	900.00
	Purple-Brown Seal at right:						
	McCavour-Saunders	25.00	50.00	80.00	150.00	300.00	750.00

FOUR DOLLARS

1882 Issue (Lorne)

Vignette: The Marquis of Lorne (Governor General 1878-1883); signatures: J.M. Courtney engraved at the right and that of various persons written at the left. As a security device the notes were printed on watermarked paper (they were the only Dominion notes that were) and bear an orange Great Seal of Canada at the right on the face side. The colour of the seal is sometimes brown due to oxidation of the ink.

		G	VG	F	VF	EF	Unc
$4	1882	150.00	275.00	400.00	700.00	1,500	5,000

1900 and 1902 Issues (Minto)

Vignettes: The Countess of Minto, the Earl of Minto (Governor General 1898-1904), the locks at Sault Ste. Marie, connecting Lakes Superior and Huron and on the back Parliament Hill as seen from the Ottawa River to the east; signatures:

J.M. Courtney (1900 and the 1902 issue with the 4s at the top) or T.C. Boville (1902 issue with the FOURs at the top) engraved at the right and that of various persons written at the left. On the initial printings (dated 1900) the U.S. side of the locks was portrayed. This error was corrected in 1902 and the design re-dated. In 1911, on the eve of the introduction of the $5 notes and the withdrawal of the $4s a third variety (with FOURs at the top for easier recognition of the denomination) was issued because of a pressing need for paper money.

1900 Issue

1902 Issue (4s at top)

1902 Issue (FOURs at top)

Back (all issues)

Major Variety / Signatures	G	VG	F	VF	EF	Unc
$4	1900	70.00	150.00	300.00	500.00	1,000	2,000
1902 Large 4s at top:						
Signed J.M. Courtney	70.00	150.00	300.00	500.00	1,000	2,000
Large FOURs at top:						
Signed T.C. Boville	65.00	140.00	275.00	500.00	1,000	2,000

FIVE DOLLARS

1912 Issue (Train)

Vignette: The "Maritime Express" travelling through the Wentworth Valley in Nova Scotia and on the back a large Roman numeral V in the centre. The first printings have a FIVE counter on each side of the vignette on the face, the written signature of various persons at the left and the engraved signature of T.C. Boville at the right. In 1922 the government switched over to countersigning the notes by printing; as a security device the seal of the Department of Finance was added with the second signature. The first printings involving machine counter-signing were with notes of the original design (FIVE at the right), so transitional notes with the seal over the FIVE were created. A signature change also occurred at this time. The final issue lacks the FIVE at the right, allowing the Finance Department seal to be more easily seen.

FIVE alone
at right

Seal over FIVE
at right

Seal alone
at right

	Major Variety / Signatures	G	VG	F	VF	EF	Unc
$5	**Plain FIVE at right:**						
	Signed T.C. Boville at right	35.00	60.00	90.00	175.00	325.00	700.00
	Blue Seal over FIVE at right:						
	Signed T.C. Boville at right	75.00	150.00	225.00	300.00	600.00	1,500
	Signed J.C. Saunders at right ...	75.00	110.00	170.00	400.00	800.00	2,000
	Seal alone (No FIVE) at right:						
	Signed Hyndman-Saunders	45.00	90.00	150.00	250.00	550.00	1,200
	Signed McCavour-Saunders	2,500	4,000	(only one known)			

1924 Issue (Queen Mary)

Vignettes: Queen Mary, wife of King George V and on the back the east block of the Parliament buildings; signatures: W. Sellar at the right and C.E. Campbell at the left, both printed on with the Department of Finance seal after the rest of the note had been printed. Although they were dated 1924, these notes were not issued until 1934, just before the withdrawal of the Dominion notes and the introduction of the Bank of Canada notes. Because of this, the notes of this issue are often encountered in high grade.

		G	VG	F	VF	EF	Unc
$5	1924	250.00	350.00	550.00	950.00	1,600	4,000

HIGHER DENOMINATIONS

The Dominion government also issued $50, $100, $500 and $1000 notes for circulation, although the two higher denominations were used almost exclusively in transactions between banks. The earliest issues were domiciled: The $50 and $100 notes came payable at Montreal or Toronto and the $500 and $1000 of 1871 came payable at Montreal, Toronto, Halifax, St. John, Victoria, Charlottetown or Winnipeg,

	Major Variety / Signatures	G	VG	F	VF	Unc	Proof
$50	1872 Only proof known to exist						2,000
$100	1872 Only proof known to exist						2,500
$500	1871 Only proof known to exist						4,000
	1911	3,500	5,000	7,500	—	—	—
	1925	—	2,500	3,500	6,000	—	—
$1000	1871 Only proof known to exist						4,500
	1911	3,500	5,000	7,500	—	—	—
	1925	—	2,500	3,500	6,000	—	—

11
BANK OF CANADA NOTES
1935 TO DATE

INTRODUCTION

The Bank of Canada was created by the Central Bank Act of 1934. Under this Act, the Bank was given sole responsibility for the issuance and management of Canadian paper money as well as being responsible for the national debt and giving advice to the government on monetary policy. The Bank of Canada while dealing directly in ordinary banking, would loan money to the chartered banks as well as accept deposits from them.

Commencing business on March 11th, 1935, the Bank of Canada assumed responsibility for all Dominion of Canada notes still in circulation, which would be replaced with the new Bank of Canada 1935 issue notes. Although chartered banks were allowed to continue issuing their own notes into the mid 1940s, they had to drastically reduce their note circulation and in fact the last date on a chartered bank issue was 1943 (Royal Bank of Canada $5). During the latter part of the 1940s, the chartered banks actively withdrew their notes and in 1950 transferred to the Bank of Canada a sum of money equal to the face value of their notes outstanding as of December 31, 1949 ($13,302,046.60). As of January 1st, 1950 the Bank of Canada assumed responsibility for redeeming these notes.

All Bank of Canada notes have been printed on blank note paper containing randomly scattered green planchettes (tiny discs of green paper embedded in the white paper during its manufacture as an anti-counterfeiting device). Two security printers in Ottawa produce the notes: the British American Bank Note Company, Ltd., and the Canadian Bank Note Company, Limited.

1935 ISSUE

Face side with portrait at left   Back with allegorical vignette

The Bank of Canada's first issue of notes was put into circulation early in 1935. The official changeover date from Dominion notes to Bank of Canada notes was March 11, 1935 and thereafter the Dominion notes were rapidly retired. The new Bank of Canada notes were small size (about 152 x 72 mm) to decrease printing costs. They consisted of two separate emissions, one English and one French, for each denomination making 18 different notes in all. The portrait on the face is positioned at the left end.

Design Details

	Basic Colour	Portrait	Back Design
$1	Green	King George V	Allegorical figure of Agriculture
$2	Blue	Queen Mary	Mercury with implements of transportation
$5	Orange	Prince of Wales, later Edward VIII, then Duke of Windsor	Allegorical figure of Power
$10	Purple	Princess Royal	Allegorical figure of Harvest
$20	Rose Pink	Princess Elizabeth, now Elizabeth II	Worker showing produce to Agriculture
$50	Brown	Duke of York later George VI	Allegorical figure of Invention with radio
$100	Dark Brown	Duke of Gloucester	Allegorical scene of Shipping with industry
$500	Tan	Sir John A. Macdonald, first Prime Minister of the Dominion in 1867	Allegorical scene showing Produce
$1000	Olive Green	Sir Wilfrid Laurier, Prime Minister 1896-1911	Allegorical figure of Security

Dates, Signatures and Numbering

All notes of this issue bear the legend ISSUE OF 1935 (or its French equivalent), the facsimile signatures of Deputy Governor (of the Bank) J.A.C. Osborne and Governor G.F. Towers, and at the right the seal of the Bank. The numbering system was the same as that used for the final issues of Dominion notes. That is, the notes were numbered in groups of four; each note within a given group received the same series letter and number (in red at top). The individual notes within a group were differentiated from each other by a black check letter, A, B, C or D. All notes of the French issue were series F, while those of the English issue were series A (except that B was also used for the $1 because the A series was completed). Within each series the numbers could go from 1 (preceded by various amounts of 0s) to 1000000.

Denomination	G	VG	F	VF	EF	Unc
English Issues:						
$1	5.00	12.00	18.00	30.00	60.00	150.00
$2	10.00	20.00	32.00	55.00	100.00	250.00
$5	20.00	35.00	65.00	125.00	250.00	550.00
$10	15.00	27.50	40.00	70.00	150.00	350.00
$20 Large Seal	70.00	125.00	200.00	350.00	700.00	1,700
Small Seal	60.00	100.00	150.00	275.00	550.00	1,400
$50	125.00	200.00	350.00	550.00	10600	2,500
$100	—	200.00	350.00	525.00	1,000	2,500
$500	—	3,000	4,500	5,500	7,000	10,500
$1000	—	—	1,250	1,400	1,500	2,000
French Issues:						
$1	9.00	17.50	25.00	40.00	80.00	200.00
$2	15.00	25.00	40.00	75.00	150.00	450.00
$5	35.00	60.00	90.00	150.00	325.00	750.00
$10	40.00	65.00	100.00	175.00	350.00	800.00
$20	100.00	200.00	300.00	500.00	1,000	2,500
$50	175.00	300.00	425.00	700.00	1,500	3,000
$100	—	320.00	500.00	900.00	2,000	4,000
$500	—	4,500	6,000	7,500	9,500	15,000
$1000	—	—	1,750	2,500	3,700	6,000

GEORGE V
Silver Jubilee Commemorative, 1935

In addition to the regular denominations, the Bank of Canada issued $25 notes to mark the 25th anniversary of the accession of George V. There were separate English and French issues like the notes of the Bank's first issue; however, the $25 notes were strictly a special commemorative issue and were not part of the first issue. This is emphasized by the different issue date on the notes (May 6, 1935) and the date span 1910-1935 at the top. The portraits of King George V and Queen Mary are shown in the centre on the face and a view of Windsor Castle appears on the back. The face tint and back colour is royal purple. The signatures and numbering are as for the regular 1935 issue.

Denomination		G	VG	F	VF	EF	Unc
$25	English issue	150.00	300.00	450.00	750.00	1,500	3,500
	French issue	225.00	400.00	550.00	1,000	1,900	4,500

1937 ISSUE

The preparation of new issue of Bank of Canada notes was begun under King Edward VIII . Upon Edward's abdication in December 1936, the portrait of his brother, the Duke of York, was substituted and work continued on the new issue. The portrait of the new monarch, King George VI, had already been used on the $50 1935 notes when he was the Duke of York. A number of major changes took place from the previous issue. The King's portrait is in the centre of the face side and was used on all denominations from $1 to $50. The $100 note has Sir John A. MacDonald (same portrait as on the 1935 $500 note) and the $1000 denomination once again had Sir Wilfrid Laurier. The $500 denomination was discontinued. The use of one bilingual note rather than two monolingual notes for each denomination was instituted, as the cost of preparing separate English and French issues had simply been too high. The text and denominations are in French on the right side and English of the left.

Back Design Details

All the allegorical back designs of the 1937 notes were the same as those used in 1935, although they did not necessarily appear on the same denominations as previously. The backs were also made bilingual and small changes in the design were made. Several denominations also changed colour from the 1935 issue.

Face with portrait in centre   Back with allegorical vignette

Denom.	Basic Colour	Back Design	Denom.	Basic Colour	Back Design
$1	Green	Same as 1935	$20	Olive Green	As $500,1935
$2	Dull Red	As $10, 1935	$50	Orange	Same as 1935
$5	Blue	Same as 1935	$100	Brown	Same as 1935
$10	Purple	As $2, 1935	$1000	Pink	Same as 1935

Dates, Signatures and Numbering

All notes bear the date January 2, 1937 but only the denominations $1 to $100 were released at that time. The $1000 note was not released by the Bank of Canada until the early fifties although the Osborne-Towers signatures indicate that they were printed much earlier. All notes bear the facsimile signature of Governor G.F. Towers at the right. Three different Deputy Governors served during the period of these notes: J.A.C. Osborne, D. Gordon and J.E. Coyne. The numbering system was changed beginning with the 1937 issue. The serial number of each note consists of a two-letter prefix, expressed as a fraction, followed by a number. The lower letter in the fraction is the denominational letter (a given letter was used on only one denomination) and the upper letter is the series letter (which could be used on any denomination). Within each series the numbers could go from 0000001 to 10000000 with the number printed twice on the face of each note.

Denomination	Good	VG	F	VF	EF	Unc
Notes signed J.A.C. Osborne at left:						
$1	8.00	12.00	15.00	25.00	45.00	100.00
$2	15.00	30.00	35.00	50.00	90.00	200.00
$5	25.00	50.00	75.00	125.00	200.00	450.00
$10	12.00	25.00	35.00	45.00	100.00	225.00
$20	40.00	70.00	100.00	125.00	250.00	550.00
$50	125.00	300.00	375.00	550.00	1,000	2,200
$100	—	150.00	190.00	250.00	550.00	1,100
$1000	—	—	1,100	1,250	1,500	2,000
Notes signed D. Gordon at left:						
$1	—	4.00	5.00	7.50	14.00	30.00
$2	—	7.00	12.00	17.50	30.00	65.00
$5	—	8.00	10.00	13.50	25.00	60.00
$10	—	10.50	12.50	15.00	30.00	60.00
$20	—	22.00	22.50	25.00	35.00	80.00
$50	—	50.00	55.00	65.00	100.00	200.00
$100	—	105.00	110.00	135.00	150.00	200.00
Notes signed J.E. Coyne at left:						
$1	—	3.50	4.50	6.50	10.00	24.00
$2	—	7.00	12.00	17.50	30.00	65.00
$5	—	10.00	12.00	17.50	35.00	75.00
$10	—	10.50	12.50	15.00	30.00	60.00
$20	—	22.00	22.50	25.00	35.00	80.00
$50	—	50.00	55.00	65.00	100.00	200.00
$100	—	105.00	110.00	135.00	160.00	225.00

1954 ISSUE

Upon the death of George VI in 1952, a new issue of Canadian paper currency was prepared for the incoming monarch, Elizabeth II with a number of marked departures from previous issues. The portrait of the Queen was positioned at the right end of the face for all denominations, where it would get less wear by folding than the centred portraits of the 1937 issue. The face tint (background colour) was more complex than previous notes and the allegorical vignettes on the backs of the 1937 issue were replaced by Canadian scenes.

This issue was withdrawn beginning in 1970 because the prefix letters were almost entirely used up. There was also a large number of counterfeits appearing on this issue, particularly on the higher $50 and $100 denominations. The later signature varieties of these denominations were replaced quickly and are relatively scarce today.

Face with Queen's portrait at right

Back with Canadian scene

Back Design Details

The basic colours for all denominations were carried over from the previous issue.

Denom.	Back Design	Denom.	Back Design
$1	Western prairie and sky	$20	Laurentian hills in winter
$2	Country valley in Central Canada	$50	Atlantic seashore
$5	Northern stream and forest	$100	Mountain, valley and lake
$10	Rocky Mountain peak	$1000	Village, lake and hills

Date, Signatures and Numbering

All notes of the first issue of Elizabeth carry the designation OTTAWA, 1954. There are five signature combinations in this issue.

J.E. Coyne and G.F. Towers (all with "Devil's Face")

J.R. Beattie and J.E. Coyne (with and without "Devil's Face")

J.R. Beattie and L. Rasminsky

G. Bouey and L. Rasminsky

R.W. Lawson and G. Bouey

For denominations of $5 and up, some of the later signature combinations were not printed.

The numbering on the notes is as previously described on the 1937 issue except that after 1968 the number range in any given series was changed to run from 0000000 to 9999999, the zero note being removed and destroyed prior to issue. Each denomination letter was used for up to 250,000,000 notes and eventually every possible denomination letter except Q was used.

Varieties

Asterisk Note (replacement)

Prior to the 1954 issue, replacement notes (to replace ones that were spoiled during printing) were individually made up with exactly the same serial numbers as those that were spoiled. In order to eliminate the nuisance of preparing new notes, a new system was devised for use with the 1954 issue. The Bank of Canada began printing series of independently numbered notes with an asterisk

(*) preceding the serial number to replace defective notes. No asterisk notes were printed for the $50, $100 or $1000 denominations.

Shortly after the 1954 issue notes appeared in circulation it was noticed that certain highlighted portions of the queen's hair created the illusion of a devil's face peering out from behind her ear. This was not an "error," nor was it the result of a prank, but was simply the faithful copying of the original photograph used as the model. The "Devil's Face" portrait created enough controversy that it was decided to modify the queen's hair thereby creating two varieties of the queen's portrait on this issue.

"Devil's face" in Queen's hair   Modified hair

Devil's Face Portrait

Denom.	Signatures	VG	F	VF	EF	Unc.
	Regular Issue					
$1	Coyne-Towers	5.00	6.00	8.00	16.00	35.00
	Beattie-Coyne	3.00	5.00	6.00	10.00	25.00
$2	Coyne-Towers	7.00	9.00	12.00	25.00	55.00
	Beattie-Coyne	3.75	5.75	8.00	16.00	35.00
$5	Coyne-Towers	—	15.00	20.00	45.00	90.00
	Beattie-Coyne	—	13.00	17.00	35.00	80.00
$10	Coyne-Towers	—	12.00	18.00	35.00	80.00
	Beattie-Coyne	—	12.00	18.00	35.00	80.00
$20	Coyne-Towers	—	25.00	30.00	60.00	160.00
	Beattie-Coyne	—	22.00	30.00	55.00	140.00
$50	Coyne-Towers	—	55.00	65.00	90.00	210.00
	Beattie-Coyne	—	55.00	60.00	75.00	175.00
$100	Coyne-Towers	—	—	110.00	125.00	225.00
	Beattie-Coyne	—	—	110.00	150.00	225.00
$1000	Coyne-Towers	—	—	—	1,200	1,500
	Asterisk Issue					
$1	Coyne-Towers	200.00	250.00	350.00	650.00	1,500
	Beattie-Coyne	100.00	150.00	200.00	350.00	800.00
$2	Coyne-Towers	550.00	750.00	925.00	1,850	4,000
	Beattie-Coyne	200.00	300.00	400.00	700.00	1,500
$5	Coyne-Towers	1,000	1,500	2,250	3,500	7,500
	Beattie-Coyne	500.00	750.00	1,125	1,700	3,750
$10	Coyne-Towers	400.00	550.00	650.00	1,300	3,000
	Beattie-Coyne	265.00	365.00	450.00	900.00	2,000
$20	Coyne-Towers	475.00	625.00	900.00	1,700	3,750
	Beattie-Coyne	400.00	500.00	750.00	1,300	3,000
$50	Coyne-Towers					Not Printed
	Beattie-Coyne					Not Printed
$100	Coyne-Towers					Not Printed
	Beattie-Coyne					Not Printed
$1000	Coyne-Towers					Not Printed

Modified Portrait

Denom.	Signatures	F	VF	EF	Unc.
	Regular Issue				
$1	Beattie-Coyne	1.25	1.75	3.00	9.00
	Beattie-Rasminsky	—	1.75	3.00	9.00
	Bouey-Rasminsky	—	1.75	3.00	9.00
	Lawson-Bouey	—	—	3.00	9.00
$2	Beattie-Coyne	4.50	6.25	10.00	30.00
	Beattie-Rasminsky	—	2.25	4.50	12.00
	Bouey-Rasminsky	—	2.25	4.50	12.00
	Lawson-Bouey	—	2.50	4.50	12.00
$5	Beattie-Coyne	9.00	14.00	20.00	60.00
	Beattie-Rasminsky	—	8.00	15.00	45.00
	Bouey-Rasminsky	—	14.00	20.00	40.00
$10	Beattie-Coyne	12.00	13.50	20.00	45.00
	Beattie-Rasminsky	—	15.00	25.00	60.00
$20	Beattie-Coyne	—	25.00	36.00	95.00
	Beattie-Rasminsky	—	25.00	30.00	65.00
$50	Beattie-Coyne	—	60.00	70.00	150.00
	Beattie-Rasminsky	—	—	65.00	150.00
	Lawson-Bouey	60.00	75.00	100.00	275.00
$100	Beattie-Coyne	—	—	125.00	175.00
	Beattie-Rasminsky	—	—	125.00	175.00
	Lawson-Bouey	—	—	125.00	175.00
$1000	Beattie-Coyne	—	—	—	2,100
	Beattie-Rasminsky	—	—	—	2,100
	Bouey-Rasminsky	—	—	—	1,100
	Lawson-Bouey	—	—	—	1,050

Asterisk Issue

Denom.	Signature	VG	F	VF	EF	Unc.
$1	Beattie-Coyne	3.00	4.50	10.00	20.00	60.00
	Beattie-Rasminsky	—	—	3.00	6.00	15.00
	Bouey-Rasminsky	—	—	3.00	6.00	15.00
$2	Beattie-Coyne	20.00	25.00	35.00	50.00	150.00
	Beattie-Rasminsky	—	—	4.00	6.00	18.00
	Bouey-Rasminsky	—	—	4.00	6.00	18.00
	Lawson-Bouey	—	—	6.00	9.00	25.00
$5	Beattie-Coyne	25.00	40.00	50.00	75.00	200.00
	Beattie-Rasminsky	—	15.00	25.00	35.00	90.00
	Bouey-Rasminsky	—	11.00	15.00	25.00	50.00
$10	Beattie-Coyne	—	18.00	30.00	45.00	120.00
	Beattie-Rasminsky	—	12.00	15.00	25.00	60.00
$20	Beattie-Coyne	—	30.00	50.00	100.00	300.00
	Beattie-Rasminsky	—	30.00	45.00	75.00	225.00
$50	Beattie-Coyne					Not Printed
	Beattie-Rasminsky					Not Printed
	Lawson-Bouey					Not Printed
$100	Beattie-Coyne					Not Printed
	Beattie-Rasminsky					Not Printed
	Lawson-Bouey					Not Printed
$1000	Beattie-Coyne					Not Printed
	Beattie-Rasminsky					Not Printed
	Bouey-Rasminsky					Not Printed
	Lawson-Bouey					Not Printed

CENTENNIAL OF CONFEDERATION
COMMEMORATIVE ISSUE, 1967

S1 - 1967 Commemorative (1867 1967 collectors' issue)

As part of the 1967 Centennial celebration, special $1 notes were issued. The face remained the same as that of the 1954 issue, except for the addition of the maple leaf symbol for Confederation and some wording changes. However, the prairie scene on the 1954 $1 back was replaced with a view of the first Parliament buildings. This vignette was originally engraved in 1872 and saw use on the face of the $100 Dominion notes. For the 1967 Bank of Canada notes certain portions (e.g. the sky) were re-engraved.

In addition to the regular serial number and asterisk issues released for circulation, a special collectors issue was prepared with the dates 1867 1967 replacing the serial numbers and were available only from the Bank of Canada at face value (although many later entered circulation). The collectors issue has remained very common, as they were hoarded by the public. The regular serial number issue are not nearly as common. All notes are signed J.R. Beattie/L. Rasminsky and bear the date OTTAWA 1967.

			EF	Unc
$1	1967	Confederation, regular serial number	$2.00	$6.00
		Confederation, Asterisk Issue	5.00	15.00
		Confederation, Collector's Issue 1867 1967	1.25	2.50

MULTICOLOURED ISSUE, 1969-1975

Face side with portrait at right   Back with Canadian Scene

In 1969 the release of a completely new and more modern series of Canadian notes began. In introducing this series, the Bank of Canada, because of the increased circulation of counterfeit notes of the 1954 series, was concerned with producing notes which would be virtually impossible to counterfeit. The most advanced security features available were incorporated into the new designs while maintaining a high artistic standard. The updated style of this series includes multicoloured printing with deeper engravings to give the notes more of a "feel."

The face of each denomination displays the multicoloured Canadian coat of arms and a red serial number on the left half, while a black portrait is on the right with the serial number repeated in blue. For the first time since the 1937 issue, portraits of former Canadian Prime Ministers replace that of the ruling

British monarch on some denominations. All denominations from $1 to $100 were released.

Design Details

Denom.	Basic Colour	Portrait	Back Design
$1	Black	Queen Elizabeth	Ottawa River and Parliament Buildings
$2	Terra cotta	Queen Elizabeth	Eskimos preparing for a hunt
$5	Blue	Sir Wilfrid Laurier	Fishing boat on the west coast
$10	Purple	Sir John A.Macdonald	Oil refinery
$20	Olive Green	Queen Elizabeth	Rocky Mountains and lake
$50	Bright red	W.L. McKenzie King	Dome formation from R.C.M.P. "Musical Ride"
$100	Dark Brown	Sir Robert L. Borden	Maritimes dock scene

Dates, Signatures and Numbering

For the first time, because of the length of time required for design and preparation of each denomination, the various notes of a Bank of Canada issue do not bear the same date. The year shown on the notes and the actual month and year of issue for each are as follows:

$1 1973 (June,1974)	$10 1971 (Nov.,1971)	$100 1975 (May,1976)
$2 1974 (Aug.,1975)	$20 1969 (June,1970)	
$5 1972 (Dec.,1972)	$50 1975 (Mar.,1975)	

The check letter system for numbering is as on the previous issue, except that the two letters are beside each other instead of in the form of a fraction. The left letter signifies denomination and the right letter indicates the series. Within each series the numbers go from 0000000 to 9999999, the zero note being removed and destroyed prior to issue. Since the series letters may include all letters from A to Z (except I, O or Q), each denomination can use 23 different series, or 230,000,000 notes. In 1981 a triple letter prefix was introduced to provide a wider range of series to be used to meet future demand.

There are four signature combinations on this issue:

J.R. Beattie and L. Rasminsky	G.K. Bouey and L. Rasminsky
R.W. Lawson and G.K. Bouey	J.W. Crow and G.K. Bouey

Replacement of defective notes by asterisk notes was continued with the multi-coloured issue on all denominations but was discontinued when the new triple letter prefix notes were introduced. Replacement notes are now indicated by using the letter X for the third letter of the prefix.

Denom.	Signature / Variety	Regular Issue Unc.	Replacement Note Issue* Unc.
$1	Lawson-Bouey / 2 letter prefix	3.50	12.00
	Lawson-Bouey / 3 letter prefix	4.50	12.00
	Crow-Bouey / 3 letter prefix	3.00	8.00
$2	Lawson-Bouey / 2 letter prefix	6.00	30.00
	Lawson-Bouey / 3 letter prefix	6.00	150.00
	Crow-Bouey / 3 letter prefix	6.00	150.00
$5	Bouey-Rasmminsky / 2 letter prefix	25.00	45.00
	Lawson-Bouey / 2 letter prefix	25.00	55.00
$10	Beattie-Rasminsky / 2 letter prefix	70.00	80.00
	Bouey-Rasminsky / 2 letter prefix	85.00	90.00
	Lawson-Bouey / 2 letter prefix	30.00	60.00
	Lawson-Bouey / 3 letter prefix	30.00	60.00
	Crow-Bouey / 3 letter prefix	25.00	75.00
	Thiessen-Crow / 3 letter prefix		

Denom.	Signature / Variety	Regular Issue Unc.	Replacement Note Issue* Unc.
$20	Beattie-Rasminsky / 2 letter prefix	55.00	120.00
$20	Lawson-Bouey / 2 letter prefix	55.00	120.00
$50	Lawson-Bouey / 2 letter prefix	125.00	225.00
	Lawson-Bouey / 3 letter prefix	100.00	200.00
	Crow-Bouey / 3 letter prefix	75.00	100.00
$100	Lawson-Bouey / 2 letter prefix	150.00	225.00
	Lawson-Bouey / 3 letter prefix	145.00	225.00
	Crow-Bouey / 3 letter prefix	145.00	150.00

*Replacement notes using 2-letter prefixes have an asterisk preceding the serial number. Replacement notes with 3-letter prefixes are designated by the use of an "X" as the third letter of the prefix.

BLACK SERIAL NUMBER ISSUE, 1979

In 1979 the Bank of Canada released $5 and $20 notes in a new format. The basic style of the multicoloured issue was retained but there were several changes. In order to make it easier to distinguish the $20 from the $1 note, the orange and pink colours on the $20 note were strengthened while the green tones were diminished, creating a greater colour contrast between the two denominations.

The major change in the design was the removal of the Words BANK OF CANADA-BANQUE DU CANADA from below the vignette on the back. New black serial numbers were put in this position replacing the red and blue serial numbers on the note faces.

These notes were introduced as an experiment to produce notes that would be machine readable but the experiment was unsuccessful and no further denominations were made in this series.

Dates, Signatures and Numbering

The black eleven-digit serial numbers differ from those of previous issues in that no letters are used as identification prefix. The first digit indicates the denomination, digits two through four indicates the series, and the remaining seven digits are the sequential note numbers from 0000000 to 9999999 as in the past. The $20 note was first issued in December 1978 and the $5 note in October 1979.

Denom.	Date	Signature	Regular Issue Unc.	Replacement Note Issue* Unc.
$5	1979	Lawson-Bouey	20.00	225.00
	1979	Crow-Bouey	30.00	750.00
$20	1979	Lawson-Bouey	90.00	225.00
	1979	Crow-Bouey	45.00	90.00
	1979	Thiessen-Crow	40.00	70.00

BAR CODE ISSUE, 1986 –

In March 1986, the Bank of Canada introduced the first of a new series of notes, completely redesigned to assist the visually impaired, increase efficiency of high speed sorting equipment, and provide improved security against counterfeiting. The $1 note was not included in the new series and manufacture of $1 notes ceased as of July 1, 1988, this denomination being replaced by the new Loon dollar coin.

Security elements include the use of microprinting. A background rainbow of wavy lines on the face of the note is composed entirely of microprinted digits corresponding to the value of the note, while the fine horizontal lines through the centre portion of the note face are actually a repeated microprinted legend (BANK OF CANADA 2 BANQUE DU CANADA on the $2 note), in which the numeral corresponds to the denomination of the note. The much larger denomination numerals and portrait are intended to assist the visually impaired and are readable by a new portable electronic device being developed for the blind.

The reverse features native Canadian birds. The serial number appears in black on each half of the reverse at the bottom of the note. A bar code is included at the bottom of the reverse side to be read by high speed sorting equipment at the Bank of Canada. The serial number consists of a three-letter prefix and a seven-digit serial. Replacement notes are identified by the letter X as the third letter of the prefix.

The notes are the same size as the previous series and are printed on the same stock. The face of the note is printed using the intaglio process combined with lithography and the reverse using lithography and letterpress.

Design Details

	Basic Colour	Portrait	Back Design
$2	Terra Cotta	Queen Elizabeth	Two Robins
$5	Blue	Sir Wilfrid Laurier	Belted Kingfisher
$10	purple	Sir John A. Macdonald	Osprey in flight
$50	Red	William Lyon Mackenzie King	Snowy Owl
$100	Brown	Sir Robert Borden	Canada Goose

Dates, Signatures and Numbering

The year shown on the note and the actual month and year of issue for each denomination are as follows:

Denom.	Year Dated	Actual Issue Date	Signature	Regular Issue Unc.	Replacement Note Issue Unc.
$2	1986	September, 1986	Crow-Bouey	4.50	15.00
	1986		Thiessen-Crow	2.50	5.00
$5	1986	April, 1986	Crow-Bouey	12.00	20.00
	1986		Thiessen-Crow	6.00	7.00
$10	1989		Thiessen-Crow	12.00	20.00
$50	1988	December, 1989	Thiessen-Crow	60.00	75.00
$100	1988	December, 1990	Thiessen-Crow	105.00	110.00

12
BULLION VALUES

Silver and gold coins are often purchased by dealers strictly for their "bullion" or "melt" value — a term which refers to the value of the precious metal contained in the coins.

The majority of Canadian coins have been struck from precious metals and the bullion grade and weight of these coins is a matter of public record. These facts have been stated throughout this catalogue. By following the examples illustrated under the bullion charts, anyone can easily determine the fair bullion val ue of coins in their possession.

Determining the Value of Gold and Silver Coins

There is usually a difference of 15% to 25% between the calculated price of gold and silver bullion coins and the actual amount paid by a dealer. There are several reasons for this. The gold or silver dealer is a middleman and must make a profit for his time, knowledge and investment. He will be faced with the additional costs of shipping the coins to (and the refined metal from) the refinery as well as the actual refining charges. Before shipping to a refinery, the dealer must accumulate a sufficient quantity of bullion coins to obtain a reasonable cost per ounce from the refinery, which will have minimum requirements as well as a fee scale which reduces as weight increases. The necessary delay in shipping to the refinery is a risk, because the value of gold and silver could drop drastically before the dealer can have the coins refined.

Silver Coins

The daily spot price of silver is always stated in troy ounces and all dealers buy and sell silver by the troy ounce. You need only know the weight and fineness of a silver coin and, using the sample calculation below, you can arrive at the melt value for any given silver price. The weight and fineness (composition) of all Canadian silver coins are listed throughout this catalogue.

To convert grams to troy ounces, multiply the weight in grams by .0321 (1 troy ounce = 31.103 grams).

Gold Coins

The daily spot price is usually given in troy ounces (although sometimes expressed in pennyweights). Again, you need only know the weight and fineness to calculate the melt value of any gold coin at any given spot price. The weight (in grams) and fineness (composition) of Canadian gold coins are listed throughout this catalogue.

To convert grams to troy ounces, multiply the weight in grams by .0321 (1 troy ounce = 31.103 grams).

To convert pennyweights to troy ounces, divide pennyweights by 20.

The fineness of gold is also often expressed in karats:

KARATS	FINENESS	PURITY	KARATS	FINENESS	PURITY
24 k	.999	99.9%	14 k	.585	58.5%
22 k	.916	91.6%	10 k	.417	41.7%
18 k	.750	75.0%			

Remember that the dealer will purchase bullion coins at a 15%-25% discount from this value in order to cover costs and show a reasonable profit.

Silver Bullion Value of Canadian Silver Coins

Coin Denom.	Years of Issue	Coin Weight Grams	% of Silver Content	Silver Troy Ounce	SILVER VALUE IN CANADIAN DOLLARS									
					$1	$2	$4	$6	$8	$10	$20	$30	$40	$50
5-cents	1858-1919	1.166	.925	.0346	.035	.07	.14	.21	.28	.35	.69	1.04	1.38	1.73
5-cents	1920-1921	1.166	.800	.0299	.03	.06	.12	.18	.24	.30	.60	.90	1.20	1.50
10-cents	1858-1919	2.333	.925	.0693	.07	.14	.28	.42	.55	.69	1.39	2.08	2.77	3.46
10-cents	1920-1967	2.333	.800	.0599	.06	.12	.24	.36	.48	.60	1.20	1.80	2.40	3.00
10-cents	1967-1968	2.333	.500	.0374	.04	.08	.15	.23	.30	.37	.75	1.12	1.50	1.87
25-cents	1870-1919	5.810	.925	.173	.17	.35	.69	1.04	1.38	1.73	3.46	5.19	6.92	8.65
25-cents	1920-1967	5.832	.800	.1498	.15	.30	.60	.90	1.20	1.50	3.00	4.50	6.00	7.50
25-cents	1967-1968	5.832	.500	.0936	.09	.19	.37	.56	.75	.94	1.87	2.81	3.74	4.68
50-cents	1870-1919	11.620	.925	.3450	.35	.69	1.38	2.07	2.76	3.45	6.90	10.35	13.80	17.25
50-cents	1920-1967	11.664	.800	.2995	.30	.60	1.20	1.80	2.40	3.00	6.00	9.00	12.00	15.00
1 Dollar	1935-1967	23.327	.800	.5990	.60	1.20	2.40	3.60	4.80	6.00	12.00	18.00	24.00	30.00
1 Dollar*	1971-date	23.327	.500	.3744	.37	.75	1.50	2.25	3.00	3.74	7.49	11.23	14.98	18.72
NEWFOUNDLAND														
5 cents	1865-1944	1.166	.925	.0346	.035	.07	.14	.21	.28	.35	.70	1.04	1.40	1.75
5-cents	1945-1947	1.166	.800	.0299	.03	.06	.12	.18	.24	.30	.60	.90	1.20	1.50
10-cents	1865-1944	2.333	.925	.0693	.07	.14	.28	.42	.55	.69	1.39	2.08	2.77	3.47
10-cents	1945-1947	2.333	.800	.0599	.06	.12	.24	.36	.48	.60	1.20	1.80	2.40	3.00
20-cents	1865-1912	4.712	.925	.1399	.14	.28	.56	.84	1.12	1.40	2.80	4.20	5.60	7.00
25-cents	1917-1919	5.832	.925	.1732	.17	.35	.69	1.04	1.39	1.73	3.46	5.20	6.93	8.66
50-cents	1870-1919	11.664	.925	.3463	.35	.69	1.39	2.08	2.77	3.46	6.93	10.39	13.85	17.32

*Collectors' Issues

Example:

To calculate the bullion value of a silver Canadian coin made of .800 silver and weighing 23.327 grams:

Multiply the weight (23.327 grams) x .0321 = .7488 Troy oz.
Multiply .7488 Troy oz. x .800 fineness = .599 Troy oz. of silver
If silver is valued at $20.00 an ounce, then the coin is worth:

$20.00 x .599 = $12.00 bullion value

(Note: Collector value may be greater.)

Gold Bullion Value of Canadian Coins

Coin Denom.	Years of Issue	Coin Weight Grams	% of Gold Content	Gold Troy Ounce	GOLD VALUE IN CANADIAN DOLLARS								
					$25	$50	$100	$200	$300	$400	$500	$600	$700	$800
CANADA														
£1 Sovereign	1908c-1919c	7.99	.917	.236	5.90	11.80	23.60	47.20	70.80	94.40	118.00	141.60	165.20	188.80
5 Dollars	1912-1914	8.3591	.900	.2419	6.05	12.10	24.19	48.38	72.57	96.76	120.95	145.14	169.33	193.52
10 Dollars	1912-1914	16.7181	.900	.4838	12.10	24.19	48.38	96.76	145.14	193.52	241.90	290.28	338.66	387.04
20 Dollars	1967	18.2733	.900	.5287	13.22	26.44	52.87	105.74	158.61	211.48	264.35	317.22	370.09	422.96
100 Dollars	1976	13.3375	.583	.2501	6.25	12.51	25.01	50.02	75.03	100.04	125.05	150.06	175.07	200.08
100 Dollars	1976-date	16.9655	.9166	.500	12.50	25.00	50.00	100.00	150.00	200.00	250.00	300.00	350.00	400.00
$50 Maple Leaf	1979-date	31.1	.999	1.000	25.00	50.00	100.00	200.00	300.00	400.00	500.00	600.00	700.00	800.00
$10 Maple Leaf	1982-date	7.77	.999	.250	6.25	12.50	25.00	50.00	75.00	100.00	125.00	150.00	175.00	200.00
$5 Maple Leaf	1982-date	3.11	.999	.100	2.50	5.00	10.00	20.00	30.00	40.00	50.00	60.00	70.00	80.00
NEWFOUNDLAND														
2 Dollars	1865-1888	3.3283	.9166	.0981	2.45	4.91	9.81	19.62	29.43	39.24	49.05	59.86	68.67	78.48

Example:
To calculate the bullion value of a gold coin made of .900 gold
and weighing 16.718 grams:
Multiply the weight (16.718 grams) x .0321 = .5366 Troy oz.
Multiply .5366 Troy oz. x .900 fineness = .4829 Troy oz. of gold
If gold is valued at $400.00 an ounce, then the coin is worth:
$400.00 x .4829 = $193.00 bullion value
(Note: Collector value may be greater.)

GLOSSARY

ALLOY: Mixture of more than one metal, usually preceded by the name of the most predominant or most important metal in the mix, such as nickel alloy.

ASSAY: The analytical test to determine the purity and weight of metal.

BAGMARKS: Slight scratches and nicks acquired by coins in contact with others in a mint bag. Most common on large and heavy silver and gold coins.

BILLON: A low-grade alloy used for some minor coin issues consisting usually of a mixture of silver and copper, and sometimes coated with a silver wash.

BLANKS: Flat round metal discs or planchets from which the coins are made.

BROCKAGE: Formerly any misstruck coin, now specifically refers to a coin having one side normal and the opposite side having the same design only as an incuse "mirror image."

BULLION: Uncoined gold or silver in the form of bars, ingots and plates. Bullion value is a term used in reference to the value of the metal content in gold and silver coins.

BUSINESS STRIKE: Any coin struck with the intention of circulating.

CAMEO-EFFECT: A description of the appearance of certain gold and silver proof coins which have frosted devices on highly polished fields.

CLASHED DIES: Damaged dies caused by the absence of a planchet at the time of striking. Each die retains a portion of its opposite's design, in addition to its own. The resulting coins show a partial impression of the reverse design on the obverse and/or vice versa.

CLIPPED PLANCHET (CLOSE PLANCHET): A planchet less than fully round, having been punched too closely to the edge of the metal sheet, or due to the adjacent planchet having been punched too closely.

DEBASEMENT: Debasement of a coin takes place when the issuing authority reduces the purity of the metal, lowering the intrinsic value of the coin but circulating it at par with the previous coins of the original purity.

DENTICLES: Tooth-like projections running inside the rim of a coin.

DEVICE: Any design feature appearing on the obverse, reverse or edge of a coin.

DIADEMED: A coin where the portrait head has a headband or fillet as a sign of royalty.

DIE: Engraved metal pieces used to impress the design of a coin on a blank planchet.

DIE AXIS: The vertical axes of the two dies when striking a coin or medal are indicated by arrows; with the obverse die assumed to be upright and the relative position of the reverse die indicated by a second arrow. Medal struck pieces have both dies upright (↑↑); coin struck, the reverse appears upside down (↑↓).

DIE CRACK: A stress crack on a die producing a raised line on the pieces struck.

DIE POLISHING LINES: Minute scratches on the die from polishing which produce very fine raised lines on some well struck coins.

ESSAI: A trial piece from dies already accepted for regular coinage. It may bear a date or mint mark other than on the coins issued for circulation or it may be a different metal.

EXERGUE: The lower part of a coin or medal which is usually divided from the field by a line under which is contained the date, place of minting or engraver's initials.

FIELD: Areas on either side of a coin not occupied by portrait, design or description.

FLAN: See BLANKS.

GEM: A relatively flawless piece of superlative quality.

HAIRLINES: Minute lines or scratches on a coin caused by cleaning or polishing.

HIGH POINTS: The highest points on the design of a coin. The first points to show wear.

INCUSE: Coins with either obverse or reverse design sunk below the coin's surface.

IRIDESCENT: Multi-coloured blending or toning usually found in older uncirculated coins.

KARAT: The degree of fineness of gold. Pure gold is 24 karats and most gold coins have a fineness of 22 karats.

LAMINATED PLANCHET: A "peeling off" of a top layer of the metal of a planchet.

LEGEND: The principal inscription on a coin.

LUSTRE: The sheen on the surface of an uncirculated coin caused by the centrifugal flow of metal on striking. Mint lustre (bloom) is somewhat frosty in appearance as opposed to the mirror-like fields of a proof. An important indicator of a coin's condition, lustre is worn through with the slightest circulation. Chemical cleaners can destroy it. Once gone lustre cannot be restored.

MAJOR VARIETY: A coin of the same date, mint mark and denomination as another, but struck from another pair of dies and having at least the major device added, removed or redesigned.

MATTE PROOF: A proof coin for which the planchet is treated in a manner other than polishing. A dull and grainy finish is achieved.

MEDAL: A commemorative metal piece in honour of a person or event. Not money.

MEDALET: A small medal, usually smaller in diameter than a fifty- cent piece.

MILLED EDGE: [1] Prior to use of collar dies the edge design was milled onto the blank before minting; [2] using collar dies, flan edges are milled so that the border or design will be adequately raised when struck.

MINOR VARIETY: A minor variety is one with all major devices the same as another, but with some easily recognizable variation.

MINT ERROR: An incorrectly struck or defective coin produced by a mint.

MINT MARK: Letter designation for a branch mint product.

MULE: A coin struck from dies not designed to be used together.

OBVERSE: The "face-up" side of the coin, regarded as more important than the reverse side and usually bearing the portrait of the monarch.

OVERDATED: The date made by an engraver at the mint punching one or more numbers on a previously dated die.

OVERSTRIKE: A coin where part of the design, particularly the date, appears over another design or date.

PATINA: Originally: a green or brown surface film (from oxidation) found on ancient copper and bronze coins; now refers to toning on any coin.

PATTERN: A design suggested for a new coinage, struck in a few examples but not adopted. If adopted for regular coinage with the same date, the piece ceases to be a pattern.

PIEDFORT: A type of pattern struck on a thick flan. Probably, piedforts were struck for use by coiners as models when making actual coins.

PLANCHET: See BLANKS.

PROOF: [1] A special striking of a coin, produced to show to those who have the right to choose the design at its best. Proofs are carefully struck by gentle pressure, usually at least twice, from carefully polished dies, on polished flans. The minutest details of the design are thus made clear. The term does NOT refer to the condition of the coin. [2] A bank note or other form of paper money specially printed as a sample or specimen but not intended for circulation.

REEDED EDGE: Minted vertical serrations on the edge of a coin.

RELIEF: Where the lettering and design are raised above the surface of the coin.

RESTRIKE: Any coin struck later than the date appearing on the coin.

REVERSE: Opposite from obverse. The back or "tails" side of a coin.

ROTATED DIE: Dies are positioned and locked on a coining press by means of a key. When these keys come loose, rotation can occur resulting in the next coin being struck with the obverse and reverse dies rotated. Coins struck from rotated dies are errors.

SPECIMEN: [1] A coin or bank note prepared, often with special care, as an example of a given issue. Sometimes, particularly with bank notes, surcharged with the word "SPECIMEN" or a similar word. [2] A synonym for a numismatic item, e.g., a very rare specimen.

SPURIOUS: A false piece made to deceive, often an original creation rather than a copy of a known item. Not genuine, counterfeit, false.

TOKEN: Usually a piece of durable material appropriately marked and unofficially issued for monetary, advertising, services or other purposes.

TRADE DOLLAR: A token used by a municipality primarily as a tourism promotion, and redeemable in most stores in the issuing municipality.

VIGNETTE: A pictorial element of a bank note design that shades off gradually into the surrounding unprinted paper or background rather than having sharp outlines or a frame.

WIRE EDGE: Slight flange on coins or medals caused by heavy striking pressure, often characteristic on Proof coins (also KNIFE EDGE). The metal is squeezed up the side of the die faces by the collar die.

WORKING DIE: Used to strike coins. Not a master die, etc.

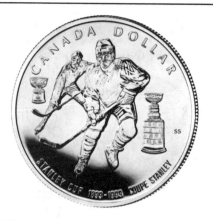

The 1993 silver dollar commemorates
the 100th anniversary of the Stanley cup.

WE CARRY ALL CURRENT
ROYAL CANADIAN MINT COINS AND SETS

**ALL OLDER ROYAL CANADIAN MINT COINS AND SETS
BOUGHT AND SOLD**

*We also buy and sell Canadian & worldwide
coins, stamps, paper money,
Franklin Mint products,
gold & silver bars and coins in any form.*

Shop in person at our retail location
PHONE & MAIL ORDERS WELCOME

COIN MARKET
710 YONGE STREET
TORONTO, ONTARIO   M4Y 2B3
(416) 964-1632

1994
OFFICIAL
CANADIAN
COIN GUIDE

DEALER BUYING PRICES

This guide is the most accurate and up-to-date publication of its kind on the market today, listing the prices currently paid by dealers for **ALL** Canadian & U.S. coins — *PLUS MUCH MORE!*

- Latest prices for all coins, tokens and paper money in the most commonly found grade
- Complete Coin series for Canada and U.S.
- All Canadian pre-confederation issues of coins and tokens
- Complete listing of paper money issued by the Dominion of Canada and the Bank of Canada
- All paper money issued by Canadian chartered banks from 1850 to date
- Complete mintage figures and other important data affecting the value of coins
- Detailed introduction including grading information.

ISBN 1-895909-01-5   RETAIL PRICE 3.95

UNITRADE ASSOCIATES
91 TYCOS DRIVE, TORONTO, ONTARIO   M6B 1W3
TEL: (416) 787-5658 • FAX: (416) 787-7104

UNIMASTER COIN ALBUMS

UNI - SAFE

The most attractive coin albums money can buy!

These attractive gold-stamped, brown-grained vinyl binders make a handsome edition to any library. Loose-leaf vinyl pages contain vinyl pocketed slides so coins can never fall out. Each slide panel contains a label strip to indicate the contents. Additional binders and pages with blank labels are also available.

ALBUM		PAGES	RETAIL	ALBUM		PAGES	RETAIL
151	1¢ Large, 1858-1920	2	11.50	161	50¢, 1870-1945	3	12.95
152	1¢ Small, 1920-date	3	12.95	162	50¢, 1946-date	4	14.50
153	1¢ BLANK	5	16.50	163	50¢, BLANK	5	16.50
154	5¢ Silver, 1858-1921	2	11.50	164	Dollars, 1935-date	5	16.50
155	5¢ Nickel, 1922-date	3	12.95	165	Dollars, BLANK	5	16.50
156	5¢ BLANK	5	15.50	166	Mint Sets	5	16.50
157	10¢, 1870-date	5	16.50	**BLANK PAGES AND BINDERS**			
158	10¢ BLANK	5	16.50	150	Blank Binder, No Titles		9.50
159	25¢, 1870-date	5	16.50	'A'	30-pocket pages (1¢ to 25¢)		each 1.95
160	25¢ BLANK	5	16.50	'B'	16-pocket pages (50¢ to $1)		each 1.95
				'C'	2-pocket pages (Mint Sets)		each 1.95

Available at your favourite coin dealer, stationery or bookstore, or through:

UNITRADE ASSOCIATES, 91 Tycos Dr., Toronto, Ont. M6B 1W3

Orders to the above address should include $2.00 postage & handling plus applicable sales tax.

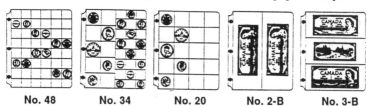

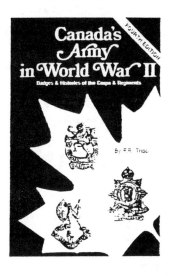

CANADA'S ARMY IN WORLD WAR II

by F.R. TRIPP

A COLLECTOR'S GUIDE TO THE BADGES
AND HISTORIES OF THE CANADIAN CORPS
AND REGIMENTS OF WORLD WAR II

- THE MOST COMPLETE GUIDE ON THE MARKET
- ALPHABETICAL LISTING OF THE CANADIAN BADGES
  OF WORLD WAR II
- OVER 200 ILLUSTRATIONS
- 128 PAGES

ISBN 0-919801-98-6   **RETAIL $10.95**

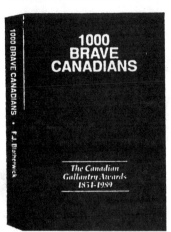